Tim Lindemann

New Rural Cinema

Film, Class, Society

Edited by
Elisa Cuter, Daniel Fairfax, Guido Kirsten
and Hanna Prenzel

Volume 2

Tim Lindemann

New Rural Cinema

Landscape, Community and Poverty
in Recent US Indie Films

DE GRUYTER

The research this book is based on was fully funded by a Queen Mary University of London Research Studentship.

ISBN 978-3-11-224748-8
e-ISBN (PDF) 978-3-11-077941-7
e-ISBN (EPUB) 978-3-11-077943-1

Library of Congress Control Number: 2023945999

Bibliographic information published by the Deutsche Nationalbibliothek
The Deutsche Nationalbibliothek lists this publication in the Deutsche Nationalbibliografie; detailed bibliographic data are available on the internet at http://dnb.dnb.de.

This volume is text- and page-identical with the hardback published in 2024.
Cover image: *Leave No Trace* (2018). Picture alliance/PictureLux/Bleecker Street/The/R4820
Typesetting: Integra Software Services Pvt. Ltd.
Printing and binding: CPI books GmbH, Leck

www.degruyter.com

Acknowledgements

This research was made possible by a Principal's Postgraduate Research Studentship for which I am grateful to Queen Mary, University of London.

This book is based on my PhD thesis which was guided by my two constructive and diligent supervisors. I am hugely grateful to Alasdair King for encouraging me from the very beginning of this project and continuously supporting me in finding new perspectives and approaches to the material. I am also indebted to Guy Westwell for his attention to detail, his inspiring knowledge of film, and for always being open to discussing any issues and uncertainties.

I would like to thank the following people for helping me access their respective work, which was instrumental in the writing of this book: Dr Kevan Feshami, Dr Marlon Lieber, and Professor Karen Wells. I am grateful to Dr Yannis Tzioumakis and Dr Mark Steven for their productive feedback as external examiners of my PhD thesis.

This book would not exist without Guido Kirsten who I thank for having faith in my research and for always being available for questions and queries. I also want to thank Myrto Aspioti at De Gruyter for being patient with my many editorial questions. I also would like to thank Elisa Cuter, Stella Diedrich, Daniel Fairfax, and Hanna Prenzel for their contribution to the publication of this book.

I cannot thank my family enough for always backing and encouraging me to follow my love for film and writing. I especially want to thank Christine Lindemann and Klaus-Dieter Bremm, who both in their own ways are role models for following one's talents and passions. I am just as grateful to Wolfram Eichler, Astrid Bremm, Gitti Gaul, Klaus Lindemann, Ulgart Höhl, Jens Bremm, Heinz-Jürgen Bremm Otti Lindemann, Ilse Bremm, Mira Faßbach, and Clara Eichler.

My heartfelt thanks go to my friends in Dortmund, Berlin, and London who have encouraged, inspired, and supported my research in various ways—from carrying books from Germany to the UK to discussing films over pints or simply being there in stressful moments: Andreas Meltl, Simon Zirzow, Sasha Danylin, Malte Siemers, Keifer Taylor, Patricia Nilsson, Mattes Teschabai, Felix Weber, Marco Paulus, Jasper Kruse, Daniela Sannwald, Kristina Jaspers, Georg Simbeni, Tashi Petter, and Lisa Duffy. I would like to thank the entire department of Film Studies at Queen Mary, an incredibly friendly bunch of people. Thank you also to Sally and Kevin Pember as well as Anna Koffer for making me feel welcome in the UK!

A very special thank you to Alice Pember, whose consistent good advice, diligent proofreading, and companionship have been a source of great strength and inspiration.

https://doi.org/10.1515/9783110779417-202

Contents

Introduction

Despite its continuous and increasing presence in both US films and the national political discourse at large, rural America remains surprisingly absent in studies of US cinema.[1] At the same time, however, the United States' urban spaces are explored again and again as the subjects of films and sites of production and exhibition in a growing number of film-geographical monographs and edited collections. Catherine Fowler and Gillian Helfield, the editors of one of the few collections explicitly dedicated to rural cinema, have summarized the "innate relationship between cinema and the city" many of these studies seem to presuppose: "Traffic, people, city life all move to the rhythm of the twenty-four-frames-per-second beat, as if celluloid is providing the heart for the metropolitan corpus."[2] The city can often seem like the geographical space cinema is meant to engage with and construct while representations of the rural "seem retrogressive and thus not worthy of the same critical and historical focus."[3]

This is particularly notable in studies focusing on the period from the 1970s onwards and its specific economic developments which are often presented as only affecting urban living, work, and culture. For example, in the introduction to their edited collection titled *The City and American Cinema: Film and Postindustrial Culture* (2019), Lawrence Webb and Johann Andersson frame the book's focus on urban spaces in post-1960 US cinema as follows:

> From the late 1960s, manufacturing decline and "white flight" accelerated, fueling an interconnected set of crises in American society that impacted on cities and culture alike. These crises—among them the urban crisis, the oil crisis, the crisis of masculinity, and Hollywood's own financial crisis—are commonly understood as ushering in a new era variously characterized, with differing emphases, as "postindustrial," "post-Fordist," "postmodern," or "neoliberal."[4]

---

1 As a general rule, I will be using "the United States" instead of "America," and "US" as an adjective instead of "American" in this book. However, I have kept the term "American" in a small number of instances: when referring to the early phase of "US" national self-conception (specifically in Chapter Three) and in established and common terms such as "Rural America" or "the American West."

2 Catherine Fowler and Gilian Hefield, "Introduction," in *Representing the Rural: Space, Place and Identity in Films about the Land*, ed. Catherine Fowler and Gillian Helfield (Detroit, MI: Wayne State UP, 2006), 1.

3 Ibid., 2.

4 Johan Andersson and Lawrence Webb, "American Cinema and Urban Change: Industry, Genre, and Politics from Nixon to Trump," in *The City in American Cinema: Film and Postindustrial Culture*, ed. Johan Andersson and Lawrence Webb (London: Bloomsbury, 2019), 5.

https://doi.org/10.1515/9783110779417-001

The authors continue by further defining the term "post-industrial" which features prominently in the volume's film analyses. They claim:

> It provides an especially productive way to position cinema within broad historic shifts in urban space, business organization, patterns of labor and consumption, as well as emerging social practices and political trends. The 1960s and 1970s can be seen as a foundational moment, then, and [. . .] the years that followed would bring cities and cinema together in new configurations.[5]

The historic connections between the American city and US cinema—be they industrial or textual—have led to an increased number of film-geographical studies of US urbanity on screen in the last twenty years.[6] What is notable about this "spatial turn" in US cinema studies is, again, that its proponents focus almost exclusively on the city, while rural spaces are mostly ignored. This is notable because, especially in the years since Donald Trump's election as US President, rural America has been key to political discussions in the United States—even if these debates are often dominated by generalizing assumptions about the supposed uniformity of rural America. Trump's upset win was at least partially credited to a growing divide between urban and rural America that was starkly visible in the exit polls, as Robert Wuthnow summarizes: "62 per cent of the rural vote went to Donald Trump, compared with 50 percent of the suburban vote and only 35 percent of the urban vote."[7] The two broad explanations put forward in the media following the 2016 election were that "rural people wanted change because they were suffering economically" or that the "predominantly white" rural population was "racist and misogynist enough" to respond positively to Trump's right-wing populist campaign.[8]

These simplified arguments determined the political discourse surrounding the Trump presidency to a significant degree. Webb and Andersson acknowledge this when they write that "long-standing geographical rifts in American society have resurfaced in which the 'liberal elites' of the coastal cosmopolitan cities are

5 Ibid.

6 Andersson and Webb list key texts such as Edward Dimendberg, *Film Noir and the Spaces of Modernity* (Cambridge, MA/London: Harvard University Press, 2004), Paula Massood, *Black City Cinema: African American Experiences in Film* (Philadelphia, PA: Temple University Press, 2003), Merrill Schleier, *Skyscraper Cinema: Architecture and Gender in American Film* (Minneapolis: University of Minnesota Press, 2009) and Pamela Robertson Wojcik, *The Apartment Plot: Urban Living in American Film and Popular Culture, 1945–1975* (Durham, NC: Duke University Press, 2010).

7 Robert Wuthnow, *The Left Behind. Decline and Rage in Small-Town America* (Princeton/Oxford: Princeton UP, 2019), 1.

8 Ibid.

pitted against the entrenched conservatism of small towns and rural areas."[9] If this is the case, it seems worthwhile to momentarily avert the gaze from the dominant US "city cinema" and investigate how the post-industrial *rural* American landscape has been represented on screen both previous to, and after 2016. After all, as we shall see, rural America *has* figured prominently in twenty-first-century US cinema. However, Webb and Andersson not only eschew even a brief consideration of rural America on screen, they also seem to suggest that such an endeavor would be pointless:

> Hollywood today is arguably more anti-rural and anti-small-town than anti-urban. The diversification of urban locations [. . .] has arguably not been matched by *any corresponding interest* in small-town America beyond recurring caricatures of rednecks and hillbillies.[10]

The authors mention a single example for this claim, *Three Billboards Outside Ebbing, Missouri* (Martin McDonagh, 2017), which is described as emblematic of contemporary Hollywood's supposed contempt for rural America and its inhabitants. One might object that *Three Billboards* is a US-British co-production, written and directed by a British-Irish filmmaker, and arguably takes on a satirical outsider view of (rural) American society. Frances McDormand's complex Oscar-winning performance as the main character Mildred seems to further limit the authors' critique that the film "flatten[s] geographical and cultural specificity in favor of well-trodden tropes of the reactionary Midwest and South."[11] Overall, the film emerges as a darkly comedic drama with a distinctly European view on established American small-town stereotypes. If authentic representation of US rurality is what one is after, McDonagh's film is certainly not be the best place to start.

Furthermore, Webb and Andersson's argument is marred by their, at least partial, equation of American cinema and Hollywood which sidelines the indie sector almost entirely. They do acknowledge that US indie productions are "frequently embedded in a bounded and highly localized diegetic world" and that they "develop more intimate connections between character and place [. . .] in contrast to the high-stakes, globalized conflicts of the blockbuster."[12] However, there is no mention of the fact that in the last two decades, US indie cinema has given rise to a significant number of prominent, award-winning films that are closely focused on rural America and have little to do with "recurring caricatures of rednecks and hillbillies." In addition, there is an equally significant number of

9 Andersson and Webb, "American Cinema," 25.

10 Ibid. Emphasis added.

11 Ibid.

12 Ibid., 13.

recent films on the borderline between indie and mainstream cinema that have brought these landscapes to ever larger audiences.

Given Webb and Andersson's focus on "city cinema," these details might appear to go well beyond its scope. What is striking, however, is the suggestion that there simply is no "rural cinema" in the United States beyond *Three Billboards* and similar films. This seems especially glaring in the context of the book's focus on "film and postindustrial culture," considering that films by Kelly Reichardt, Debra Granik, Jeff Nichols, David Gordon Green, Chloé Zhao, and others have delivered impressive portraits of the deindustrialized landscapes of rural America and the precarity their inhabitants experience. Regardless of their potential use of stereotypes, then, these films, too, reflect the social, political, and economic crises that have engulfed the United States since the 1970s and are thus worthy of analysis. Indeed, close analyses of the cinematic representations of rural spaces are just as revealing of postindustrial culture, precisely because they are largely relegated to the margins of US cinema. Such an investigation of the "intimate connections between character and place" within a rural context necessarily demands a different analytical framework than those of studies of "city cinema." Such an approach would have to, firstly, grasp how these contemporary rural films make visible the close interaction between rural inhabitants and their physical environment. Secondly, these cinematic representations of contemporary rural America need to be understood within the context of the historic significance of rural landscape within US visual culture and specifically the cinema.

This book suggests exactly such a novel way of looking at landscape in cinema by closely analyzing four recent US indie films, which form part of a larger cycle of films focused on rural poverty and marginality. *Winter's Bone* (Debra Granik, 2010), *Ballast* (Lance Hammer, 2008), *Beasts of the Southern Wild* (Benh Zeitlin, 2012), and *Leave No Trace* (Debra Granik, 2018) usher in a new substantive understanding of rural landscape in US cinema that has gradually emerged over the last decade, roughly stretching from the 2008 financial crisis to the outbreak of the Covid-19 pandemic. This cycle is thus closely associated with crises that have exacerbated pre-existing economical, regional, and racial inequalities in the United States and arises from a socio-political context of infrastructural devastation, joblessness, racial division, and violence. It stands in sharp contrast to a large part of US film history which identifies the rural as pastoral idyll associated with a romanticized past and instead presents a much bleaker picture. I therefore suggest the term New Rural Cinema for this loosely connected cycle.

The term cycle might appear counterintuitive in the context of US indie cinema at first. In her monograph *American Film Cycles: Reframing Genres, Screening Social Problems, and Defining Subcultures*, Amanda Ann Klein mainly discusses the cycle as a phenomenon of either Hollywood mainstream or exploitation cinema and suggests that the relative absence of the term in academic analyses is based on the wide-spread assumption that "film cycles are simply cultural ephemera cranked out to capitalize on current events, trends, fads, and the success of other films."[13] While Klein argues that cycles are usually "made in reaction to a particular social anxiety, problem, or crisis,"[14] she mainly focuses on 'low-brow' genre films such as teen comedies and the "ghetto action films" of the nineties. An "indie cycle" like the New Rural Cinema, partially defined by its distance to the mainstream, therefore falls slightly outside of her understanding of the term. Annette Kuhn and Guy Westwell allow for a broader definition in the *Oxford Dictionary of Film Studies*. They argue that behind the term cycle stands the question "of the relationship between cinema and society: to what extent do films mirror social concerns of the day, and to what extent do they shape debate and discourse around such issues? [. . .] These questions are perhaps best answered through investigations of particular cases."[15] As will become clear, this is precisely the interest of this book: to investigate how poverty and rurality have been addressed in recent US indie cinema and to draw attention to shared narrative and visual similarities between the films, particularly in relation to cinematic landscape.

However, it is not the main interest of this book to compile a definitive corpus of films under the label "New Rural Cinema." This is because unlike most film cycles, the New Rural Cinema is not an obviously coherent "group of *genre* films that enjoy significant popularity and influence over a defined period time," but a looser, homogenous trend in contemporary US indie cinema that started around the turn of the millennium and intensified just before and in the aftermath of the 2008 financial crisis. Questions of genre are not insignificant in its analysis, as will become clear in Chapter Three, yet while some of the films of the New Rural Cinema might be clearly recognizable as genre entries, others remain more ambiguous. It is also important to note here that none of the filmmakers have ever publicly claimed to belong to any such movement or trend. Nevertheless, an indicative, if not exhaustive list of films—some of which will be mentioned throughout—is included at the end of this book. These include *George Washington* (David Gordon Green, 2000), *Undertow* (David Gordon Green, 2004), *Shotgun Stories* (Jeff Nichols, 2007), *Frozen River* (Courtney Hunt, 2008), *Joe* (David Gordon Green, 2013), *Songs My Brothers Taught Me* (Chloé Zhao, 2015), *Dayveon* (Amman Abasi, 2017), *Nomadland* (Chloé Zhao, 2020), *War Pony* (Riley Keough and Gina Gammell, 2022) and others.

13 Amanda Ann Klein, *American Film Cycles: Reframing Genres, Screening Social Problems, and Defining Subcultures* (Austin: University of Texas Press, 2011), 6.

14 Ibid., 20.

15 Annette Kuhn and Guy Westwell, *Oxford Dictionary of Film Studies*, 2nd ed. (Oxford: Oxford UP, 2020), 126. Emphasis added.

The films' distinctive difference in picturing rural America is reflected on a thematic as well as on a structural, spatial level. Firstly, these films seek to center poor rural Americans from diverse backgrounds without either demonizing them or depicting their struggles as something to be resolved on an individual level. While there are certainly earlier examples of this kind of representation, this new cycle constitutes a particular concentration. Secondly, and more importantly for this book, these films chime with an understanding of (rural) landscape that goes beyond notions of landscape as scenery, setting, or background. Instead, they illustrate an interactive relationship between rural communities and their environment that foregrounds custom, solidarity, and cooperation. Whilst the films of the New Rural Cinema portray this relationship in different ways and reach different outcomes, they all suggest alternative, communal forms of social organization that contest the injustices of the underdeveloped rural environments surrounding them.

This book will focus in detail on the four previously mentioned case studies yet draw on examples of landscape representation from across the cycle when necessary. The selection of the four case studies arises, firstly, out of their respective depictions of rural landscape which serve especially well to highlight distinctive aspects of the approach to cinematic landscape suggested by this book. These aspects concern the significance of community, interactivity, and marginality, the intersections of class, race, and gender, as well as connections to specific national and regional landscape histories. The four films will form a representative corpus illuminating the distinctive concept of landscape I am suggesting here. Chapter Three contains an extensive discussion of the historical depictions of rural landscape in US cinema and will thereby provide cross-references to thematic and stylistic elements of landscape representation across both US cinema history at large and the recent New Rural Cinema cycle more specifically. Therefore, it will become apparent how the four case studies are embedded within a long and ongoing thematic tradition in both mainstream and independent US cinema, while at the same underlining their unique, novel visions of landscape, polity, and solidarity.

Chapter One
Against the "Propertied Gaze" – Rural Poverty in the United States and its Cinematic Representations

In this chapter, I will establish some of the larger discourses with which this book engages. I will give a brief overview of the main problem the New Rural Cinema approaches, namely the reality of deep rural poverty in the United States, its current scope, and the political discourse surrounding it. This leads to, secondly, an evaluation of the specific context of rural poverty today, which can be identified in what Neil Brenner and Nik Theodore call "actually existing neoliberalism."[1] According to the authors, "each round of capitalist development is associated with a distinctive, historically specific geographical landscape in which some places, territories, and scales are systematically privileged over and against others as sites for capital accumulation."[2] The section will therefore consider some of the concrete policies and developments that have amplified rural poverty and determined its geography since the late 1970s. Thirdly, I will summarize how discourses surrounding (rural) poverty have historically been addressed in US cinema and how they relate to notions of class. Finally, I will offer a brief overview of the category of US "indie cinema," its contested position in relation to mainstream Hollywood, and its ability to critique and subvert hegemonic ideologies.

1 The metrics of poverty

In 2017, Philip Alston, a Special Rapporteur to the United Nations, visited some of the poorest areas in the United States to evaluate if the level of poverty affected the basic human rights of citizens living in these areas. The visit coincided with the implementation of a controversial tax plan by the Trump administration that included vast cuts in welfare programs aimed specifically at such underdeveloped regions. Alston's findings were damning. Two major concerns stand out in his report. Firstly, he notes the immense inequality between rich and poor Americans that not only persists but is continuously exacerbated by policies such as Trump's

1 Neil Brenner and Nik Theodore, "Cities and the Geographies of 'Actually Existing Neoliberalism'," *Antipode* 34:3 (2002), 355.
2 Ibid.

https://doi.org/10.1515/9783110779417-002

Tax Cuts and Jobs Act of 2017. He comments that this recent policy development "stakes out America's bid to become the most unequal society in the world, and will greatly increase the already high level of wealth and income inequality between the richest 1% and the poorest 50% of Americans."[3] This growing internal inequality between the lives of the rich and the poor—from education, debt, sanitation, incarceration, and housing conditions to death rates—is contrasted with an external contradiction: the extreme discrepancy between the United States' role as a global hegemon of cultural, political, and economic power and the persistence of extreme poverty in the country. His report continues: "The United States is one of the world's richest, most powerful and technologically innovative countries; but neither its wealth nor its power nor its technology is being harnessed to address the situation in which 40 million people continue to live in poverty."[4] Alston suggests that these findings stand in harsh contrast to the idea of "American exceptionalism" which, traditionally, claims that the United States is unparalleled in its promotion of equality and possibility. He observes:

> The United States is alone among developed countries in insisting that while human rights are of fundamental importance, they do not include rights that guard against dying of hunger, dying from a lack of access to affordable healthcare, or growing up in a context of total deprivation.[5]

Alston's second major concern addresses the prevalent ideology that conceals this discrepancy between claimed social mobility and real-life inequality: the demonization of the poor. Since, in theory, all citizens are supposed to be able to economically thrive in the United States, a failure to do so is seen as personal shortcoming—a testament to irresponsible, idle behavior. Welfare as a means to prevent severe deprivation is therefore constantly undermined through a "drumbeat of allegations of widespread fraud in the system".[6] The prevalent notion is that "the poor are inherently lazy, dishonest, and care only about their own interests."[7] The grave effects of this ideology are not only the ongoing marginalization of poor Americans but also its internalization by many poor people "who proudly resist applying for benefits to which they are entitled."[8] In sum, Alston stresses that "particularly

---

3 Phillip Alston, "Statement on Visit to the USA, by Professor Philip Alston, United Nations Special Rapporteur on Extreme Poverty and Human rights," *The Office of the High Commissioner for Human Rights* (2017), https://www.ohchr.org/en/statements/2017/12/statement-visit-usa-professor-philip-alston-united-nations-special-rapporteur. 1.

4 Ibid.

5 Ibid., 2.

6 Ibid., 7.

7 Ibid.

8 Ibid., 6.

in a rich country like the USA, the persistence of extreme poverty is a political choice made by those in power."[9] These political choices will be explored further below, however, it is essential to firstly define what is meant when we talk about poverty in the United States. The following summary mostly relies on the 2021 report by the US Department of Agriculture's Economic Research Service (ERS), which collects and interprets data gathered by the American Community Survey (ACS) of the Census Bureau, as well as on related articles from the ERS website.

Officially, poverty in the US is defined by the Census Bureau through the application of income thresholds. In 2019, two of the various thresholds were, for example, defined as an annual income of $13.300 for a single individual under the age of 65 and as $30.510 for a family with two adults and three children. This differs, for example, from the approach to poverty followed by the European Union (EU) where, as Ann Tickamyer and Emily Wornell point out, "poverty is defined in relative terms that emphasize its relationships to inequality [. . .] [by assessing] poverty relative to median income" in the EU member countries.[10] The official US poverty measure in 2018 was 13.1% of the whole population, which accounts for almost 42 million people living under their respective income threshold. "Deep" or "extreme" poverty is defined as living on less than half of this respective income—in 2017, an estimated number of 18.5 million Americans were living in such conditions, about half of the overall poverty measure.[11] Areas where a majority of residents live in deep poverty, as the ERS clarifies in an article on their website, "more often lack availability of healthcare, healthy and affordable food, safe and affordable housing, quality education, and adequate protective service and transportation systems compared with more affluent localities."[12] In 2018/19, the article continues, "all of the extreme poverty counties were in rural America."[13] Therefore, the ERS' numbers render visible a clear and demonstrable concentration of extreme poverty in the United States' rural areas while, however, remaining vague concerning the causes of this phenomenon.

Rural poverty rates (or "nonmetro", as they are termed in official census data) have been consistently higher than "metro" poverty rates since they were

---

9 Ibid., 3.

10 Ann R. Tickameyer and Emily Wornell, "How to Explain Poverty?" in *Rural Poverty in the United States*, ed. Ann R. Tickamyer, Jennifer Sherman, and Jennifer Warlick (New York/Chichester: Columbia UP, 2017), 104.

11 See: Alston, "Statement on Visit to the USA," 3.

12 Tracey Farrigan, "Extreme Poverty Counties Found Solely in Rural Areas in 2018," *Amber Waves (ERS)* (May 4, 2020), https://www.ers.usda.gov/amber-waves/2020/may/extreme-poverty-counties-found-solely-in-rural-areas-in-2018.

13 Ibid. Emphasis added.

first recorded in the 1960s, even though the gap has generally narrowed over time. Rural poverty reached a 30-year peak in 2012/13 with a rate of 18.4% of the rural population and an even higher rate of child poverty (26.7%), a development which is largely identified as the aftereffect of the 2008 housing and financial crisis.[14] This period of soaring rural poverty coincides with the production and release of the first notable cluster of New Rural Cinema films: *Winter's Bone, Frozen River, Ballast, Beasts of the Southern Wild, Wendy and Lucy* (Kelly Reichardt, 2008), *A Single Shot* (David M. Rosenthal, 2013) and others were all conceived and released during this time. From the highpoint of 2013 until 2019, rural poverty rates have declined by about 3%. However, in many rural areas, poverty is persistent. The ERS defines counties "as being persistently poor if 20 percent or more of their populations were living in poverty" over the past forty years and finds that "the large majority (301 or 85.3 percent) of the persistent-poverty counties are nonmetro."[15] Strikingly, many of these counties serve as the settings for the films of the New Rural Cinema: for example, the recent ERS report specifically mentions the Mississippi Delta—where *Ballast* takes place—as well as the Native American reservations of South Dakota—the setting of *Songs My Brothers Taught Me* and *The Rider* (Chloé Zhao, 2017)—as areas with some of the most severe poverty rates in the country.

Furthermore, it is important to note in this context that counties in which deep poverty persists, such as the Mississippi Delta, "are not evenly distributed, but rather are geographically concentrated and disproportionately located in regions with above-average populations of racial minorities," particularly Native American and Black communities.[16] Overall, rural African Americans had "the highest incidence of poverty in 2019 (30.7 percent), while nonmetro American In-

14 An ERS article from the following year states: "The 2007–2009 recession and subsequent slow recovery have resulted in substantial increases in poverty, especially among children" (Tracey Farrigan, "Poverty and Deep Poverty Increasing in Rural America," *Amber Waves (ERS)* (March 4, 2014), https://www.ers.usda.gov/amber-waves/2014/march/poverty-and-deep-poverty-increasing-in-rural-america.).

15 Tracey Farrigan, "Rural Poverty and Well-Being," *ERS* (2021), https://www.ers.usda.gov/topics/rural-economy-population/rural-poverty-well-being/#howis.; ibid.

16 Ibid.: I will capitalize the word Black throughout this book when it refers to African Americans. I am doing this in order to distinguish the term from its use as a mere color and instead have it refer to the shared cultural identity of African Americans. *The New York Times*, which has recently adopted the same spelling, cite the US and Ghanaian sociologist W.E.B. du Bois in their editorial article, who once stated that "the use of a small letter for the name of twelve million Americans and two hundred million human beings [is] a personal insult." (W.E.B. Du Bois, quoted in Nancy Coleman, "Why We're Capitalizing Black," *The New York Times* (July 5, 2020), www.nytimes.com/2020/07/05/insider/capitalized-black.html.)

dians/Alaska Natives had the second highest rate (29.6 percent). The poverty rate for nonmetro Whites in 2019 was less than half as much (13.3 percent) of both of those other groups."[17] Thus, race remains a fundamental determining factor of poverty in the United States, which points towards enduring systemic racism and injustice. Black rural poverty can be traced back to plantation slavery and the "extraordinary power [. . .] whites had over Blacks [which] has maintained this inequality and long-term poverty," yet is only very rarely addressed in films surrounding present-day rurality.[18] A similar point can be made with regards to the intersection of poverty and gender. As Tickamyer points out "the greater representation of women householders with children among the poor" speaks for the aggravating influence of patriarchal structures on poverty such as "labor market and wage discrimination, gendered family roles that assign women major responsibility for [. . .] household and family reproduction, and lack of social support for these tasks."[19] This is reflected in the overall predominance of female characters in the films discussed here as well as in the New Rural Cinema at large, which foregrounds the pressures of performing care-work within an environment lacking a social safety net.

Finally, it seems crucial to question how a wealthy country in which over forty million people live in poverty or extreme poverty can display such dismissive attitudes towards the poor as compiled by Alston in his report. In her study on rural poverty, Cynthia Duncan delivers a concise summary of the popular and academic discourse surrounding poverty in the United States since the 1960s. She argues that the influential "culture of poverty" thesis developed by anthropologist Oscar Lewis in the 1960s remains a powerful tenet in current right-wing ideology and works against the progressive notion that structures and systems such as capitalism and racism perpetuate poverty, not poor people themselves. The thesis conveys that "the poor, discouraged by their own failures, do not teach their children the values they need to succeed," thus accounting for persistent poverty in certain regions.[20] Lewis' original intention was to shift the blame from the poor individual's personality towards the "slum community and family," as he put it, but instead

17 Farrigan, "Rural Poverty and Well-Being."

18 Cynthia Duncan, *Worlds Apart. Poverty and Politics in Rural America*. 2nd ed. (New Haven/ London: Yale UP, 2014), 234.

19 Ann R. Tickameyer, "Rural Poverty: Research and Policy for U.S. Families," in *Rural Families and Communities in the United States: Facing Challenges and Leveraging Opportunities* (National Symposium on Family Issues, 10), ed. Jennifer E. Glick, Susan M. McHale, and Valarie King (Cham, Switzerland: Springer Nature, 2020), 11.

20 Duncan, *Worlds Apart*, 234.

he created one of the most harmful justifications against welfare intervention.[21] Duncan argues that "the culture-of-poverty thesis became part of a victim-blaming analysis that attributed poverty's persistence to the poor's cultural values. For some conservative social theorists and policymakers [. . .] the obvious implication is that no policy will reduce poverty."[22] Thereby, poverty becomes naturalized, a simple fact of life, unchangeable by government decisions. Rural poverty in particular is very easily naturalized because of its confusion with romanticized ideas of supposedly "simple" life in the picturesque countryside—it is incorporated into the scenic landscape.

2 A "passively rotting mass"? Class and poverty under neoliberalism

Poverty in the United States is influenced by a myriad of demographic factors such as race, gender, marital status, age, ability, and many more. Therefore, generalizing statements concerning the sources of poverty are difficult to make. Considering once again that according to the most recent data, "all of the extreme poverty counties were in rural America," it seems reasonable to follow Tickamyer's argument that "a spatial perspective is useful in locating sources of poverty."[23] Furthermore, she claims that while the rural poor have come to share many characteristics with the urban poor since the 1960s—for example "increasing minority share, weak labor force attachment, nonmarital births [. . .] female-headed households—[. . .] the larger underlying causes combine to create a profile for rural poverty dissimilar to its urban counterparts."[24] She goes on to argue that some of these underlying factors include "the spatial clustering of poor places, the historical legacies of these places and their residents, the economic structure and conditions of the rural U.S., particularly deindustrialization, and the sources and impacts of social welfare policies for the rural poor."[25] As we will see, most of these conditions are visible in the New Rural Cinema.

Duncan identifies the structural causes for some of these factors in "the economic restructuring that has enveloped the nation since the late 1970s."[26] While

21 Oscar Lewis, "The Culture of Poverty," *Scientific American* 215 (1966), 19.

22 Duncan, *Worlds Apart*, 235.

23 Tracey Farrigan, "Extreme Poverty Counties Found Solely in Rural Areas in 2018"; Tickameyer, "Rural Poverty: Research and Policy for U.S. Families," 11.

24 Ibid., 13.

25 Ibid.

26 Duncan, *Worlds Apart*, 234.

never using the term in her analysis, she is referring to the *neoliberal* deregulation of industries and labor, as well as the termination of Keynesian social welfare politics in response to slowed-down growth rates and high inflation rates at the end of the 1970s. The term “neoliberalism” will be used throughout this book in the sense of its complex double-meaning, succinctly framed by Wendy Brown: “it names a historically specific economic and political reaction against Keynesianism and democratic socialism, as well as a more generalized practice of ‘economizing’ spheres and activities heretofore governed by other tables of value.”[27] These developments can be understood as a continuation of established capitalist principles of accumulation. The geographer David Harvey argues in a 2007 article:

> If the main effect of neoliberalism has been redistributive rather than generative, then ways had to be found to transfer assets and channel wealth and income either from the mass of the population toward the upper classes or from vulnerable to richer countries. I have [. . .] provided an account of these processes under the rubric of accumulation by dispossession. By this, I mean the continuation and proliferation of accretion practices that Marx had designated as “primitive” or “original” during the rise of capitalism.[28]

His following list of these practices include the “commodification and privatization of land,” “suppression of rights to the commons” as well as “colonial, neocolonial, and imperial processes of appropriation of assets.”[29] We will see how these specific practices are both explicitly and implicitly visible in the landscapes of the films at hand. It is thus important to stress here that I use term neoliberalism in this book to refer to a continuation of earlier strategies of dispossession identified by Marxist analyses.

The implementation of neoliberal policies in the United States is mostly identified with President Ronald Reagan, who took office in 1981. Reagan began his tenure with the introduction of laws (later dubbed “Reaganomics”) such as OBRA (Omnibus Budget Reconciliation Project), which dramatically reduced welfare spending, and ERTA (Economic Recovery Tax Act), which offered some of the largest tax breaks for wealthy Americans in the country’s history. Writing at the time, Thomas Edsall claimed that Reagan’s economic policies constituted “an across-the-board drive to reduce the scope and content of federal regulation of industry, the environment, the workplace, healthcare, and the relationship between buyer and

27 Wendy Brown, *Undoing the Demos. Neoliberalism’s Stealth Revolution* (New York: Zone Books, 2015), 21.

28 David Harvey, “Neoliberalism as Creative Destruction,” *The Annals of the American Academy of Political and Social Science* 610 (2007), 34.

29 Ibid., 34–35.

seller."[30] While rural poverty certainly existed before this period in the United States, Reagan's presidency can be seen as the point of origin of many of the conditions and developments seen in rural America today. Anthropologist Marc Edelman argues in an article for *Jacobin* magazine that "since the turn to [. . .] free-market policies in the 1980s, American capitalism has systemically underdeveloped rural and small-town regions of the United States."[31] I want to specifically focus here on how neoliberal capitalism has affected the landscape of rural America as it appears on screen in the New Rural Cinema.

Firstly, the deindustrialization of rural America and the accompanying decline of "extractive and goods-producing jobs" is perhaps the most obvious factor shaping the landscapes of the New Rural Cinema.[32] As argued in Chapter Three, this is by no means the first cycle of films to address this development—in fact, the rural horror cycle of the 1970s first indexed the violence and paranoia emerging from the closing of factories and mines without any contingency plans for the laid-off workers. Concrete references to such practices are rare in the New Rural Cinema—*Nomadland* is a notable exception as it takes the gradual disappearance of an entire town build around a sheetrock factory as the explicit starting point of its narrative. The four films discussed in this book certainly do not address the closure of manufacturing industries directly—yet their landscapes, often strewn with ruined buildings, rusted metal parts, and abandoned cars, are clearly indicative of this ongoing process. Edelman argues that "the deindustrialization of the United States reached a crescendo after the 2008 crash," and that after 2008, "non-metro areas outpaced the rest of the country in industrial job losses, with a 35 percent drop in manufacturing employment."[33] Compared to urban regions, Tickamyer claims, rural communities' economies "are less diversified in employment options, and a plant closing or layoff will be devastating to both the community and its residents," resulting in joblessness and rural flight.[34] One of the main reasons behind this devastating development is, as has been widely argued, neoliberal financialization.

The term describes the process "whereby finance capital and financial institutions account for a greater share of all economic activity," diverting money

30 Thomas Edsall, *The New Politics of Inequality* (London/New York: Norton, 1985), 128.

31 Marc Edelman, "How Capitalism Underdeveloped Rural America," *Jacobin* (January 26, 2020), https://jacobinmag.com/2020/01/capitalism-underdeveloped-rural-america-trump-white-working-class.

32 Duncan, *Worlds Apart*, 234.

33 Ibid.

34 Tickameyer, "Rural Poverty: Research and Policy for U.S. Families," 10.

away from productive economy activity.[35] Edelman further describes financialization as "the ownership of assets not for what they might produce but for how they might be stripped to generate shareholder value" as well as "an opaque process" taking place "far away from the affected communities."[36] While this is true, Tickamyer and Wornell add that "many remote and persistently poor places are not left behind by the modern world. Rather, *they are poor precisely because they are part of the world capitalist system.*"[37] This is a crucial point because it underlines how the narratives of the New Rural Cinema, while not directly concerned with global processes such as deindustrialization or financialization, nevertheless take place in environments that are shaped by these neoliberal market trends. As such, they are indicative of Brenner and Theodore's aforementioned concept of "actually existing neoliberalism," meaning that they demonstrate how "each round of capitalist development is associated with a distinctive, historically specific geographical landscape in which some places [and] territories [. . .] are systematically privileged over and against others as sites for capital accumulation."[38]

A second aspect that is even more directly visible in the films at hand, is the relative absence of social welfare and infrastructure. A core tenet of neoliberal ideology is, as Carolyn Gallaher summarizes, "to redirect state subsidies from broad public programs (e.g., food stamps for the poor [. . .]) to private enterprises. [. . .] Neoliberals believe state spending on social needs is inefficient."[39] Under these conditions, as Tickamyer points out, "all poor people are subject to serious material deprivation, [. . .] [yet] the experiences, causes, and consequences may vary by location" insofar as the experience of poverty in rural America today is a specifically isolated one.[40] She goes on to argue that some of the main aggravating circumstances in rural poverty today result from "the limited or even total lack of availability of public and social services."[41] Examples of these conditions are plentiful and are depicted in a variety of ways in the four films discussed here and in the cycle at large. For instance, the absence of adequate education is a central narrative element in several of the films. Tickamyer argues that rural "schools are often inadequate in facilities and curricula" which chimes with the depiction

35 Alisdair Rogers, Noel Castree and Rob Kitchin, *Dictionary of Human Geography* (Oxford: Oxford UP, 2013) doi: 10.1093/acref/9780199599868.001.0001.

36 Edelman, "How Capitalism Underdeveloped Rural America."

37 Tickameyer and Wornell, "How to Explain Poverty?", 93. Emphasis added.

38 Brenner and Theodore, "Cities," 355.

39 Carolyn Gallaher, "Anti-Statism," in *Key Concepts in Political Geography*, ed. Carolyn Gallaher (London/Los Angeles: Sage, 2009), 263–264.

40 Tickameyer, "Rural Poverty: Research and Policy for U.S. Families," 10.

41 Ibid.

of deficient schools in *Winter's Bone* and *Ballast*.[42] The same goes for institutions such as libraries, care facilities, hospitals, post offices, and many other infrastructural elements which either do not appear in the New Rural Cinema's environments at all or are depicted as deeply dysfunctional.

This infrastructural decline is closely linked to neoliberal austerity politics. Edelman points out how "in recent decades, federal and state governments have slashed funding for social services" in rural areas.[43] He provides the striking example of "rural hospital closures [which] doubled between 2011–12 and 2013–14."[44] The New Rural Cinema presents its viewers with environments in which bare survival is at stake because the experiences of homelessness, illness, hunger, and explosive violence are not, or insufficiently mitigated by any of the State's institutions. This chimes with Wendy Brown's identification of neoliberalism as "an order of normative reason that [. . .] takes shape as a governing rationality extending [. . .] economic values [. . .] to every dimension of human life."[45] Brown argues that, as these free-market values and practices are extended to all human endeavors, subjects under neoliberal capitalism inevitably become "human capital," as she puts it, "tasked with being responsible for ourselves in a competitive world of other human capitals."[46] At the same time, however, "we have no guarantee of security, protection or even survival. [. . .] This jeopardy reaches down to minimum needs for food and shelter insofar as social-security programs of all kinds have been dismantled by neoliberalism."[47] While this is a global trend, neoliberal ideology in the United States is exacerbated, Brown claims, by its amalgamation with "a strange brew of long-established antistatism" which stokes rejection of government support even among those most gravely affected by its absence.[48]

How does this notion of human capital figure the experiences of poverty depicted in the New Rural Cinema as experiences of class? It is difficult to conceive of these films as "working-class-films" because traditional forms of labor are generally absent from their narratives. The rural protagonists either scarcely live off the land in ways that markedly do not evoke romanticized notions of pastoral life, or they are dependent on their neighbors' and communities' kindness and solidarity. A small minority of films focus on traditional wage labor or farming

42 Ibid.
43 Edelman, "How Capitalism Underdeveloped Rural America."
44 Ibid.
45 Brown, *Undoing the Demos*, 30.
46 Ibid., 37.
47 Ibid.
48 Ibid, 20.

(*Shotgun Stories, Frozen River, Undertow*) and only a slightly larger number follows itinerant protagonists in precarious employment (*Wendy and Lucy, Joe, Nomadland*). From this perspective, they differ from contemporary urban- or suburban-centered films which often explicitly foreground what Guy Standing has termed "the precariat."[49] Standing defines the precariat as a "class-in-the-making" in which he locates vocations such as call center workers and fast-food service employees that lack a clear class identity and are often not represented by trade unions.[50] Aside from *Ballast*'s Marlee, who works in a precarious cleaning job at the outset of the film's narrative, none of the protagonists of the four case studies would even fall into this new class category and its labor-based notion of precarity: Standing clearly distinguishes the precariat from the even lower ranks of, as he puts it, the "unemployed [. . .] and [the] [. . .] socially ill misfits living off the dregs of society."[51] Indeed, the protagonists of the New Rural Cinema mostly fall into the category of the *Lumpenproletariat* which Marx and Engels described as a "passively rotting mass [. . .]. Its conditions of life prepare it far more for the part of a bribed tool of reactionary intrigue [than for proletarian revolution]."[52] Seen as disorganized, unpredictable, and lacking class-consciousness, the non-working poor have no place in Marxist class struggle. If anything, they are even seen as a threat to organized labor in that they may constitute the "industrial reserve army" for capital, meaning cheap labor forces that can be "drafted" in case of a strike or similar industrial action.[53]

The political scientist Clyde Barrow has recently reaffirmed the significance of the concept *Lumpenproletariat* specifically for the poor in the United States. He claims that the term was abandoned in left-wing discourses due to its classist undertones around the 1980s, paradoxically at the time when deindustrialization and "the global spread of neoliberalism [. . .] [in] capitalist economies were replacing proletarians with *lumpenproletarians* in unprecedented numbers."[54] He

49 Recent examples of such films include *Sorry We Missed You* (2019), director Ken Loach's portrait of a British delivery driver and his family, and, in the US, *The Florida Project* (2017), an exploration of precarious work and everyday life in the impoverished Florida suburbs surrounding the Disney World theme park. Furthermore, the surrealist US-satire *Sorry to Bother You* (2018) follows a Black call-centre worker who becomes a success after he pretends to be white on the phone.

50 Guy Standing, *The Precariat: The New Dangerous Class* (London: Bloomsbury Academic, 2016), 8.

51 Ibid.

52 Karl Marx and Friedrich Engels, *The Communist Manifesto*, trans. L.M. Findlay (Minneapolis, MN: First Avenue Editions, 2018), 13.

53 Karl Marx, *Capital Volume 1*, trans. Ben Fowkes (London: Penguin Books, 1990), 797.

54 Clyde Barrow, *The Dangerous Class. The Concept of the Lumpenproletariat* (Ann Arbor: University of Michigan Press, 2020), 10.

further argues that the debate "has attained renewed salience with the election of [. . .] Donald Trump and the rise of right-wing populist movements throughout the world, which are often seen as [. . .] [drawing support from] a burgeoning lumpenproletariat."[55] His analysis reveals that the demonization of these "deindustrialized Americans" by both conservative and liberal media figures dismissively positions them as "not the industrial working class of the 1950s and 1960s, but [as] something lower, meaner, cruder, and less stable—both economically and mentally—as their predecessors."[56] Barrow challenges this discourse by offering a pessimistic re-reading of Marx that points "to a scenario where the proletariat is actually destined to decay into an ever-burgeoning lumpenproletariat [. . .] This post-industrial capitalist development may pose insurmountable obstacles to a theory of revolutionary agency."[57] Brown makes a similar point when she argues that "when everything is capital, labor disappears as a category, as does its collective form, class, taking with it the analytic basis for alienation, exploitation, and association among laborers."[58] In a neoliberal world, in which experience of work is atomized and every individual is solely responsible for their own well-being, the concept of class does not offer any hope for resistant agency to the poor.

Therefore, this book focuses on poverty as a visible outcome of neoliberal marginalization or, as Harvey puts it, on "how capitalism produces poverty."[59] Seen from this perspective, the term "poverty" serves to describe the material outcome of structural dispossession and deprivation under capitalism in relation to people and, crucially, *place*. Structural explanations of poverty enable discussions of class as well as gender and race because they "identify systems of structured social inequality such as institutional racism, gender discrimination, patriarchy, and a number of other structures of domination and subordination determined by economic position."[60] These stratification systems, as Tickamyer and Wornell highlight, "vary by location" and their spatial analysis is therefore helpful in locating the reasons for rural poverty—and how they are mediated in the construction of the filmic landscape.[61]

The films of the New Rural Cinema emerge as fitting representations of the instability and spatial inequality that is distinctive of class relations under neolib-

55 Ibid., 2.
56 Ibid., 14.
57 Ibid.
58 Brown, *Undoing the Demos*, 38.
59 David Harvey, *A Companion to Marx's Capital* (New York: Verso, 2018), 274.
60 Tickameyer and Wornell, "How to Explain Poverty?", 90.
61 Ibid., 91.

eralism. They suggest that their impoverished protagonists are indicative of a growing, heterogenous US underclass which forms a significant social factor in the contemporary United States. Thereby, they complicate Barrow's pessimistic suggestion of the impossibility of the poor's "revolutionary agency" under neoliberal capitalism. The films identify a perhaps not revolutionary, but certainly collective, solidary agency in the interactive relation between marginalized rural inhabitants and their environments. The rural communities depicted in these films are not characterized by labor union struggles as featured in US films such as *Norma Rae* (Martin Ritt, 1980) or *North Country* (Niki Caro, 2005) yet are (to varying degrees) endowed with the potential of resistance and change. Furthermore, films like *Ballast, Beasts of the Southern Wild, Songs My Brothers Taught Me,* and *Dayveon* expand the limiting notion of the "disintegration of the *white* working class" which dominates the discourse surrounding Trump's election and his voter base by explicitly foregrounding the intersection of class and race in rural America.[62]

3 Rural poverty in US (indie) cinema

Mainstream US films generally tend to avoid overt illustrations of working-class life, let alone poverty. In his study of depictions of poverty and homelessness in US cinema, Stephen Pimpare concludes that "American film has a blind spot when it comes to poor and homeless people" since there are "relatively few films that take poverty or homelessness as their subject."[63] Claire Perkins also identifies this tendency and describes it as "an ideological effect of the myth of America as a classless society, where everyone is perceived to be pursuing a version of the American Dream in a universal—if multifaceted—middle class."[64] When mainstream films do engage with experiences of poverty, they usually illustrate successful attempts at escaping these conditions. One of the most fundamental cinematic fables of US cinema, for example, is the so-called "Horatio Alger myth," a narrative archetype that follows a "simple" man or woman who overcomes his or her unprivileged upbringing by working hard, achieving economic success,

62 Barrow, *The Dangerous Class*, 12. Emphasis added.

63 Stephen Pimpare, *Ghettos, Tramps, and Welfare Queens. Down and Out on the Silver Screen* (New York: Oxford UP, 2017), 331; ibid., 333.

64 Claire Perkins, "Life During Wartime: Emotionalism, Capitalist Realism, and Middle-Class Indie Identity," in *A Companion to American Indie Film*, ed. Geoff King. Oxford: Wiley-Blackwell, 2017, 351.

and thus bettering his or her social standing.[65] While such a narrative may include the adversity of a greedy capitalist elite, such a critique is usually aimed at a few "bad apples," not at the capitalist class system as such. As Perkins puts it, the desire of the hero or heroine "to transcend working-class life suggest[s] acute dissatisfaction with the limitations that capitalism imposes, but is expressed in individualist terms that tend to reinforce the legitimating ideology of the class system."[66] Classic examples of this narrative tradition can be found in the films of director Frank Capra; a more recent example is the film *Joy* (David O. Russell, 2015) which adapts the real-life "rags-to-riches" tale of self-made multimillionaire Joy Mangano (played, interestingly, by Jennifer Lawrence who portrays Ree in *Winter's Bone*).

Pimpare therefore suggests to describe this specific perspective of US cinema as "the propertied gaze," meaning that "the viewer is never assumed to be poor or homeless, and films are never meant for them, even when they are ostensibly about them."[67] He continues by arguing that "the cinematic language used to describe poor and homeless people is constrained [. . .] because the people making movies are trying to appeal to a broad audience, one with the time and money required to invest in a movie."[68] US cinema history is therefore not abundant with films exploring poverty in a way that eschews the tendency towards the Horatio Alger myth or attempting to take the conditions of poor people seriously. This is especially true for *rural* poverty since, as Pimpare points out, "films about poverty set in New York and other big cities exist radically out of proportion to the actual poverty we find there."[69] Pimpare then goes on to offer brief synopses and analyses of several films which, in his opinion, do genuinely acknowledge rural poverty and its causes—including several films identified as belonging to the New Rural Cinema in this book, yet markedly leaving out the rural horror cycles of both the 1970s and 2000s.

Pimpare's central example is one of the most famous depictions of poverty in US film history: John Ford's 1940 adaptation of John Steinbeck's novel *The Grapes of Wrath*. Both novel and film revolve around the hardship of the Joad family, a Midwest farming family, who are evicted from their land during the Great De-

65 The term refers to Horatio Alger Jr. (1832–1899), a US American children's author whose popular novels about impoverished boys overcoming their dire situation through virtuous behavior provided a template for the "rags-to-riches" narrative structure central to the ideology of meritocratic capitalism.

66 Ibid., 350.

67 Pimpare, *Ghettos, Tramps, and Welfare Queens*, 331.

68 Ibid.

69 Ibid., 155.

pression by the deed holding bank. They consequently begin a strenuous journey towards California, where they hope for a better future that does not materialize. While the film arguably disarmed Steinbeck's anti-capitalist critique of banks and agricultural companies and turned its poor protagonists into saint-like figures, its bleak depiction of poverty and marginalization of migrant workers still stands in harsh contrast to much of the cinematic output of the 1930s Hollywood studio system. Appearing at a time when the US economy had just overcome the shock of Depression a decade earlier, as Peter Stead points out, *The Grapes of Wrath* "chose rural America [. . .] as a symbol of what had gone wrong."[70] It developed a cinematic aesthetic of poverty associated with waste and dust that is closely related to the landscapes this book is concerned with.

The same can be said for the so-called New Hollywood period of the 1970s and early 1980s. After the end of the studio system, young directors influenced by European film movements and the US counterculture were able to produce, as Derek Nystrom describes, "narratively, visually, and politically adventurous films," which were released to mainstream audiences.[71] In his study, Nystrom identifies this cinematic period as a time in which Hollywood became more interested in working-class culture and connects this to the "the worldwide economic slump that began in 1973," and the early onset of neoliberal policies. He argues that "U.S. businesses responded to the slump [. . .] by working together to thwart pro-labor legislation while promoting corporate-friendly changes in tax, regulatory, and antitrust law."[72] His main argument is that many of the working-class-films of the New Hollywood era—for example *Five Easy Pieces* (Bob Rafelson, 1970), *Walking Tall* (Phil Karlson, 1973), and *Deliverance* (John Boorman, 1972)—can be understood as displaced representations of middle-class anxiety in response to these developments. He thus claims that "American films of the 1970s—produced in the midst of profound shifts in the national political and economic terrain, and during a period of aesthetic and industrial change in Hollywood—often testify to a vivid sense of class difference not seen since the 1930s."[73]

Only a few, not particularly prominent, films of the 1980s addressed the impact of Reaganomics on deindustrialization and the decline of farming in rural America. Pimpare mentions two films released in 1984—*Country* (Richard Pearce) and *The River* (Mark Rydell)—which focused on the contemporary crisis of agriculture and

70 Peter Stead, *Film and the Working Class: The Feature Film in British and American Society* (London: Routledge, 1989), 95.

71 Derek Nystrom, *Hard Hats, Rednecks, and Macho Men: Class in 1970s American Cinema* (Oxford: Oxford UP, 2009), 3; ibid., 4.

72 Ibid.

73 Ibid., 5.

exhibited a landscape iconography of "closed factories, abandoned buildings and [. . .] teetering shacks."[74] Notably, these films, as well as all other films mentioned in this section so far, were either produced or at least distributed by major Hollywood studios or their offshoots. This seems to change from the 1990s onwards, if we take Pimpare's comprehensive list of films on rural poverty as orientation. The list excludes several prominent earlier films, however, which were produced outside of the studio system and fall into a category of regional independent films made before the consolidation of the indie movement in the mid- to late eighties. These include *Spring Night, Summer Night* (Joseph L. Anderson, 1967), *Northern Lights* (John Hanson and Rob Nilsson, 1978) and *Heartland* (Richard Pearce, 1979).[75]

These films can be understood as more direct predecessors of the indie films of the New Rural Cinema: in addition to their industrial position outside of the studio system, they similarly use local non-professional actors, largely eschew spectacular, scenic landscape shots, and focus on prosaic everyday interactivity between impoverished rural inhabitants and their environment. In a detailed discussion of *Heartland* and the phenomenon of regional independent film production, Cynthia Baron and Yannis Tzioumakis argue that the film can be understood as "one of the paradigmatic films that kick-started [. . .] what is widely recognized as contemporary American independent cinema."[76] It heralded the end of the dispersed appearance of independent feature films and the beginning of "a more formal organization of the independent film sector" in the mid-eighties which came to be accepted as an artistic register offering "naturalistic low-key stories normally shunned by Hollywood cinema."[77]

It is perhaps unsurprising, then, that from the 1990s, rural poverty seems to be a topic mostly addressed in US indie films. Pimpare mentions films such as *Gummo* (Harmony Korine, 1997), *George Washington, Frozen River, Ballast, Winter's Bone, Wendy and Lucy*, and the documentary *Rich Hill* (Andrew Droz Palermo and Tracy Droz Tragos, 2014), all of which fall into the category of indie. This category is far from stable, however. Geoff King's definition of the term crucially distinguishes between "indie" and "independent" cinema. The central question that arises here is whether indie cinema is better equipped than Hollywood

74 Ibid., 164.

75 One could further mention prominent documentaries of the time such as *Harlan County, USA* (Barbara Kopple, 1976) as potential influences.

76 Cynthia Baron and Yannis Tzioumakis, *Acting Indie. Industry, Aesthetics, and Performance* (London: Palgrave Macmillan, 2020), 133.

77 Ibid.

films to address the issue of rural poverty in a way that enables a radical critique of its determining factors—and, thus, of neoliberal capitalism.

King begins his definition of indie with an *ex negativo* argument; he claims that "indie is not Hollywood [. . .] But neither is it the avant-garde or the experimental, or the most exploitation oriented of non-Hollywood American film. It is not 'independent,' either, in the broader use of this important cognate term."[78] While the terms "independent" and "indie" have often been used conterminously, there is a distinction to be made. King rejects the idea, however, that this is a distinction of quality: the diminutive "indie" does *not* suggest, in his opinion, "something that claims some of the virtues of independence while having some attachment to Hollywood institutions or values, or a more general sense of softening [. . .] or 'selling out' certain values and principles associated with independence."[79] Instead, he defines indie as a mode of film-making that is linked to a specific period of U.S. film history. He gives the following definition:

> A particular range of non-Hollywood cinema that came to prominence, crystallized, and achieved a particular form of institutionalization in the period from approximately the mid- to late 1980s into the 1990s, when it grew significantly to the point at which some of the issues of co-optation cited above were raised.[80]

The vast majority of films of the New Rural Cinema fall into this particular cinematic tradition in terms of their mode of production, distribution, and marketization. What are the key features, however, that might be applied to decide whether or not a film belongs to this mode or not? King suggests a form of analysis that is well suited for the purposes of this book:

> [Such an analysis] entails the particular *textual* qualities of the works involved, individually or collectively. Independence might also be defined, that is, by the subject matter of films, including how they tackle particular sociocultural issues, and thus how they are implicitly positioned in a political—ideological sense.[81]

To identify typical textual features of indie films is, however, not entirely unproblematic. While it is true, as Tzioumakis argues, that indie films usually "depart from the conventions that characterize mainstream filmmaking" in some narrative, visual, or ideological form, "it is also clear that several aspects of the classical narrative and style remain in place."[82] He continues: "This means that in terms of

78 Geoff King, "Introduction: What Indie Isn't . . . Mapping the Indie Field," in *A Companion to American Indie Film*, ed. Geoff King (Chichester: Wiley & Sons, 2014), 1.

79 Ibid., 2.

80 Ibid.

81 Ibid.

82 Yannis Tzioumakis, *American Independent Cinema* (Edinburgh: Edinburgh UP, 2017), 8.

aesthetics, independent films retain a certain grounding on mainstream traditions, the extent of which varies from film to film."[83] Nevertheless, the New Rural Cinema can be identified as assuming a certain "indie style"; key narrative and stylistic elements include the refusal of clear-cut happy endings, sparse dialogue, slow pace, casting of non-professional actors, and a naturalistic visual style.

Of course, this focus on textual qualities does not mean that industrial features do not matter at all. King argues:

> The limits that are set on the approaches available to films in sociocultural or formal terms remain in general terms closely related to the industrial dimension. [. . .] scope for radical departure is usually closely tied to an industrial position at a distance from the more commercial mainstream, as manifested by either Hollywood or the more commercially oriented parts of the indie sector.[84]

While this renders the category indie as ambiguous and hard to pin down, it offers the possibility of identifying a certain formal and textual "radicalism," meaning in this case a departure from US mainstream cinema's aesthetic, narrative, or political conventions, as the defining component of indie cinema.

King's definition of indie is useful for this book because it suggests that the radically different perspective on landscape and poverty the New Rural Cinema displays is partly possible due to the films' indie status. Indeed, King has directly commented on the initial wave of the New Rural Cinema in his book *Indie 2.0* (2014), which addresses Kelly Reichardt's films, *Frozen River*, *Winter's Bone*, and *Ballast* and argues for their alignment with "classic" indie values in terms of both their themes and production. He writes:

> On release, these films seemed timely in their own ways, often depicting struggle of life on the social margins, a dimension that seemed especially resonant for those which opened during the deep recession of the late 2000s. In many respects, however the films [. . .] emerging in this period marked a strong vein of continuity with the indie cinema of the 1980s and early 1990s, in their maintenance of something like the classic independent recipe of low-resource production and traditional smaller-scale release beyond the orbit of the studio specialty divisions.[85]

Furthermore, he mentions that these films' stylistic heritage is based in "the realm of international art cinema, ranging from earlier reference points such as Italian neo-realism [. . .] to more contemporary figures."[86]

---

83 Ibid.

84 King, "Introduction," 4.

85 Geoff King, *Indie 2.0: Change and Continuity in Contemporary American Indie Film* (London: IB Tauris, 2014), 170.

86 King, *Indie 2.0*, 170.

Returning to Pimpare's list of films and the previous observation that from the early 1990s onward—which, according to King, signals the beginning of the indie movement as he understands it—rural poverty seems to be a topic largely limited to the indie realm, one can make the assumption that US indie cinema seems indeed to be the locus in which these issues can be best addressed. Sherry B. Ortner supports this notion in her book *Not Hollywood. Independent Film at the Twilight of the American Dream* (2013). She argues that "the independent film movement that emerged in the late 1980s represented a critical cultural movement, an attempt to critique the dominant culture (represented by 'Hollywood') through their films."[87] She suggests a connection of the emergence of this movement to the economic crisis of the 1970s and the neoliberal policies passed by the Reagan administration: "With the downturn of the economy starting in the 1970s, and registering strongly by the late 1980s, people could no longer take the American Dream for granted."[88] The loss of trust in the upward mobility promised by the American Dream was part of what Ortner describes as "major transformations in the class structure" of American society.[89]

More than just mere mediations of difficult economic times, however, Ortner argues that "within the world of [. . .] independent film [. . .] every act of representation is at the same time meant to be a challenge to viewers—to think differently, to feel differently, and even [. . .] to get off our bottoms and act back on the real world."[90] From this perspective, indie cinema becomes a vital form of cultural critique directed at the neoliberal restructuring of society that even has the potential to inspire and affect real-world change. Ortner concludes:

> When the class structure starts moving in any major way, as it has been doing since the late 1970s, the impact is enormous for everyone. Independent film is one of the sites in which these seismic shifts have registered, often as forms of violence, which they are. And independent film is one of the sites in which these shifts have been—again often violently—exposed for critique and challenge.[91]

While I agree with Ortner that indie cinema can enable such forms of critique, it is important to also qualify its independence from Hollywood and to stress that its potential challenge to neoliberal politics is not inherently given. Its effectiveness is bound to funding and production practices as well as textual and stylistic choices.

---

87 Sherry B. Ortner, *Not Hollywood. Independent Film at the Twilight of the American Dream* (Durham/London: Duke University Press, 2013), 190.

88 Ibid., 16.

89 Ibid., 261.

90 Ibid., 260.

91 Ibid., 264.

Kevan Feshami approaches the issue of indie's political value from such a more sceptical perspective and specifically complicates both notions of 'independent' cinema mentioned here, namely a supposed industrial, and textual independence. He argues:

> Highlighting US independent cinema's freedom, even in a relative sense, from the commercial intentions of the major studios overlooks the fact that the majority of films designated as independent are nevertheless commodities and, as such, are influenced by the commercial pressures of our capitalist mode of production.[92]

Undoubtedly, none of the films discussed in this book are produced outside of capitalist mode of film production. In fact, several of them turned out to be financial success stories: *Winter's Bone*, as the trade publication IndieWire reported in 2010, "has gone on to claim the title as arguably the runaway indie success of the year, earning $6 million and counting at the box office"[93] with a budget of only 2 million dollars; *Beasts of the Southern Wild*, according to the online viewing figure database *The Numbers*, with an even lower budget of (estimated) 1.5 million dollars made 12 million in the US alone.[94] I certainly agree with Feshami when he posits that "just as with all other facets of life, independent cinema is not autonomous in relation to the determinations of capitalism."[95]

However, it is worth noting that there is nevertheless a substantial amount of industrial independence to be observed throughout the New Rural Cinema until the gradual absorption of its themes into films positioned closer to the mainstream which will be discussed in this book's conclusion. Two aspects are worth stressing in particular: firstly, most of the New Rural Cinema's films were produced outside of the direct influence of a major studio and emerged from a status of complete "creative control" on the filmmakers' part; secondly, many associated filmmakers also took explicit influence on the distribution of their films in order to specifically ensure that the films not only reached a typical urban, middle-class "indie audience," but rural areas as well. *Ballast* is a particularly telling example of the latter characteristic. After winning two awards with the film at the 2008 Sundance film festival, director Lance Hammer backed out of "a post-Sundance

---

92 Kevan Feshami, "US Independent Cinema and the Capitalist Mode of Production: Complicating Discourses of Independence and Oppositionality," in *Contemporary Cinema and Neoliberal Ideology*, ed. Eva Mazierska and Lars Kristensen (London: Routledge, 2018), 42.

93 *IndieWire*, "Toolkit Case Study: How Indie Hit Winter's Bone Came to Be." (November 4, 2010), https://www.indiewire.com/2010/11/toolkit-case-study-how-indie-hit-winters-bone-came-to-be-244485.

94 *The Numbers*, "Beasts of the Southern Wild." https://www.the-numbers.com/movie/Beasts-of-the-Southern-Wild#tab=summary.

95 Feshami, "US Independent Cinema," 51.

deal with IFC Films for the distribution of *Ballast*" and instead decided to release the film using his own money, without the backing of a major distributor.[96]

Feshami's second point relates to "how some of the most celebrated aspects of [independent cinema's] discourse actually reinforce a key narrative of the neoliberal worldview."[97] Feshami argues that the romantic notion of the autonomous indie auteur who does not have to bow to the pressures of the system falls into line with one of the core tenets of neoliberal ideology—individualism. He continues: "Lost in this equation are the interdependence and mutual constitution of human beings as they cooperate in the making and living of life."[98] Strikingly, this assertion serves well to describe exactly the approach to rural landscape that is so distinctive in the indie films discussed in this book. They foreground interdependence, solidarity, and interaction with the environment on both a narrative and a formal level, in order to challenge individualism and atomization as key symptoms of neoliberal ideology and policies.

In addition, most of the films of the New Rural Cinema have been produced in close cooperation with the local population, incorporating both local non-professional actors in major and minor roles as well as local crew members. They constitute collective efforts in which—to varying degrees—the cast and crew had major input. For *Songs My Brothers Taught Me*, Chloé Zhao spent several months on the Pine Ridge Indian Reservation in southwestern South Dakota and deployed an "experimental, collaborative writing approach that drew heavily on the lives and personalities of the [Lakota Sioux] cast members."[99] In a recent interview on the occasion of *George Washington*'s 20th anniversary, David Gordon Green described the close interaction with the local community during the shoot.[100] *Ballast* is "derived from two months of on-set rehearsals and improvisations with the [non-professional] leads."[101] Producer Nina Parikh elaborated on the process in an interview explaining that the director Lance Hammer "didn't want to pretend he came up with the right words. He developed the scenarios [. . .] but the actors

96 Nelson, Rob, "Down in the Delta," *Film Comment* 44.5 (2008), 41.

97 Ibid.

98 Ibid., 52.

99 Lee Purvey, "Navigating Fact and Fiction: Chloé Zhao on Songs My Brothers Taught Me," *Walker Art Center Magazine* (March 1, 2016), https://walkerart.org/magazine/navigating-fact-and-fiction-Chloé-zhao-on-songs-my-brothers-taught-me.

100 Sam Spence, "David Gordon Green talks history of *George Washington*, 20 years later," *Charleston City Paper* (November 18, 2020), https://charlestoncitypaper.com/2020/11/18/david-gordon-green-talks-history-of-george-washington-20-years-later.

101 Nelson, "Down in the Delta," 41.

really found the words to convey the ideas."[102] Examples like these can be found in relation to most films of the New Rural Cinema.

Secondly, the films do not fit in with the individualist celebration of Indie auteur filmmakers that Feshami mentions for several distinct reasons. For example, *Beasts of the Southern Wild*, while directed by Benh Zeitlin, was developed by his New Orleans-based independent filmmaker's collective, Court 13. Only after its Sundance premiere was it acquired by the major studio Fox. Notably, the film had its first official premiere in Montegut, Louisiana, a town near the film's main setting on the Isle de Jean Charles mainly in front of, as Andrew Lapin reported for IndieWire, "locals who, in some way or another, became closely, fundamentally tied to the production."[103] *Ballast's* director Lance Hammer functions even less than Zeitlin as a representative of individualist auteur culture: *Ballast* remains at the time of writing his only film as a director. In fact, he seems to have withdrawn from the film industry altogether. Debra Granik has acquired some acclaim for her three critically celebrated features to date, yet arguably still remains a figure on the margins of US indie cinema.

The New Rural Cinema in various ways contradicts Feshami's skepticism towards indie culture as a site of alternative filmmaking. In his conclusion, Feshami asserts: "If that filmmaking we deem independent [. . .] is to realize an oppositional potential, then a rejection of this [individualist] outlook in favor of an oppositional collectivity is a necessity."[104] These films meet this criterion to different degrees from an industrial perspective, and as will become clear, centrally challenge the notion of individualism on a textual level as well. While this obviously does not presuppose their effectiveness in criticizing the effects of neoliberal capitalism, it clearly positions them within King's assumption of indie as a textual quality, meaning the way in which films "tackle particular sociocultural issues, and thus how they are implicitly positioned in a political-ideological sense."[105] This is first and foremost linked to their unique construction and representation of landscape, the analysis of which requires an understanding of landscape that arises from the very notions of collectiveness, interactivity, and solidarity.

102 Nina Parikh, "An Interview with Mississippi Film Producer Nina Parikh," Interview by Phillip Gentile. *Southern Quarterly* 49:2/3 (2012), 91.

103 Andrew Lapin, "The Real Bathtub: Back To The Bayou With Beasts Of The Southern Wild," *IndieWire* (June 27, 2012), https://www.indiewire.com/2012/06/the-real-bathtub-back-to-the-bayou-with-beasts-of-the-southern-wild-46302.

104 Feshami, "US Independent Cinema," 54.

105 King, "Introduction," 2.

Chapter Two
From *Landschaft* to Landscape: Perspectives and Transformations in Geography and the Cinema

This book suggests an approach to landscape in cinema that seeks to transcend a solely visual understanding of landscape as scenery. Instead, it rests upon a novel, substantive way of analyzing cinematic landscapes that foregrounds both the historicity and the aliveness of landscape, which is understood as the product of a continuous interactivity between inhabitants and their environment. At the same time, from this perspective landscape is inherently political. The term is, as we shall see, inseparable from notions of community and polity and is, thus, instrumental in interpreting landscape as a primarily social category. Such an understanding carries with it the potential of countering neoliberal mechanisms of marginalization through solidarity and cooperation. This approach to landscape rests to a large degree on the writings of geographer Kenneth Olwig, particularly his book *Landscape, Nature, and the Body Politic* (2002). In this seminal work, Olwig suggests that the original social meaning of landscape as connected to polity and custom has gradually been supplanted by a scenic, visual understanding that serves both autocratic and nationalist ideologies.

Furthermore, I make use of the related, anthropological concept of landscape suggested by phenomenologists Tim Ingold and John Wylie which foregrounds dwelling in the sense of everyday activity and custom as crucial in understanding the interactivity of landscape. Finally, since this book is concerned with poverty and class, I am incorporating aspects of Marxist geography into my theoretical approach to landscape, in particular the writings of Don Mitchell. This serves to analyze the conditions of possibility the films' characters find themselves in and to understand them as the outcome of historic and current spatial processes determined by the capitalist notion of landscape as property and commodity.

1 "Conditions of possibility" — Marxist understandings of landscape as veil and way of seeing

The primary source of confusion when discussing landscape is what John Wylie has described as the term's inherent tension—an ambiguity with regards to the spectator's position to it: "It is a tension between proximity and distance, body and mind, sensuous immersion and detached observation. Is landscape the world

https://doi.org/10.1515/9783110779417-003

we are living *in*, or a scene we are looking *at*, from afar?"[1] An understanding of landscape as objective, material reality has historically been central to geographical analyses of topography, as Stephen Mills relates:

> [It] consisted of an examination of environmental changes effected by human activity, starting with those background features of general relief, climate, vegetation, and soils that existed prior to any human impact upon plants and animals. Physical geography is followed by the impact made by agriculture, trade and, finally, industry.[2]

This topographical approach has served to map, survey, and study natural and cultural phenomena and, therefore, relied on the assumption that "landscapes are real: in other words, they are really out there: solid, physical, and palpable entities."[3] However, in both the fields of cultural and human geography as well as in art history, landscape "while being linked in one way to what are usually called objective facts, to the real world 'out there', landscape is also found in the eye of the beholder."[4] It is assumed here that the artificiality we attribute to the visual rendition of a landscape is already inherent in the original "view" of it: as art historian Malcolm Andrews puts forward, "a 'landscape', cultivated or wild, is already artifice before it has become the subject of a work of art. Even when we simply look, we are already shaping and interpreting."[5] From this perspective, landscape is quintessentially visual: it "can be thought of as both something seen and a particular 'way of seeing' the world—both the land and the gaze upon it."[6]

The term "way of seeing" is generally attributed to art critic John Berger who used it as the title of both a television series he co-created as well as his accompanying study of art history. In this influential book, Berger claimed that "sometimes a landscape seems to be less a setting for the life of its inhabitants than a curtain behind which their struggles, achievements, and accidents take place."[7] This is a fitting summary of Marxist views on landscape which gained traction in the larger field of geography in the mid-1980s. They rest upon the assumption that the mechanisms of order which form the basis of both topographical measurements *and* perspectival landscape art, as Don Mitchell puts it, "are the result and reflection of the cultural imperatives of those who make and represent the

---

1 John Wylie, *Landscape* (London: Routledge, 2007), 1.

2 Stephen Mills, *The American Landscape* (Edinburgh: Keele UP, 1997), 3.

3 Wylie, *Landscape*, 6.

4 Ibid., 7.

5 Malcom Andrews, *Landscape in Western Art* (Oxford: Oxford UP, 1999), 1.

6 Wylie, *Landscape*, 55.

7 John Berger, *Ways of Seeing* (London: Penguin, 2008), 41.

landscape."[8] Landscape in this view is ideology made space—"both the result of and an input to specific relations of [capitalist] production and reproduction."[9] The "curtain" that Berger speaks of symbolizes the deceptive pretense of capitalist ideology suggesting that spatial principles such as ownership of land are a "natural" part of the landscape, not man-made principles enacted by the ruling class.

Cultural geographer Denis Cosgrove has argued for the crucial role perspectival landscape art has historically played in this endeavor of deception. He claims that the composition of landscape paintings is expressive of this property-based perspective and thus of a particular way of seeing the world—namely, a controlling view based on geometrical authority. As Wylie summarize, in this Western visual tradition, the representation of landscape signals "the transformation of *land* into *private property*."[10] Cosgrove argues that linear perspective, which came into being in Renaissance Italy of the fifteenth century, "was regarded as the discovery of the inherent properties of space itself."[11] Thus, he concludes, modern landscape representation and its claim of realism originated as a "composition and structuring of the world so that it may be appropriated by a detached, individual spectator to whom an illusion of order and control is offered through the composition of space according to the certainties of geometry."[12] In other words, landscape represented in linear perspective is a way of seeing that is "accomplice and expression" of the ruling class and their notion of property. Furthermore, it "covered up and concealed the actual material conditions" of its inhabitants.[13] Cosgrove therefore concludes that "there is an inherent conservatism in the landscape idea, in its celebration of property and of an unchanging status quo, in its suppression of tensions between groups *in* the landscape."[14] For him landscape remains a largely unquestioned term in geography which ensures that the term's history of "presenting an image of natural and social harmony" in the interest of capital is uncritically preserved in most geographical discourses.[15] We will encounter a similar notion in Olwig's concept of "mindscaping" below.

Don Mitchell builds on Cosgrove's ideas when he claims that "landscapes work ideologically to establish the very conditions of what is 'natural' or 'right' in a par-

---

8 Don Mitchell, "Landscape," in *Cultural Geography*, ed. David Atkinson (London: I.B. Tauris, 2005), 49.

9 Ibid.

10 Wylie, *Landscape*, 59.

11 Denis Cosgrove, "Prospect, Perspective and the Evolution of the Landscape Idea," *Transactions of the Institute of British Geographers* 10:1 (1985), 51.

12 Cosgrove, "Prospect, Perspective and the Evolution of the Landscape Idea", 55.

13 Wylie, *Landscape*, 59; ibid., 62.

14 Cosgrove, "Prospect," 58.

15 Ibid.

ticular place."[16] Mitchell further stresses how the idea of landscape as developed through the invention of linear perspective is not merely a visual representation, but a representation that takes on "physical form, a concrete materialization of social relations" through capitalist processes of production and consumption.[17] This makes "the form of the land [. . .] enormously hard to change," for not only is landscape under capitalism an incredibly vast, interconnected system of values and (property) laws, capitalist ideology also actively works to disguise and naturalize the very existence of this system.[18] He continues: "People work very hard to maintain, to reproduce, the already existent landscape. The landscape—its very built form, in other words—has enormous inertia, an inertia made real not only in bricks and stone but also in people's livelihood and homes."[19] In the context of this book, this leads to the question of how neoliberalism as the current form of capitalism has influenced contemporary "concrete manifestations" of landscape. The answer can be found in Theodore and Brenner's concept of "actually existing neoliberalism".

In their article, Brenner and Theodore aim to "explore the path-dependent, contextually specific interactions between inherited regulatory landscapes [of Keynesian capitalism] and emergent neoliberal, market-oriented restructuring projects at a broad range of geographic scales."[20] They base their analysis on Joseph Schumpeter's notion of "creative destruction" as the motor of capitalist innovation when they describe neoliberalism's "uneven, socially regressive, and politically volatile trajectories of institutional/spatial change."[21] In essence, the idea of creative destruction in this context

> illuminates the ways in which the geographies of actually existing neoliberalism are characterized by a dynamic transformation of capitalist territorial organization from the nationally configured frameworks that prevailed during the Fordist-Keynesian period to an increasingly "glocalized" configuration of global-national-local interactions in which no scale serves as the primary pivot for accumulation, regulation, or socio-political struggle.[22]

In particular, the notion of uneven regional development is significant for the films at hand and their deeply impoverished rural settings. In order to highlight the "destructive character of neoliberal policies," the authors identify some of its

16 Mitchell, "Landscape," 50.
17 Ibid.
18 Ibid.
19 Ibid., 51.
20 Brenner and Theodore, "Cities," 351.
21 Ibid.
22 Ibid., 363.

major forms of “creative destruction” and their spatial effects.[23] The most crucial aspect here is their observation that “cities have become strategically crucial arenas for neoliberal forms of [. . .] institutional restructuring” and are “systematically privileged over and against other [. . .] [geographical landscapes] as sites for capital accumulation.”[24] Mitchell makes a similar point when he argues that “the development of some areas is made possible only through the creative destruction of other places. In turn, such regional creative destruction—or, less spectacularly, local underdevelopment—sets people in motion, people often with little left to survive on.”[25] As discussed in the previous chapter, this results in joblessness, rural flight as well as in devastation of rural welfare infrastructure.

This Marxist perspective on landscape is useful for this book as an analytical point of departure, for it enables, firstly, an understanding of the economic factors determining the protagonists’ conditions of possibility in my corpus of films. It draws attention to the fact that neoliberal policies are not solely reflected in mainly urban phenomena such as gentrification, the “gig economy,” and others, yet also in rural underdevelopment and infrastructural decline. Secondly, it also enables a recognition of landscape’s function as “veil” and “way of seeing” which symbolizes capital’s “dominion over the land in the very act of ‘naturalizing’ it, of making its particular representation seem the natural order of things.”[26] How can we determine, however, if the four films discussed in this book do not fall into the same ideological trap of covering up the “actually existing” conditions prevailing in the environments they display? Mitchell argues that “the landscape ‘tells’ us—when we read it (or when others read it for us)—what is possible, what must be overcome, what is to be struggled for and against.”[27] This can be applied both to the close readings of the cinematic landscapes that will be undertaken in this book as well as to the revelatory work the films themselves undertake. The films in question, or rather their landscapes, either actively work to disrupt the “image of natural and social harmony” that is often attributed to rural America in particular, or draw attention to the ideological “veil”—this is especially striking in *Leave No Trace*’s comparison of park and wilderness spaces.[28] Finally, Mitchell argues that “to see the power at work in the landscape requires attention not just to the landscape (as form, representation, or set of meanings) in and of itself, but

23 Ibid., 353.
24 Ibid., 357; ibid., 355.
25 Mitchell, “Landscape,” 51.
26 Wylie, *Landscape*, 69.
27 Mitchell, “Landscape,” 51.
28 Cosgrove, “Prospect,” 58.

to the social relations that give rise to [. . .] the landscape's ability to do work [. . .] in capitalist societies."[29] This next crucial step in reading the landscape of the films will be undertaken here by taking into account phenomenological approaches to landscape.

2 "Embodied acts of landscaping" — Dwelling and everyday activity in phenomenological approaches to landscape

Marxist approaches to landscape as a way of seeing have been contested since about the 1990s from a phenomenological perspective. Cultural anthropologist Tim Ingold in particular is seen as a prominent figure in this phenomenological rebuttal. In his influential article "The Temporality of the Landscape" (1993), he proclaims that "the landscape [. . .] is not a picture of the imagination, surveyed by the mind's eye, nor however is it an alien and formless substrate awaiting the imposition of human order."[30] Ingold points out that the Marxist approaches and their idea of landscape as a mainly visual space produced by a dominant perspective reproduced the very dualistic relation of subject-object it sought to criticize. Marxist critiques of Western capitalist practices of landscape representation and formation were, in Ingold's opinion, weakened by their own assumption of landscape as a cultural image which is projected "on to the bare matter of the world."[31] This theory, Wylie summarizes, reproduced the same "spectatorial epistemology which severs subject from object."[32] Particularly the model of culture and its imposition on the environment through ideology seems problematic to Ingold. He termed this limited view of material surroundings and bodies the "building perspective."[33] In his opinion, this perspective, which he defined as the limited notion that "worlds are made before they are lived in," ignored the fact that human beings are unavoidably enmeshed in their natural surroundings: they are not able to remove themselves from the material world their bodies exist in, and therefore cannot observe it from a neutral, self-conscious position.[34] He criticizes that Marxist geographers suggest the possibility of a distanced gaze detached from material surroundings. Instead, he proposed a "dwelling perspective" and therefore aligned himself with the

29 Mitchell, "Landscape," 51.

30 Tim Ingold, *The Perception of the Environment: Essays on Livelihood, Dwelling and the Skill* (London: Routledge, 2000), 191.

31 Wylie, *Landscape*, 157.

32 Ibid.

33 Ingold, *The Perception of the Environment*, 179.

34 Ibid.

phenomenological approaches of Maurice Merleau-Ponty and Martin Heidegger, both of which "set out from the premise that every person is, before all else, a being-in-the-world."[35]

What is important to point out here is the contrast to a Cartesian worldview, which takes, as Ingold puts it, "as its starting point the self-contained subject confronting a domain of isolable objects [and] assumes that things are initially encountered in their pure occurrentness."[36] Instead, Ingold's dwelling perspective adapts Heidegger's suggestion that, as Ingold summarizes, "self and world merge in the activity of dwelling, so that one cannot say where one ends and the other begins" and combines it with Merleau-Ponty's focus on bodily perception which leads to the conclusion that "the intentional presence of the perceiving agent, as a being-in-the-world, must also be an *embodied* presence."[37] Landscape is no longer understood as a view from a certain perspective but is inextricably bound to embodied experience: it is, as Wylie summarizes, "the fact that I belong to the landscape of visible things that enables my seeing—it is my seeing which enables me to witness that belongingness."[38] The subject gazing at landscape is no longer understood to be constructing its meaning, instead "it is a self assembled and performed via bodily practices of landscape."[39]

What exactly are those bodily practices, however, that constitute "dwelling"? Geographers Paul Cloke and Owain Jones describe it as "the rich intimate ongoing togetherness of beings and things which make up landscapes and places, and which bind together nature and culture over time."[40] For Ingold, who approaches landscape from an anthropological perspective, dwelling is also centrally connected to practical activity: "It is through being inhabited that the world becomes a meaningful environment."[41] Phenomenological approaches such as Ingold's move away from a visual perspective towards a tactile appreciation of landscape. This is expressed in the analysis of what cultural geographer Hayden Lorimer has termed "embodied acts of landscaping," or bodily experiences of engagement with the material world.[42] Crucially, this interaction is reciprocal: according to Ingold, "the world emerges with its properties alongside the emergence of the per-

35 Ibid., 168.

36 Ibid.

37 Ibid., 169.

38 Wylie, *Landscape*, 152.

39 Ibid., 153.

40 Paul Cloke and Owain Jones, "Dwelling, place, and landscape. An Orchard in Somerset," *Environment and Planning* A33 (2001), 651.

41 Ingold, *The Perception of the Environment*, 173.

42 Hayden Lorimer, "Cultural Geography: The Busyness of being 'More-Than-Representational'," *Progress in Human Geography* 29:1 (2005), 85.

ceiver as person, against the backdrop of involved activity."[43] In geography, as Wylie concludes, there "has been both a rhetorical and substantive shift, from studies of representations of landscape [. . .] to studies instead investigating various *performances*" such as, for example, the landscaping act of orchard-growing in Cloke and Jones' above quoted work.[44] In studies such as theirs, the rhythmic and performative quality of everyday activity comes into focus.

How does this phenomenological perspective relate to artistic representations of landscape? Ingold argues:

> Far from dressing up a plain reality with layers of metaphor, or representing it, map-like, [. . .] songs, stories, and designs serve to conduct the attention of performers *into* the world. [. . .] At its most intense, the boundaries between person and place, or between self and the landscape, dissolve altogether.[45]

Such moments, as I shall argue, that dissolve the boundaries between self and landscape are central to the New Rural Cinema. This is illustrated through performances of custom (dancing, music-making, hunting, cooking, etc.), the interaction with animals, yet also in more ambiguous activities such as the sinister conclusion of *Winter's Bone*. They demonstrate a deep connection between land and community that forms the basis, as we shall see, of any potential contestations of marginalization these films suggest.

Some authors have already noticed the prevalence of such an interactive understanding of landscape in the New Rural Cinema—and often explicitly distinguish it from the Western genre's scenic depiction of landscape. For example, Sue Thornham has commented on *Winter's Bone*'s focus on the performance of everyday activities and the resulting tactile, interactive qualities of the film's landscape when she writes that "Granik's film [. . .] has reversed the practices of the Western genre it references, overturning its relentless linear drive and substituting a sense of space as at once immense and intensely, and tactily, *lived*."[46] In his analysis of *Songs My Brothers Taught Me*, which follows two young Lakota Sioux siblings' everyday lives on the impoverished Pine Ridge Reservation, Hervé Mayer comments on the film's powerful final scene. It consists of a hand-held shot of the central character, the teenager Johnny Winters (John Reddy) who, after having considered leaving the reservation for Los Angeles, has finally decided to stay with his younger sister. Alone in the surrounding Badlands, he drops to the

---

43 Ingold, *The Perception of the Environment*, 168.
44 Wylie, *Landscape*, 163.
45 Ingold, *The Perception of the Environment*, 56.
46 Sue Thornham, *Spaces of Women's Cinema. Space, Place and Genre in Contemporary Women's Filmmaking* (London: BFI/Bloomsbury, 2019), 46.

ground, slowly takes a handful of dry soil, and throws it into the air where the whitish dust lingers in the still desert air (see Fig. 1). Mayer points out how the scene portrays "Native intimacy to a land he [. . .] loves, understands and inhabits. The mythic imagery of the West is still present, Western landscapes and an esoteric connection to them are still celebrated, but the myth has been appropriated and redefined by the indigenous population at the center of the narrative." Johnny and his sister Jashaun (Jashaun St. John) "embrace the Western desert as their home, and their connection with it is intimate as much as historical."[47]

Fig. 1: Final scene of *Songs My Brothers Taught Me* (Chloé Zhao, 2015) Johnny (John Reddy) picks up a handful of soil in the Badlands National Park, South Dakota.

Marlon Lieber's article on *Beasts of the Southern Wild* brings up "dwelling" in its Heideggerian sense and poses the question if the German philosopher's affiliation with Nazism and its fascist *Lebensraum* ideology are somehow secretly integrated into the film's communal landscape vision. Lieber writes: "the film's commitment to place rests on what one could call a Heideggerian notion of an essentialist relationship between land and people."[48] He quotes Heidegger's text "Buidling Dwelling

47 Mayer, Hervé. "Neo Frontier Cinema: Rewriting the Frontier Narrative from the Margins in *Meek's Cutoff* (Kelly Reichardt, 2010), *Songs My Brother Taught Me* (Chloé Zhao, 2015) and *The Rider* (Chloé Zhao, 2017)," *Miranda* 18 (2019), http://journals.openedition.org/miranda/16672, 7.

48 Marlon Lieber, "Spaces of Communal Misery: The Weird Post-Capitalism of Beasts of the Southern Wild," in *Spaces and Fictions of the Weird and the Fantastic – Ecologies, Geographies, Oddities*, ed. J. Greve and F. Zappe (London: Palgrave Macmillan, 2019), 188.

Thinking" to illustrate this claim: "To dwell, to be set at peace, means to remain at peace within the free, the preserve, the free sphere that safeguards each thing in its nature."[49] The way Heidegger, according to Lieber, "equates being free not with an ability to freely develop but with the imperative to remain the same,"[50] fits in, in Lieber's opinion, with the film's skepticism towards state intervention. He concludes: "Thus, the film's woke Heideggerianism—after all, the Bathtub [the film's fictional setting] is not the Black Forest, and the beasts are more diverse than what he conceived of as the *Volksgemeinschaft*—proves deeply compatible with a libertarian rejection of the federal government."[51] I will interrogate this position in more detail in Chapter Five.

It is important to note, however, that phenomenological approaches to landscape have generally come under scrutiny for "lacking the critical purchase provided by the argument that historical and material circumstances hold the key to understanding both individual and social worlds."[52] Lieber's argument is symptomatic of the criticism levelled at phenomenological landscape studies. Wylie summarizes these criticisms as follows:

> Attending to individual human emotion and perceptions inevitably reifies such emotion and perceptions [. . .] and thus failing to recognize that the very notion of the free, autonomous individual is to some degree an ideological fabrication essential to the functioning of a capitalist socio-economic system.[53]

Particularly the Heideggerian notion of "dwelling" has been criticized to be based on a "sinister [. . .] rustic romanticism" that entails nostalgia for a supposedly more wholesome rural past.[54] At its worst, it might, as Wylie summarizes, install a "false boundary between the 'traditional' and the 'modern'."[55] While an interactive perspective on landscape and the focus on the performance of everyday tasks is essential for this book, it is Olwig's theory of landscape, which can be seen as a synthesis of traditionally Marxist and phenomenological approaches that provides the missing link. It allows us to reintroduce the notion of *power* that is largely absent from phenomenological approaches to landscape whilst holding on to the realm of community, custom, and everyday activity as the point of origin for landscape.

---

49 Martin Heidegger, "Building Dwelling Thinking," in *Poetry, Language, Thought*, translated by Albert Hofstadter (New York: Harper Perennial, 2001), 147.

50 Ibid.

51 Ibid., 189.

52 Wylie, *Landscape*, 180.

53 Ibid., 180–181.

54 Cloke and Jones, "Dwelling, place, and landscape," 661.

55 Wylie, *Landscape*, 182.

3 From *Landschaft* to landscape — Kenneth Olwig's substantive approach to landscape

Olwig's theory of landscape is based on two presuppositions. Firstly, Olwig follows the distinction between space and place famously made by geographer Yi-Fu Tuan. Place, as Tuan argues in his influential study on space and place, "is a unique entity [. . .] [that] has a history and meaning. Place incarnates the experiences and aspirations of a people."[56] Space, on the other hand, denotes the realm of perspectival representation, of maps and mainstream landscape art, and thus of hegemonic power. Secondly, Olwig traces the English term "landscape" back to its Germanic root, *Landschaft*. He claims that, originally, *Landschaft* did not denote a scenery or view but a very concrete political entity: *Landschaften* were communities or "polities" in Renaissance Northern Europe independent from the rule of monarchs. They referred to themselves as *Landschaften* not in a physical, spatial sense but in order to describe their representative political, and social assemblies that decided on the interpretation of local customary law. He concludes:

> A *Landschaft* was more than a place; it expressed the very idea of political representation as manifested in the representative body that stood for a political community. The *Landschaft* as place was thus defined not physically, but socially, as the place of a polity. The physical manifestation of that place was a reflection of the common laws that defined the polity as a political landscape.[57]

The *Landschaften* were defined by their shared custom and culture as well as by kinship and communal organization—not, as Olwig repeatedly reaffirms, by geographical features. The very notion of a *Land*, Olwig claims, was based on "a given body of customary law that would have developed historically from within through the workings of the judicial bodies of a given legally defined community."[58] The word "body" in "body politic" is central here, because it is not used solely in the abstract, as it is commonly used today, but as a literal reference to the bodily practices of custom as well as to the physical presence of a polity's members in the assembly. Olwig argues that "the representative body of the *Landschaft* was a body of actual bodies, and the precedent of customary law rooted in bodily practice constituted its power."[59] This is the point of origin for

---

56 Yi-Fu Tuan, "Space and Place: Humanistic Perspective," *Progress in Geography* 6 (1974), 213.

57 Kenneth Olwig, *Landscape, Nature, and the Body Politic* (Madison: University of Wisconsin Press, 2002), 10.

58 Ibid., 17.

59 Ibid., 218.

Olwig's argument in *Landscape, Nature and the Body Politic*. The book then outlines how and why this original, "substantive," as Olwig calls it, understanding of landscape was gradually supplanted by the scenic understanding we mainly know today.[60]

The study follows the mounting tension between an understanding of representational community and the top-down authority of monarchies that, in the Christian tradition, saw the "state in terms of a mystic body that incorporated its member parts" and sought to fuse the independent *Landschaften* with their sovereign empires.[61] He gives the example of a *Landschaft* on the German-Danish border that was conquered in 1559 by the Danish King Frederick II because it "was a thorn in the side of a consolidating monarchical state"—not only for its independent existence and special legal rights within the superior authority of the monarchy but also because it "could have inspired dreams of a representative form of government at a time when such a system was rare."[62] Military conquests and punitive measures were, however, not the only way monarchs and local nobility used to counter the representative ideology of the *Landschaften*.

The Danish Field Marshall Henrik Rantzau (1526–1598), Olwig notes, "brought the humanism and science of his time to bear upon the task of appropriating the independent-minded *Landschaften* under the authority of the state" through the commission of maps as graphic representations of the kingdom.[63] Such cartographical representations eventually found their way into art, offering an authoritative view—and here Olwig calls to mind Cosgrove's afore mentioned argument —that ideologically supported and naturalized the concept that the state and its smaller regional units "together constituted a unity of people and territory, tied together by geography."[64] This is where Olwig's central claim emerges: he proposes that, gradually, the original socio-political understanding of *Landschaft* was transformed and "eventually emptied of its place-bound meaning and came to refer to the make-believe space of scenery," a scenery viewed from the elevated perspective associated with the controlling gaze of the monarch.[65] Olwig specifically mentions theatre as an art form that helped spread the notion of landscape as a unifying scenery "masking" the previously heterogeneous communities and their customs: "the theatre made it possible for the lord to make believe that the polity of the *Landschaft* was embodied [. . .] within the illusory bodily space of his

60 Ibid., 18.
61 Ibid., 218.
62 Ibid.
63 Ibid., 28.
64 Ibid., 30.
65 Ibid., 216.

state as body politic."[66] In the theatre, the *literal* scenery was often aligned with the elevated view of the lord's view from his box. Olwig terms this process of transformation of landscape from a communal *place* into a scenic, representational *space* "mindscaping."[67]

This is where Olwig's argument fuses with recent writings on the origins of nationalism, particularly Benedict Anderson's concept of the "imagined community," "an amalgam of ethnicities and cultures living within a large territorial entity."[68] Olwig argues that "the scenic illusion of landscape made it easier to believe that different historically constituted polities and places could be unified within the space of a body politic as embodied by a geographical body [. . .] bound by mystical bonds of soil and blood."[69] As we will see in Chapter Three, Olwig understands this process as particularly pronounced in the history of the consolidation and unification of Britain and, consequentially, in the emergence of the United States as one "American" nation. He summarizes: "Whereas the *Landschaft*, as place and polity, was built on a law opposed to the bonds of blood that threatened to destroy the peace of the land, the nation-state sought to reconstitute blood-like ties at a higher level of abstraction and spatial scale."[70] This, Olwig argues, is the foundation of modern nationalism and, pursued to its logical endpoint, paves the way for fascism. He argues that by "jumping" from the scenery of theatre into physical landscape designs such as "landscape parks", the idea of landscape as scenery became "a particular worldview."[71] This worldview was "reified to the point that in Germany, those thought to be without bonds of blood to the landscape, like the Jews and gypsies [sic], were eventually removed from the scene by violence."[72] Again and again, this is the ultimate danger in an understanding of landscape where "the space of scenery has [. . .] appropriated the place of a people."[73] I shall return to this part of Olwig's argument in Chapter Three in relation to the genocide of Native Americans that was justified and driven by a similar hegemonic landscape vision.

How does Olwig's focus on the origins of landscape as a term for an autonomous polity, the *Landschaft*, relate to the present day, fictional rural communities

66 Ibid., 218.

67 Ibid.

68 Kenneth Olwig, "'Natural' Landscapes in the Representation of National Identity," in *The Routledge Research Companion to Heritage and Identity*, ed. Brian Graham and Peter Howard (London: Routledge, 2008), 73.

69 Olwig, *Landscape, Nature and the Body Politic*, 218–219.

70 Ibid., 219.

71 Ibid., 220.

72 Ibid.

73 Ibid.

seen in the films, such as the Bayou community called the Bathtub in *Beasts of the Southern Wild* or the communal trailer park in *Leave No Trace?* Going back to his initial example of the Northern European *Landschaften*, Olwig notes:

> The polity of the land [. . .] found concrete expression in the physical place of the polity and its physical environment, shaped under the governance of its laws. The shape of the material environment of the land reflected the condition of the polity that formed it.[74]

The response of imperial power was, as Mitchell comments in his review of Olwig's book, to change the physical environment from the common to the scenic "and in the process to instill a new relationship between land, law and justice."[75] Olwig's approach thus opens up various productive routes of investigation into the relation of communities, land, and power under neoliberalism.

Firstly, his observation that "the meaning of landscape changed from common*places* to scenic *spaces*" rings particularly true in an economic era which, as we have seen, has been characterized by the usurpation of common goods, including places, and by the economization of every aspect of human life.[76] However, Olwig himself distances himself from an outright critique of capitalism. While his work is outspokenly anti-racist and anti-fascist, he is reluctant to identify capitalism as the "culprit" of the transformation of landscape from commonplace to scenic space. In *Landscape, Nature, and the Body Politic*, he writes:

> The tendency in much modern scholarship is to give some abstraction, like "capitalism" or "the State," the active role in creating history. [. . .] I find the idea that flesh and blood people, rather than abstractions, make history to be somehow comforting. People make abstractions that then take on a life of their own, seeming to make history for us. But perhaps by recognizing these abstractions for what they are, maybe then we can remake history.[77]

I find this statement evasive: Olwig makes use of "abstractions" throughout his book, particularly of nationalism which, unlike his throwaway mention of capitalism in scare quotes, he actually takes the time to explain and contextualize. Furthermore, while he convincingly explains how the scenic use of landscape, for example in maps, was used to justify imperial conquest, he fails to mention the certainly as important commercial aspect of these representations.

Nevertheless, this is where his work is most compatible with critics of neoliberalism such as Wendy Brown. Brown, like Olwig, points out that the privatization of

---

74 Ibid., 20.

75 Don Mitchell, "Cultural Landscapes: Just Landscapes or Landscapes of Justice?" *Progress in Human Geography*, 27: 6 (2003), 788.

76 Olwig, *Landscape, Nature, and the Body Politic, 214.*

77 Ibid., 220–221.

former public spaces is not a trifle, but a fundamental attack on democratic values and human political existence. She argues that

> When the domain of the political itself is rendered in economic terms, the foundation vanishes for citizenship concerned with public things and the common good. Here, the problem is not just that public goods are defunded, and common ends are devalued by neoliberal reason [. . .] but that citizenship itself loses its *political* valence.[78]

The New Rural Cinema illustrates how the lack or endangerment of common places reduces communities to impoverished, lawless, and violent environments and Olwig's approach allows us to analyze how this is spatially manifested in the landscape the characters inhabit. For example, *Frozen River, Ballast*, and *Winter's Bone* all display a disrupted mise-en-scène—the absence of establishing shots, endless stretches of country road crosscut with claustrophobic interiors, characters often simply appearing at locations, their journeys having been omitted—that never allows the viewer to form a coherent image of the environment in their mind. The films' landscapes thereby illustrate the experience of existing in the scenic space created by neoliberal capitalism.

Secondly, Olwig's approach also enables an appreciation of the traces of polity and community visible in the landscapes of the films to varying degrees. In his review of Olwig's book Mitchell writes: "beneath the dreamwork [. . .] of empire lies a very different relationship between people and their landscape, one that is never fully repressed: there is a struggle for landscape and it is at the same time the struggle for justice."[79] This form of struggle takes shape in "embodied acts of landscaping" and communal cooperation that is visible in all four films, if, again, to varying degrees. For example, while *Beasts* features a rebellious community that exists in close connection to their environment and even commits a radical act of resistance when they blow up a dam, *Ballast* displays a barren, empty stretch of the Mississippi Delta where resistance seems only possible in the tiniest, everyday acts of solidarity. It is these small acts of cooperation, communality, and hospitality however, that emerge here as the lingering traces of landscape as polity.

Susan Braedley and Meg Luxton argue that one of neoliberal ideology's main weaknesses is that it is based on "macro analyses and broad [. . .] economic arguments [and disregards] effects on differently located people, their motivations and social relations more generally."[80] Indeed, a totalizing, scenic vision of land-

---

78 Brown, *Undoing the Demos*, 39.

79 Mitchell, "Cultural Landscapes," 788.

80 Susan Braedley and Meg Luxton, "Competing Philosophies. Neoliberalism and Challenges for Everyday Life," in *Neoliberalism and Everyday Life*, ed. Susan Braedley and Meg Luxton (Montreal: McGill-Queen's UP, 2010), 11.

scape that obscures, on the one hand, histories of marginalization, colonialism, and racism as well as, on the other hand, local customs and social relations thus works in favor of neoliberalism's "governing rationality."[81] The cinematic reconstruction of an interactive environment, of landscape as a "living land of the people" based on custom and history can therefore invite a rethinking of landscape as a social concept.[82] It serves to disrupt a disembodied, rational understanding of landscape as scenery which, in this case, serves neoliberalism's overarching extension of economic values. This constitutes a way of looking at landscape in cinema that, as the next section will show, goes beyond the common practice of either condemning it to mere backdrop or merely granting it symbolic and metaphorical qualities.

4 Landscape in cinema — Beyond the pictorial

Olwig's approach to landscape identifies the perspectival representation of the environment, and particularly the map as a central tool of installing a landscape image that envisions a top-down relation to landscape and is heavily associated with nationalism and imperialism. Olwig elaborates on the significance of naturalizing national identity:

> "Natural" landscapes are central themes in representations of national identity. Their power lies in the idea that nature, commonly understood as the opposite of culture, can nevertheless provide a source of human identity. National identity can thereby be seen to be a heritage of nature, rather than culture, and this, in turn, lends legitimacy to national identity by suggesting that it is natural, rather than artificial.[83]

If this is successful, Olwig argues, "it is possible to create a unified national identity as part of an imagined national community that, simultaneously, can be opposed to the identities of other nations."[84] He goes on to claim that since "governments have often had explicit educational policies regarding the propagation of national identity," the map takes a central position in such policies.[85] He continues:

81 Brown, *Undoing the Demos*, 30.
82 Olwig, *Landscape, Nature, and the Body Politic*, 220.
83 Olwig, "'Natural' Landscapes," 73.
84 Ibid.
85 Ibid., 74.

> [The map] typically represents the world in terms of bounded organic shapes, so that school pupils, who see the map of their nation on the wall of the schoolroom, soon form a mental image of the shape of that nation, and the territories it encloses within it.[86]

He goes on to give the example of the Swedish map which, he argues, covers up the fact that the northern parts of the country were originally settled by the indigenous Sami peoples yet are now seamlessly integrated into the map. This takes physical shape in the declaration of these stretches of land as Swedish national parks. I am including this detour here because it eventually leads to one of the few instances in which Olwig directly addresses *cinema* as a form of representing the environment. Strikingly, he compares the techniques and mise-en-scène of cinema to the functioning of the map. He suggests that the map enfolds its true power in combination with perspectival landscape images in that nature and national identity are mentally synthesized. He argues:

> [This process] is close, in form, to the illusion that we experience in a cinema, where a series of framed pictures is moved so rapidly in front of our eyes that we seem to experience a flow of continuous movement in time within a contiguous space. The illusion is enormously effective, but it is an illusion. The ability to create an illusion that is as convincing as that in a modern cinema is something that took centuries [sic] to develop. It was not just a question of technique but also one of developing the public's ability to comprehend and want such an illusion.[87]

Later in the text, he returns to the cinema and this time identifies a specific genre, the Western, which in his view undertakes a very similar ideological work as the maps in schoolrooms:

> Today, the more sophisticated technology of the "Western" movie endlessly repeats the central mythic elements of the birth of American nation: the struggle with the wild Indians; the settlement by pastoralist cowboys; the supplanting of the cowboys by farmers; and the growth of great cities.[88]

I will return to the Western and its ideological implications in Chapter Three. What I want to point out here is that Olwig sees cinema solely as part of "the linking of national identity and nature [which] is accomplished using illusions like that of perspective" and which, as he correctly identifies, feeds into outgrowths like racism, imperialism, and even fascism.[89] What is absent in this article is the idea that cinema might also be able to counter such a hegemonic perspective—which Olwig *does* indeed suggest elsewhere for specific forms of landscape paint-

86 Ibid., 77.
87 Ibid., 75.
88 Ibid., 83.
89 Ibid., 86.

ing, as we will see. Since Olwig is a geographer, not a film scholar, it seems pressing to turn to other views on landscape and cinema.

In their introduction to their edited collection *Cinema and Landscape* (2010), Graeme Harper and Jonathan Rayner seemingly come to a similar conclusion as Olwig. At the very beginning of their article, the authors state that "map-making is analogous to the cinematic endeavor."[90] They explain this analogy as follows:

> Both maps and films assume and position audiences, ideologically as well as geographically. The interaction between mapmakers/filmmakers and their audiences can be akin to a shared pilgrimage, in which the individual, or the group, or a culture, moves through a familiar or newly discovered landscape.[91]

It gradually becomes clear, however, that Harper and Rayner's concept of both landscape and map is quite different from Olwig's. Whereas at the basis of Olwig's understanding is an interactive concept of landscape, one that emerges through bodily acts of custom, Harper and Rayner mainly seem to subscribe to the Cartesian notion of a fully formed topographic landscape onto which culture is projected. Cinema, in their sense, is map-like because it makes the features and meanings of landscape visible through its framing of landscape images. This becomes especially clear when they argue:

> Like a map, the cinematic landscape is the imposition of order on the elements of landscape, collapsing the distinction between the found and the constructed [. . .] Cinema, as the twentieth century's most successful art form, worked in an analogous way to the globe produced by Behaim in the fifteenth century, in that it delineated and disseminated images and ideas about landscape, and promoted them for further discovery.[92]

While I generally agree with Harper and Rayner's "inescapable truth that cinema has itself contributed to the imagining of national landscapes and communities," I find the exclusive understanding of cinema as map reductive.[93] Surely, there are differentiations to be made between different genres, modes, periods, styles, etc. regarding the way they relate to the landscapes they depict. If the concept of the map, with its imperial, colonial, rational history, were to be the only possible way of making sense of cinematic landscapes, a humanist, social, and progressive interpretation of landscape in both filmmaking and film analysis would be impossible.

Similarly, this book is not particularly concerned with cognitive approaches to cinematic landscapes, what Harper and Rayner call the "typology of landscape

90 Graeme Harper and Jonathan Rayner, "Introduction — Cinema and Landscape," in *Cinema and Landscape*, ed. Graeme Harper, Jonathan Rayner (Bristol: Intellect, 2010), 15.

91 Ibid.

92 Ibid., 16.

93 Ibid., 24.

perceptions" in cinema.[94] This relates to the argument that "film can be both metaphoric in its depictions [of landscape], as well as metonymic."[95] Metonomy in this context relates to how cinematic landscapes can "indicate further and larger concepts and relevance and [. . .] encapsulate rather than suggest inclusivity."[96] The authors give the example of "the framing of a ramshackle farmer's hut [. . .] [which suggests] the transference of the idea of labor, of pastoralism, of the pre-industrial or agrarian existence."[97] The metaphoric dimension, on the other hand, "entails the transference to an alternate plane of reference."[98] Thereby, landscapes such as the Monument Valley in John Ford's Westerns enable "the audience to extend its relationship with the text [by] [. . .] offering displaced representations of desires and values, so that these can be expressed by the filmmaker and shared by the audiences."[99] In his book *Landscape Allegory in Cinema* (2010), David Melbye has referred to this process when he writes that "the landscapes of our natural world become the landscapes of our minds."[100] While these concepts will be taken into account in Chapter Three in relation to landscape images and their role in the forming of US national identity, they still rest on a mainly visual, scenic understanding of landscape that this book seeks to complicate.

More suited to the objectives of this book therefore is the understanding of cinematic landscapes put forward by Martin Lefebvre. His contribution to the edited collection *Landscape and Film* (2006) still follows a more traditional, scenic approach to landscapes in cinema. In the chapter, he argues for the difference between *setting* and *landscape* in a film on the basis of different modes of viewing. Setting, in his model, is part of the "narrative mode" of classical cinema according to which "everything must be subordinated to the narrative."[101] He argues that in classical narrative cinema, "each element of the film ought to be able to be integrated into the narrative process. This is especially true for the setting [. . .] which situates the action and events related by the film."[102] Landscape, on the other hand, is, he argues, related to the "spectacular mode" of the cinematic experience. This specific form of the gaze occurs when the narrative is mo-

94 Ibid., 20.
95 Ibid.
96 Ibid.
97 Ibid.
98 Ibid.
99 Ibid., 20–21.
100 David Melbye, *Landscape Allegory in Cinema – From Wilderness to Wasteland*. New York: Palgrave Macmillan, 2010, 2.
101 Martin Lefebvre, "Between Setting and Landscape in the Cinema," in *Landscape in Film*, ed. Martin Lefebvre (London: Routledge, 2006), 28.
102 Ibid.

mentarily interrupted by pure, visual spectacle. It is this same principle of the autonomous gaze that "enables the notion of filmic landscape in narrative fiction [. . .]: it makes possible the transformation of setting to landscape."[103] This argument suggests the possibility of "breaking through" the view of landscape as mere setting, or scenery that reminds us of Olwig's concept. Lefebvre's claim that "landscape in narrative film possesses the peculiar ability to appear and disappear before the spectator's very eyes" certainly calls to mind the notion that landscape needs to be *read* in order to be understood.[104]

What is absent in this particular text by Lefebvre is the logical next step, to collapse the boundary between action and setting/landscape. It is, following Ingold and Olwig's approaches, precisely the characters' actions, their interactive engagement with their environment that produces the landscape. Cinema, because of its addition of movement and sound to the tradition of artistic representation of landscape, offers a unique possibility to portray "land as polity and place, and nature as a complex, historically constituted concept imbued with social values."[105] This is only hinted at in Lefebvre's text when he describes cinematic landscape as a "*doubly temporalized landscape* [. . .] [in that it is] subjected simultaneously to the temporality of the cinematographic medium and to that of the spectator's gaze which is given to shifting from the narrative to the spectacular mode and back again."[106]

However, in his 2011 article "On Landscape in Narrative Cinema," Lefebvre does explore how the temporality of filmic landscape also enables an understanding of landscape as something constantly evolving through continuous social interaction Lefebvre begins by recapitulating his argument concerning setting and landscape and its implications regarding narrative and visual spectacle. In the text's final section, however, he considers a more immersive, interactive concept of landscape. Lefebvre gives the example of Alexander Sokurov's film *Mat i Syn (Mother and Son,* Aleksandr Sokurov, 1997), which follows a young man and his ailing mother on a long walk through a rural landscape using long shots and other techniques to foreground slowness and duration. These techniques, Lefebvre argues, support "our ability to 'arrest' the landscape image" and create different "feelings" from the ones experienced in a more traditional film where landscape mainly works as setting.[107] He then argues that "these feelings [. . .] can help draw us *into*

103 Ibid., 29.

104 Ibid.

105 Ibid., 226.

106 Lefebvre, "Between Setting and Landscape in the Cinema," 29.

107 Martin Lefebvre, "On Landscape in Narrative Cinema," *Canadian Journal of Film Studies* 20:1 (2011), 71.

the landscape, so that our experience of it may not be as *distanced*—and therefore as purely *visual*—as we might think."[108]

In this text, Lefebvre therefore *does* establish the connection from his previous conception of the temporality of cinematic landscape to Ingold's notion of the "dwelling perspective." He argues that "it would seem logical to assume that any *specific* contribution narrative film might make to the idea of landscape [. . .] would stem from the medium's ability to *temporalize* the landscape and move us *into* it."[109] He continues:

> In narrative film, as in painting or photography, our ability to experience and interpret the landscape—to discover *in it* or think through *with it* all sorts of symbolic meanings, from purely aesthetic themes to political ones [. . .]—finds its source in the way it can come to occupy the center of our attention.[110]

Narrative, he concludes, can thus be experienced in two ways:

> Either as that which conceals landscape or that which may be interpreted to reveal it. For though a tension often exists in a film between the pictorial experience of landscape and narrative, that experience [. . .] may in turn bring the narrative to further reveal the landscape as dwelling. [. . .] under these conditions, it is now narrative that serves the landscape.[111]

This is a fundamental prerequisite requirement for the approach to landscape broached by this book. The New Rural Cinema articulates a current tendency in US indie film-making that attempts a representation of landscape that is in line with Ingold's immersive concept of the dwelling perspective and, by extension, Olwig's understanding of "land as polity and place."[112] While the pictorial aspect of landscape is, of course, of undeniable importance, it is particularly the social, interactive origin of landscape that I want to focus on here.

108 Ibid., 71–72.
109 Ibid., 74.
110 Ibid., 75.
111 Ibid., 76.
112 Olwig, *Landscape, Nature, and the Body Politic*, 226.

Chapter Three
Wild Country – National Identity and Landscape in the United States

The idea of national community has always been contested in the United States—for a multitude of reasons. As the country prides itself, as the anarchist Voltairine de Cleyre wrote in 1909, on anti-statist "American traditions, begotten of religious rebellion, self-sustaining communities, isolated conditions, and hard pioneer life," any examination of the country's national identity is necessarily complicated.[1] Experiences of extreme inequality reinforce this sentiment as the socialist historian Howard Zinn remarked in his anti-nationalist study *A People's History of the United States* (1980):

> The pretense is that there really is such a thing as "the United States", subject to occasional conflicts and quarrels, but fundamentally, a community of people with common interests. [. . .] Nations are not communities and never have been. [. . .] The history of any country, presented as the history of a family, conceals fierce conflicts of interests [. . .] between conquerors and conquered, masters and slaves, capitalists and workers, dominators and dominated in race and sex.[2]

As Zinn's reflection suggests, the US American experience has always been a fractured one, highly dependent upon the many power scales defined among others by class, race, gender, ability, and sexual orientation. While one might agree with Zinn that such injustices can be found in the history of any country, the United States are measured on their exceptional foundational claim to universalism and, as historian John Higham outlines, "our egalitarian ideology [. . .] molded by the Enlightenment and forged in the revolution [. . .] simultaneously a civic credo, a social vision and a definition of nationhood."[3] The idea of a civic nation, a nation of immigrants, which stands out from the European concept of nationalism rooted in ethnic conceptions, continues to promise equality and inclusiveness. It is a national origin narrative that has long been central to US identity and continues to be told and retold—for in its performative retelling, as Nikhil Pal Singh

1 Voltairine de Cleyre, "Anarchism and American Traditions," in *Exquisite Rebel: The Essays of Voltairine de Cleyre*, ed. Sharon Presley and Crispin Sartwell (New York: State University of New York Press, 2005), 91.

2 Howard Zinn, *A People's History of the United States. 1492 to Present* (New York: Harper Perennial, 2010), 9–10.

3 John Higham, "Multiculturalism and Universalism: A History and Critique," *American Quarterly* 45 (1992), 197.

https://doi.org/10.1515/9783110779417-004

argues, it helps "resolve a special problem for the liberal-democratic or 'civic' nation: the production and reproduction of a people who recognize themselves as consenting to a common enterprise."[4]

The constant repetition of this narrative of equality and universalism, however, as countless resistant voices have demonstrated over the last centuries, has also been an instrument in the suppression of any divergence from the supposed white, male, Christian norm. The genocide of the indigenous population as well as African American slavery in particular raise questions on the validity and aim of US universalism. Singh argues that if the "individuals and communities who benefit from national belonging are [. . .] constituted in white supremacist terms [. . .] [American universalism is] not merely an apology for racist practice but implicated in creating and sustaining racial division."[5] Silvia Federici puts forward a similar argument:

> No major political change will [. . .] be possible in the United States unless the two grand injustices on which this country is based—the dispossession and genocide of the Native Americans and the enslavement of millions of Africans [. . .]—are confronted.[6]

Most recently, the Black Lives Matter protests that re-ignited in 2020 in cities all over the country in response to the murder of George Floyd, a Black man, by a Houston police officer, demonstrate that these racial injustices continue to shape the US political landscape.

Nancy Isenberg notes a similar "gnawing contradiction" in relation to poverty.[7] Class as a category, she argues, is commonly concealed in the United States by the hegemonic insistence on equality: "the problem is that popular American history is most commonly told [. . .] without much reference to the existence of social classes. [. . .] How does a culture that prizes equality of opportunity explain, or indeed accommodate, its persistently marginalized people?"[8] Such considerations chime with the New Rural Cinema's exploration of rural poverty at the intersection of class, race, and gender in the twenty-first century United States. These films suggest that, in light of growing inequality, deep poverty, and persistent systemic racism, a totalizing narrative of the United States as a national community seems increas-

---

4 Nikhil Pal Singh, *Black is a Country. Race and the Unfinished Struggle for Democracy* (Cambridge, MA: Harvard UP, 2005), 19.

5 Ibid., 20.

6 Silvia Federici, *Re-enchanting the World. Feminism and the Politics of the Commons* (Oakland, CA: PM Press, 2019), 91.

7 Nancy Isenberg, *White Trash: The 400-Year Untold History of Class in America* (London: Penguin, 2017), 2.

8 Ibid., 1–2.

ingly disjointed from reality. For this reason, they bring into focus marginal, destitute communities—both white, Black, and ethnically diverse—which appear sealed-off from the US mainstream and illuminate the discrepancies between the unifying tropes of nationalism and the atomizing experience of poverty under neoliberal capitalism. Furthermore, they also suggest, to varying degrees, if and how they can be countered through communal organization.

As suggested in Chapter Two, the four case studies discussed in this book work through these discrepancies by employing a specific focus on landscape as a social concept. Historically, landscape as a pictorial representational model has been intrinsically connected to US national identity. While many other nation states have defined their identity through their characteristic terrain, the role landscape has played in US history from the country's colonial beginnings is especially pronounced, yet also clearly indebted to the concept's European origins. This chapter will give an overview of the relation of national identity and landscape in the United States through its presentation as scenery in visual art, specifically film. I will then contextualize the New Rural Cinema within a cinematic tradition that interrogates the landscape of the United States as a social construct and, at times, suggests alternative, more inclusive landscape visions.

1 "A country of countries" — The colonial transition of the scenic landscape

As has been established in the previous chapter, cultural geographer Kenneth Olwig describes how the concept of landscape in Renaissance Northern Europe underwent a shift from describing a self-reliant community or polity (a *Landschaft*) to a scenic representation of rural space. This transformation was not arbitrary but was advanced by lords and monarchs in order to unify their realms, invoke proto-nationalist sentiments of belonging, and squash the independent minded communities' resistance to their sovereignty. The overall aim was to prevent the formation of a representative political body of these independent communities. Apart from violent conquest, a means to achieve such a reframing of landscape "was to represent the *Landschaft* by means that [. . .] [were] more suited to the top down power of the Lord."[9] Among these means were maps as well as landscape paintings in the linear perspective common to the Italian school of painting.

9 Olwig, *Landscape, Nature, and the Body Politic*, 26.

Olwig contrasts these perspectival representations of landscape with an earlier European artistic tradition that sought to represent the land as shaped by custom and bodily interaction with the terrain. Northern European paintings of artists such as Pieter Brueghel the Elder (ca. 1525–1569), were committed to the original meaning of landscape—"customary law [. . .] inscribed and memorized in the material fabric of the *Landschaft*"—and visualized a democratic vision of rural life, namely "the process by which members of the non-noble estates of emerging national bodies sought to establish cultural identities as [. . .] politically engaged [. . .] citizenries."[10] According to Olwig, landscape in Brueghel's paintings seems to emerge through the interaction of people with the rural environment, not through a masterful gaze. By contrast, linear perspective, he argues, created the illusion of a centralized geography which served to illustrate a vision of landscape under the centralized law of the monarch. This controlling gaze escalated in the hierarchic landscaping of the physical terrain: "the scenic conception of landscape as nature moved from the arena of art [. . .] out into the garden before leaping the garden fence," as Olwig puts it.[11]

How were these competing continental-European notions of landscape transferred to the American continent and how did they contribute to the development of the "New World's" national identity? Olwig writes:

> The ideas of landscape, country, and nature that had initially developed within a European context provided an important basis for the creation of an American national identity. This identity was wedded, on the one hand, to the idea of the nation as a political landscape making up a country of countries and, on the other, to the idea of a manifest destiny tied to the landscape of the American continent's geographical body.[12]

Olwig's term "a country of countries" suggests a degree of heterogeneity that chimes with Zinn's skepticism towards the United States as a homogeneous national community. Similarly, the term also conjures up images of the fractured map detailing French, Spanish, British, and other colonial claims and influences in North America throughout the seventeenth and eighteenth century. Undoubtedly, a "country of countries" also calls to mind the period of sectional divide that would eventually lead to the Civil War. Finally, it may also allude to the fundamental racial inequality and normative positioning of a white, male national subject built in to the fabric of American politics and society that, according to Singh, "casts a healthy skepticism on the notion that there exists a universalizing ten-

10 Ibid., 27–28.

11 Olwig, *Landscape, Nature, and the Body Politic*, 149.

12 Ibid., 176.

dency within this nation that inevitably wins out."[13] Singh opens his study of US nationalism and racism with a quote by African-American poet Amiri Baraka that concisely encapsulates the marginalizing, racially charged notion of the term "country" in the American context: "In America, 'Black' is a country."

How is the concept of "country", however, related to the already established term "landscape"? Country is the English translation of the Germanic words *Land* and *Landschaft* and, similarly, it also took on a variety of levels of meaning throughout its history. On the one hand, "country" in Britain referred to a polity or political community and was used interchangeably with the word "county," the "place of a people." In this sense, it was associated with a local community defined by its specific customary law and people, the countrymen and -women, as well as with the political representation of this local community in Parliament. On the other hand, "country" came to be used in reference to "the entire English "commonwealth": a country founded on law and united by compact or tacit agreement of the people for the common good" and often in opposition to the centralized understanding of sovereignty represented by the court.[14]

Olwig argues that these levels of meaning were transported to England's North American colonies, where they were eventually used to voice the conflict between colonizers and revolutionaries. He quotes the Declaration of Independence, which documents that one of the injustices the revolutionaries accused the British king of was forcing "our fellow Citizens [. . .] to bear Arms against their *Country*, to become the executioners of their friends and Brethren."[15] Even before the revolution had taken its course and independence was proclaimed, the "United States" were thus perceived as a country. The term was used by the revolutionaries, Olwig claims, in a similar way to how it had been used in the English Civil War about a century before—the people, the countrymen, rose up against the autocratic rule of the royal tyrants: "country was part of the vocabulary of the American revolutionaries [. . .] [because] they were inspired by the ideas and rhetoric of the Englishmen who had revolted, in the name of Parliament, against the Stuart kings in the mid-seventeenth century."[16]

Therefore, the term "country of countries", on the one hand, refers to the continuation of a certain understanding of the term country in Britain's American colonies that was deeply connected to community identity as expressed through local customs, law, and tradition as well as political representation. On the other

---

13 Singh, *Black is a Country*, 14.

14 Olwig, *Landscape, Nature, and the Body Politic*, 46.

15 Thomas Jefferson, *Declaration of Independence* [1776] (Jackson, MS: Applewood Books, 1997), quoted in Olwig, *Landscape, Nature, and the Body Politic*, 43. Emphasis added.

16 Olwig, *Landscape, Nature, and the Body Politic*, 43.

hand, it also refers to the problem every evolving nation state faces, but which seemed especially momentous in the context of the colonization of an immense geographic space such as the North American continent: the transition from "the customs of a small community to ideologies that bind the imaginations of a people to the land of vast states [. . .] these two dimensions of social existence must necessarily link if a state is to function."[17] As has already been established, one of the instruments that had historically been used to induce such a top-down-link is the scenic representation of landscape. Stephen Daniels, making use of Benedict Anderson's term, writes in his study of landscape imagery and national identity that "the symbolic activation of time and space [. . .] gives shape to the 'imagined community' of the nation. Landscapes [. . .] provide visible shape; they picture the nation."[18] The specific landscape picture that emerged in the nineteenth century in the context of the US nation-building process was one of wilderness—a wilderness that is instrumental in US national identity as a source of pride and inspiration and, at the same time, as a symbolic enemy of progress that needed to be conquered.

This notion was specifically broadcast by means of Manifest Destiny—the belief that the colonial, westward expansion was divinely preordained. Roderick Nash argues that after an initial response to the hardships of frontier life resulted in widespread depictions of wilderness as a realm of "anarchy and evil to which the Christian mind was unalterably opposed," it gradually began to form the basis of what would become known as American exceptionalism, the association of America with a chosen country, a new Eden:[19]

> Americans sought sustenance for their national ego. They needed something valuable and distinctive that could transform embarrassed provincials into proud and confident citizens. Gradually cultural nationalists began to sense that in one respect their country was different: nature in the New World had no counterpart in the Old. Specifically, it was wilder.[20]

The elevation of wilderness to a source of nationalist pride had to overcome a fundamental paradox, however: the presumed wilderness had already been inhabited and shaped as a *Landschaft* by generations of indigenous people. In fact, as Sarah Bonnemaison and Christine Macy suggest, "the first wave of Europeans who settled North America did not experience wilderness at all."[21] The authors claim:

---

17 Ibid., 58.

18 Stephen Daniels, *Fields of Vision: Landscape Imagery and National Identity in England and the United States* (Oxford: Princeton UP, 1993), 5.

19 Roderick Nash, *Wilderness and the American Mind.* 4th ed. (New Haven, CT: Yale UP, 2001), 34.

20 Ibid., 66.

21 Sarah Bonnemaison and Christine Macy, *Architecture and Nature: Creating the American Landscape* (London: Routledge, 2003), 1.

> The forests of New England, for example, were so well maintained by controlled annual burning that one could drive a carriage under the canopy of trees. One might even say that far from destroying pristine wilderness, European settlers created it. As European diseases devastated human populations in the Americas and Native communities could no longer carry out controlled burning, wilderness quickly took over.[22]

Cultural theorist Henry Nash Smith, writing about the symbolism of the American West, recognized this ideological paradox as "two distinct Wests," a concept that entails both the idea of an untouched Edenic garden waiting to be appropriated and, at the same time, the notion of a dangerous wilderness that must be tamed, conquered, and subdued.[23] In the end, however, both perspectives served to justify the murder and displacement of North America's indigenous peoples, as Olwig writes: "The wilderness ideal helped naturalize a colonial imperialism that simultaneously required the removal, and even extermination, of the previous native population, often deemed to be racially inferior, and the obliteration of the memory of this population."[24] The promotion of a scenic understanding of landscape, as opposed to an interactive, embodied understanding, was instrumental in facilitating this obliteration of indigenous culture.

An effective tool which helped to transform the formerly indigenous *Landschaften* into US landscape scenery was the notion of the "frontier." The United States defined itself and, to a certain degree, derived its national identity through the ongoing conquest of wild landscape, the heroic advancement of the so-called frontier between "civilization" and "savagery." The contemporary historian Frederick Jackson Turner is most prominently associated with this "frontier hypothesis," the notion that the struggle against wilderness, which encompassed impassable terrain as well as indigenous inhabitants, was crucial for the process of transforming vast amounts of supposedly empty space into a new nation. In his influential essay *The Significance of the Frontier in American History* (1894), Turner claimed that the advancement of the frontier not only supported the United States' disengagement from European influences, it also facilitated the transformation of heterogeneous communities of immigrants into a unified nation state: "If one would understand why we are to-day one nation, rather than a collection of isolated states, he [sic] must study this economic and social consolidation of the country [on the frontier]."[25] The transition from the term "country" to "nation" is telling here. According

---

22 Ibid.

23 Henry Nash Smith, *Virgin Land: The American West as Symbol and Myth* (Cambridge, MA: Harvard UP, 1971), 55.

24 Olwig, *The Meanings of Landscape*, 12.

25 Frederick Jackson Turner, *The Significance of the Frontier in American History* [1894] (London: Penguin, 2008), 14.

to Turner, the advancement of the frontier reconfigures the heterogeneous collection of isolated countries as, to use Benedict Anderson's term, the "imagined community" of the US American people, the nation.

In his influential study of nationalism, Anderson prominently used the attribute "imagined" "because the members of even the smallest nation will never know most of their fellow-members, meet them, or even hear of them, yet in the minds of each lives the image of their communion."[26] Turner's essay—which has been called "the single most influential piece of writing in the history of American history"[27]—can therefore be considered one of the most central cultural representations of American landscape as scenery, or as Anderson puts it, as the image of the national communion. Historian Greg Grandin is only the most recent of many critics throughout American history to point out, however, that its focus on finding new horizons, this "constant fleeing forward allowed the United States to avoid a true reckoning with its social problems, such as economic inequality [and] racism."[28] The ongoing influence of Turner's thesis on US national identity underlines Singh's suggestion that "Americans have largely lived in denial about the centrality of their racial-imperial project to national self-conceptions."[29] Like the Renaissance maps which helped the courts of Europe to visually claim authority over formerly independent polities, the influential notion of the frontier framed genocidal colonialism as an abstract, scenic battle between "wilderness" and "civilization".

Without the conceptual transformation of landscape from polity into *visual* scenery, however, the notion of the frontier and its supposed integrative qualities could hardly have caused such fundamental reverberations. Olwig claims that "the scenic illusion of landscape made it easier to believe that different historically constituted [. . .] places could be unified within the space of a body politic as embodied by a geographical body."[30] Early US landscape painting, especially the Romantic paintings of the emigrated Englishman Thomas Cole (1801–1848), assumed exactly this role. Cole's migration from England to the United States,

26 Benedict Anderson, *Imagined Communities. Reflections on the Origin and Spread of Nationalism* (London/New York: Verso, 2003).

27 John Mack Farragher, *Rereading Frederick Jackson Turner. "The significance of the frontier in American history", and Other Essays* (New Haven, CT: Yale UP, 1998), 1.

28 Greg Grandin, *The End of the Myth. From the Frontier to the Border Wall in the Mind of America* (New York: Metropolitan Books, 2019), 4.

29 Singh, *Black is a Country*, 29–30.

30 Olwig, *Landscape, Nature, and the Body Politic*, 218.

where he was to become a major influence on the nationalist understanding of landscape, perfectly encapsulates Olwig's claim that "the United States, as a former British colony, ha[d] inherited the British scenic idea of landscape."[31] Cole's paintings of US landscapes can be seen as performing a similar task as Turner's writings in establishing a scenic image of the environment that served as an ideological tool of nation-building.

Cole became a celebrated artist in the United States early in his life—by the mid-1820s he was already a well-known public figure and the figurehead of a young artists' collective later known as the Hudson River School which included other prominent figures such as Albert Bierstadt and Frederic Church. The focus of Cole's work lay on the transformation of wilderness into developed land which he portrayed in overwhelming, monumental landscape scenes. While his paintings also subtly suggested the ecological destruction entailed in the United States' expansion as well as the presence of indigenous inhabitants, they mostly conveyed the inevitable march of progress inherent in the idea of a Manifest Destiny. Such representations were particularly popular in the eastern cities at the time and fostered an "emergent sense of exceptionalism: the idea that America was different than Europe because of its nature."[32] Both the vast landscapes of the East, such as the Catskill Mountains and Niagara Falls, and later the even more impressive Western landscapes, such as Yosemite Valley, as well as their ongoing discovery and industrial subjugation became objects of national pride.

Crucially, Cole's own contribution as an artist to a nationalist discourse surrounding landscape is reflected in some of his paintings. For example, *View from Mount Holyoke, Northampton, Massachusetts after a Thunderstorm (The Oxbow)* (1836) depicts "the moment of transformation to civilization by reference to an exactly determinable geographical situation"[33] (see Fig. 2). The right side of the panoramic canvas shows cultivated farmland, bathed in bright sunlight whereas the left side depicts a still wild landscape covered in dark rain clouds. Right in the middle between wilderness and civilization, in the liminal space of the frontier, the artist has pictured himself, working on his canvas, both documenting and, apparently, facilitating the unstoppable force of progress—and, by implication, what Turner called the "consolidation" of the country.

31 Olwig, *The Meanings of Landscape*, 45.

32 Angela Miller, "The Fate of Wilderness in American Landscape Art," in *American Wilderness — A New History*, ed. Michael Lewis (New York: Oxford UP, 2007), 92.

33 Julia Galandi-Pascual, *Zur Konstruktion amerikanischer Landschaft* (Freiburg: Modo, 2010), 75, My Translation.

Fig. 2: *View from Mount Holyoke, Northampton, Massachusetts after a Thunderstorm (The Oxbow)* (Thomas Cole, 1836).

While paintings such as the cycle *The Course of Empire* (1833–1836) suggested greed and violence as drivers of capitalist development, Cole’s paintings generally portrayed a country on the march into a bright future. In his aptly titled *Essay on American Scenery* (1836), which implied that the United States’ nature was unrivalled in its potential for artistic reproduction, he wrote: “American associations are not so much of the past as of the present and the future [. . .] Where the wolf roams, the plough shall glisten; on the gray crag shall rise temple and tower—mighty deeds shall be done in the now pathless wilderness.”[34] Carefully avoiding any obvious reminiscence of European masters, Cole created a realist aesthetic that produced an uplifting atmosphere of a young nation on the rise. As Angela Miller comments, Cole’s “landscape paintings offered aesthetic solutions to problems whose origins were social—an imaginary stage on which to explore the role of nature in the nation’s evolving identity.”[35] Cole’s paintings were instru-

34 Thomas Cole, “Essay on American Scenery,” [1836] *University of Virginia*, http://xroads.virginia.edu/~HYPER/DETOC/hudson/cole.html.

35 Miller, “The Fate of Wilderness,” 110.

mental in promoting this self-conception and, by extension, in transforming dispersed communities into a consolidated nation state.

The nascent artistic discipline of photography intensified the pictorial construction of US self-conception through landscape as its technological development coincided with the westward exploration in the mid-nineteenth century. Early US photographers like Carleton E. Watkins and Ansel Adams produced pastoral images of wondrous Western landscapes such as Yosemite Valley that portrayed pristine and, significantly, unpopulated landscapes and thereby illustrated the boundless economic possibilities of the American West (see Fig. 3). As Karen Current describes, "photography and the West came of age in post-Civil War America"; both westward expansion and the exciting new technology "offered a new frontier to master, and each exerted an immense magnetism on the war-weary American mind."[36] More so than painting, however, early landscape photography also included an economic aspect: its claim at first was not primarily artistic but served to advertise Western landscapes as commodities for tourists, settlers, and investors.

Railroad, mining, real estate, and other companies employed photographers to accompany westward expeditions in order to both document the respective topographical conditions and at the same time produce aesthetic images which could be used for advertisement.[37] What may be perceived today as a glaring inconsistency—the celebration of pristine nature *and* its industrial transformation—did not register as such in the nineteenth century: "extraction of resources from even the most singular sites was rarely a problem, providing that industry did not disturb those elements of the landscape that gave European-Americans visual confirmation of their cultural values."[38] The camera, as Galandi-Pascual writes, "played a special role in the historical process of appropriation" that was the westward expansion of the nineteenth century.[39] These early photographs of the imperialist appropriation of land and resources solidified the idea of Manifest Destiny by offering its viewers a photorealistic presence of the newly exploited, yet seemingly untouched territories. As photography was perceived to be "the nearest approach to a truthful delineation of nature," as the expedition leader Ferdinand V. Hayden wrote in his report in 1870, it "proved to be the ideal medium for the documentation and commu-

36 Karen Current, *Photography and the Old West* (New York: Abradale Press, 1986), 16.
37 See: Galandi-Pascual, *Zur Konstruktion amerikanischer Landschaft*, 88.
38 Martin A. Berger, "Overexposed: Whiteness and the Landscape Photography of Carleton Watkins," *Oxford Art Journal* 26:1 (2003), 14.
39 Galandi-Pascual, *Zur Konstruktion amerikanischer Landschaft*, 89, My Translation.

Fig. 3: *View from Inspiration Point, Yosemite* (Carleton E. Watkins, 1879).

nication of this process of appropriation."[40] The endless expanse of wilderness became more accessible, at least visually, and the idea of a collective national identity simultaneously more plausible.

The apparent scientific realism of photography heralded a new level in the transformation of landscape from a place of community to a scenic category. Julia Galandi-Pascual makes the following point concerning the photographic documentation of westward expansion:

> [It] visualized Manifest Destiny and the inherently connected pioneer myth [. . .] The geological findings were still assigned to a specific place on a map, but only through photography did the thus named place, until then only seen by members of the expedition, really become visible. [. . .] therefore, these photographs of expeditions must not be thought of as mere illustrations but as analogical to the symbolic form of a *map*. As such, they become

40 Ferdinand V. Hayden, *Sun Pictures of Rocky Mountain Scenery* (New York: J. Bien, 1870), quoted in: Galandi-Pascual, *Zur Konstruktion amerikanischer Landschaft*, 88; Galandi-Pascual, *Zur Konstruktion amerikanischer Landschaft*, 88.

> instruments of visualization in both a tangible and an abstract sense: they name something that, at the same time, they visualize for the first time.[41]

Galandi-Pascual's comparison of landscape photography and the map is striking because it links back to Olwig's understanding of the map as one of the central ways to represent the Renaissance *Landschaften* that were "more suited to the top down power of the lord."[42] The map itself had of course continued to function as a tool of hegemonic (colonial) power in the New World, too: as J.C.H. King points out in his study of Native history, it was "colonial maps", created by means of the "gradually regularized measurement systems [. . .] [that] ensured proper disposal of land alienated from aboriginal peoples."[43] To summarize, the US understanding of landscape, nature, and country cannot be considered in isolation from its European and specifically British inheritance: both the etymological roots of country and *Landschaft* in the sense of polity, community, and customary law as well as their reinterpretation as consolidating spatial scenery have been transferred to the New World. The exceptional prominence of landscape in the formation of US national identity rests to a large degree on the frontier myth and its renditions as has been argued thus far for painting, photography, and the use of landscape as national symbol in Turner's famous essay. The following section expands this focus by taking into account cinema as perhaps the most influential visual medium in recent US history, particularly the nexus of landscape and nationalism on display in the classical Western film.

2 Landscape as "blank space" in the classical Western

Ever since reflections on its structure and meaning gained influence in the 1950s, the Western film, its protagonists, and its landscapes have been widely understood as expressions of ideas about US national identity. An early advocate of these ideas was French film theorist André Bazin who in 1953 published a formative essay with the telling title "The Western, or the American Film par excellence" in which he writes: "the continuous movement of the characters [. . .] is inseparable from its geographical setting and one might well define the Western by its set—the frontier town and its landscapes."[44] As will become apparent, the Western genre's conflation of rural landscape, identity, violence, law, and com-

41 Ibid., 89–90. Emphasis added, My Translation.

42 Olwig, *Landscape, Nature, and the Body Politic*, 26.

43 J.C.H. King, *Blood and Land. The Story of Native North America* (London: Penguin, 2017), 134.

44 André Bazin, *What is Cinema? Vol. 2*, trans. Hugh Gray (Los Angeles/Berkeley: University of California Press, 2004), 141.

munity form such a towering influence in US film-making—and therefore, also on the New Rural Cinema—that it is necessary to take it into consideration as a primogenitor, and sometimes as an explicit point of reference. Some of the films of the New Rural Cinema either include overt references to the Western's iconography (*Winter's Bone, Nomadland, A Single Shot,* etc.) or can even be directly understood as (Neo-)Westerns (*Meek's Cutoff, First Cow, The Rider, Shotgun Stories*).

When the study of popular Hollywood genres as recognizable structures of film production and distribution emerged in film studies from the 1960s, the Western was of central importance. With its easily identifiable iconography, narratives, and themes, it was used to establish the formerly literary concept of genre for the analysis of Hollywood cinema. Landscape scenery was a key factor in classifying the Western genre throughout, as a few examples will demonstrate. In 1969, Jim Kitses published the structuralist study *Horizons West,* in which he developed an interpretative framework of binary oppositions central to the "narrative and dramatic structure" of the genre which included spatial categories such as "wilderness/civilization", "nature/culture", "West/East."[45] Film critic Philip French, writing in 1973, asserted in his book *Westerns* that "landscape has been an integral part of the Western both as an ingredient in the genre's popular appeal and for its role in shaping the dramatic action."[46] In his canonical study (1981) of classical Hollywood genres, Thomas Schatz defined the genre by implicitly referring to its importance in the transformation of landscape from *Landschaft* into scenery: "the Western projects a formalized vision of the nation's infinite possibilities and limitless vistas, thus serving to 'naturalize' the policies of westward expansion and Manifest Destiny."[47] More recent studies still include explicit references to landscape, if with a decidedly more ecocritical thrust, as can be seen in Mary Lee Bandy and Kevin Stoehr's genre study *Ride, Boldly, Ride* (2012):

> It [the Western] is about control of the land, land for the white man's community to tame, nurture, and establish as homestead and town. It is about taking from the earth its riches, its gold and silver, its trees and beavers and buffalo—about making the land yield itself to human desire.[48]

Finally, Sue Thornham notes that "through its invocation of landscape, the Western continues the ideological themes of nineteenth-century American popular culture, with its repeated working through of a national creation narrative."[49] To an

45 Jim Kitses, *Horizons West.* 2nd ed. (London: BFI Publishing, 2004), 25.

46 Philip French, *Westerns: Aspects of a Movie Genre* (London: Secker and Warburg, 1977), 100.

47 Thomas Schatz, *Hollywood Genres* (New York: McGraw-Hill, 1981), 47.

48 Mary Lee Bandy and Kevin Stoehr, *Ride, Boldly Ride: The Evolution of the American Western* (Berkeley: University of California Press, 2012), 14.

49 Thornham, *Spaces of Women's Cinema,* 21.

extent, however, the genre also stands in contrast to narrative cinema's visual media predecessors. The appeal of early nature photography, for example, was the seemingly objective visual accessibility of the country's most impressive landscapes—both for mapping, entertainment, and advertising purposes—and film at first followed this principle. In his book on the origins of the Western, Scott Simmon asserts that "the early 'moving picture' could revel in the mere discovery of landscape" as it offered "glimpses of the West in motion."[50] Soon, however, the new medium added not only movement but also narrative to its formalization of the frontier aesthetic. Very early genre entries such as *The Great Train Robbery* (Edwin S. Porter, 1903) and *The Battle at Eldersbush Gulch* (D.W. Griffith, 1913) offered cinematic versions of historic events or, as David Lusted describes it, "a history refracted through the fiction of folklore and romance narratives."[51] By building on earlier forms of narrative representation of the Western expansion—such as folk music and pulp novels—the Western film genre, to cite Schatz, "began to develop the story of the American West as popular mythology."[52] What is striking, as Simmon notes, "in looking back at the Westerns that began to explode in popularity around 1908 is how often their stories center on Native Americans [. . .] at a time when American Indians were not particularly prominent in popular culture."[53] Such being the case, the landscape images of the early and classical Western can largely be read as a glorification of the white settlers' colonial exploits.

In continuation of the already established pictorial tradition of US painting and photography, landscape scenery took on an especially prominent role in this context. Vast, overwhelming views of empty landscapes defined the genre's iconography from the very beginning, and were, as Virginia Wright Wexman points out, hardly just a backdrop for the action but a vital ingredient in the genre's retelling of the nation's imperialistic beginnings: "The implications of such visions of vast territories embraced in a *single possessive gaze* are far from egalitarian; they rather suggest the more hierarchical, dominating dimension of American imperialist aspirations."[54] This notion of a "single possessive gaze" reproduces the logic of

50 Scott Simmon, *The Invention of the Western Film — A Cultural History of the Genre's First Half-Century (*Cambridge/New York: Cambridge UP, 2003), 3.

51 David Lusted, *The Western* (London: Routledge, 2003), 21.

52 Schatz, *Hollywood Genres*, 45.

53 Simmon, *The Invention of the Western Film*, 3–4.

54 Virginia Wright Wexman, "The Family on the Land: Race and Nationhood in Silent Westerns," in *The Birth of Whiteness — Race and the Emergence of U.S. Cinema*, ed. Daniel Bernadi (New Brunswick, NJ: Rutgers UP, 1996), 142. Emphasis added.

Olwig's assessment of the cartographic representations and perspective drawings of landscapes first used by Renaissance European courts in order to "mirror their authority [visually in the] pictorialized space," i.e. the landscape as scenery.[55]

Furthermore, the Western landscape as "blank space," a concept developed by Jane Tompkins, chimes with Olwig's understanding of landscape as the scenery for the performance of national consolidation. Tompkins argues that "the typical Western opens with a landscape shot. [. . .] All there is, is space, pure and absolute."[56] The landscape's openness, she continues, "flatters the human figure by making it seem dominant and unique, dark against light, vertical against horizontal, solid against plane, detail against blankness."[57] Therefore, she argues, "the apparent emptiness makes the land desirable not only as a space to be filled but also as a *stage on which to perform* and as a territory to master."[58] This chimes with Olwig's identification of the masque, "a play and festivity held on customary holidays" at the Stuart courts of Renaissance Britain, as a major factor in the enforcement of the representation of landscape as perspectival scenery.[59] He argues:

> The masque used the same sort of means to create a sense of community solidarity amongst the elite as did customary festivities amongst the commoners. In the masque, however, custom was replaced with costume [. . .] just as, through the representation of landscape as perspective scenery, unchanging geometrical principles replaced the evolving laws of custom.[60]

Again calling to mind Wexman's notion of the "single possessive gaze" in the Western's landscapes, the masque's perspectival representation of landscape scenery was specifically calibrated so that "the focal point for the lines of perspective was the seat of 'state,' or royal throne. This throne of state was elevated above the public [. . .] so that the king's eye was at the focal point of the lines of perspective."[61] Therefore, the Western shares with this earlier performative, visual tradition that the landscape, while remaining a central element, "ceased to be [. . .] an environment shaped through customary practices and bodily activity [and] instead [. . .] became the scene" on which the national origin myth could be performed in order to be naturalized, "masked," and centralized.[62]

---

55 Olwig, *Landscape, Nature, and the Body Politic*, 30.

56 Jane Tompkins, *West of Everything: The Inner Life of Westerns* (Oxford: Oxford UP, 1992), 69–70.

57 Ibid.

58 Ibid., 74. Emphasis added.

59 Olwig, *Landscape, Nature, and the Body Politic*, 61.

60 Ibid.

61 Ibid., 80.

62 Ibid.

The visual aspect of this performance—the landscape as "blank space" and stage—is closely connected to the genre's recurring thematic negotiation of law and lawlessness. Neil Campbell describes how from "the 'blank spaces' of the western lands was created, forged, and inscribed a grid of human inhabitation, settlement, and narrative."[63] The "grid" is, of course, a visual concept that links back to the perspectival representation and mapping of the land, which, as Olwig argues, is also instrumental in the emergence of a statutory law. Returning to his distinction between landscape paintings in "Italian single-point perspective and [. . .] styles, identified with northern Europe, that sought to reflect the laws of custom that shaped the land," he argues that the changing visual representation of landscape propelled the appropriation of independent *Landschaften* and their customary law under the statutory, "natural" law of the royal elites.[64] The visual representation of landscape in the single-point landscape paintings as well as in maps is constructed, he claims, on the basis of "a rational, lawful framework that is not unlike the principles of [. . .] natural statutory law. Customary law, on the other hand, is built up through a process of development based upon the precedence [. . .] of particular concrete cases."[65]

The geometrical "blank space" of the Western's landscapes can be understood as a similar signifier of the hegemonic "natural" law of the United States, specifically in its relation to land as private property, a further transfer of European landscape ideas to North America. J.C.H. King points out that "European ideas of rights to land in North America derive from seventeenth-century political thinking," referring specifically to John Locke (1632–1704) and his theory of property as a natural right which he first laid out in *Two Treatises of Government* (1689).[66] Faced with the fact that the land to be purchased was already inhabited and therefore, from a European perspective, potentially owned by indigenous peoples, early British settlers qualified Lockean notions of property "with the proposition that land unused or underused by its inhabitants could be appropriated."[67] The "natural" law of property largely functioned as part of the white dominion over indigenous *Landschaften* as it provided, according to Stuart Banner, "the power to establish the legal institutions and the rules by which land transactions would

63 Neil Campbell, *Post-Westerns: Cinema, Region, West* (Lincoln/London: University of Nebraska Press, 2013), 11.

64 Olwig, *Landscape, Nature, and the Body Politic*, 36.

65 Ibid., 37.

66 King, *Blood and Land*, 113.

67 Ibid.

be enforced."[68] From the colonizers' perspective, this worked particularly well, Banner argues:

> [While] the threat of physical force would always be present, [. . .] most of the time it could be kept out of view [. . .] [as] it was not needed. Anglo-Americans could sincerely believe, for most of American history, that they were not conquerors, because they believed they were buying land from the Indians in the same way they bought land from each other.[69]

The law and the landscape, understood as both scenery and property, are thus inseparable in US history.

Therefore, the early and classical Western's fascination with landscape is, as Wexman argues, "a function of its larger concern with the sanctity of private property and its relation to the law. Outlaws [in the classical Western] are typically defined by their crimes against property rather than persons."[70] By closely associating "lawlessness" with disrespect for private property and the ownership of land with idealized settings such as the family farm, the Western, according to Wexman, further naturalizes the idea of right to land: "the concept of the family farm could be used to rationalize not only the Anglo pioneers' abandonment of the aristocratic heritage of Europe but also their seizure of land from other, competing groups in the New World."[71] Wexman concludes that hereby "the European tradition of the family farm could be held up as superior to the patterns established by Indian societies, where land was held communally."[72] Indeed, as Federici relates, the Native peoples' understanding of land and law was generally based around their "lack of attachment to private property" which resulted in "a communal outlook that valued cooperation, group identity, and culture."[73] In order to discredit such competing approaches to land ownership, Western films often "appropriated a particular discourse on racial difference that flourished from the nineteenth to mid-twentieth century," namely a hierarchical racism that was thinly veiled behind ideas concerning the strength and weaknesses of the different races.[74]

It is for this confluence of a scenic understanding of landscape, the propagation of a "natural" law, and the adaptation of racist discourses that the Western helped to retroactively "naturalize a colonial imperialism that simultaneously re-

68 Stuart Banner, *How the Indians Lost Their Land: Law and Power on the Frontier* (London/ Cambridge, MT: Harvard UP, 2005), 6.

69 Ibid.

70 Wexman, "The Family on the Land," 157.

71 Ibid., 158.

72 Ibid., 159.

73 Federici, *Re-Enchanting the World*, 80.

74 Wexman, "The Family on the Land," 158.

quired the removal, and even extermination, of the previous native population, often deemed to be racially inferior, and the obliteration of the memory of this population."[75] While there are examples, even in the classical period, that sought to complicate this perspective on Native Americans, the majority of films "align[ed] the values and achievements of their heroes with those of the growing social order and with the dominant national ideology—usually identified with the ideal of Manifest Destiny, a conviction in the inevitable progress of [. . .] capitalism."[76] Only with the end of the studio era and the beginning of the counterculture-influenced New Hollywood movement did the genre's outlook on the country's imperial past begin to change on a broader scale: many Westerns from the late 1960s onwards, such as *The Wild Bunch* (Sam Peckinpah, 1969), *Little Big Man* (Arthur Penn, 1970), or *Heaven's Gate* (Michael Cimino, 1980), as Nystrom relates, "engaged in a systematic deconstruction of the genre's ideological underpinnings, utilizing the form to critique its racialized narratives of national/imperial Manifest Destiny."[77] I do not aim to chart the historical development of the Western genre in detail here; however, a brief analysis of a recent film that can be understood as a hinge between the Western and the style and focus of the New Rural Cinema, Kelly Reichardt's *Meek's Cutoff* (2010), shall illuminate the relevance of the Western for the larger cycle.

Meek's Cutoff (2010)

The setting of *Meek's Cutoff* harks back to early epic Westerns such as *The Iron Horse* (John Ford, 1924) and *The Covered Wagon* (James Cruze, 1923) as well as later renditions such as John Ford's *Wagon Master* (1950) which dramatized the westward migrations of the mid-1800s. It follows three families of settlers on the Oregon Trail in 1845 as they attempt to cross the high plain desert in their covered wagons under the guidance of a dubious mountain man, Stephen Meek (Bruce Greenwood), who has apparently led them astray. The story is based on historic reality: Meek was a historical figure and his disastrous cut-off as well as many of the events in the film are related in journals and letters of the time. As food on water supplies grow short, tensions among the group constantly mount; when they encounter a Native man (Rod Rondeaux), they must decide whether they

75 Olwig, *The Meanings of Landscape*, 12.

76 *Broken Arrow* (Delmer Daves, 1950), *The Searchers* (John Ford, 1965), and *Apache* (Robert Aldrich, 1954) are three examples which strive for a more nuanced depiction of Native American protagonists whilst, however, still relying heavily on established racist stereotypes; Bandy and Stoehr, *Ride, Boldly Ride*, 230.

77 Nystrom, *Hard Hats, Rednecks, and Macho Men*, 55.

trust him to lead them to a water source and, eventually, their western goal. While Meek is against trusting the Native, one of the women, Emily Tetherow (Michelle Williams), attempts to form a temporary alliance with the stranger.

The slow and quiet film's focus rests on the characters' struggle with the mercilessly dry, monotonous terrain—a struggle that, as quickly becomes obvious, is not presented as heroic, as in many classical Westerns, but as a strenuous, corporeal fight for survival in a surrounding hostile to life. This becomes especially tangible in the detailed scenes of everyday routine activity the film accentuates in frequent shots of the preparation of meagre meals, the careful rationing of water as well as the constant readjustment and redistribution of the precious cargo in the wagons. This establishes a tactile style which draws the viewer into the dangerous reality of the emigrants' temporary community as well as into their experience of the environment surrounding them. Three aspects of this approach align the film with the understanding of landscape found in the New Rural Cinema. Firstly, the landscape here is stripped of the mythical, scenic qualities the classical Western—with which Reichardt's film is conversing—has endowed it with. Mayer comments on the landscape in *Meek's Cutoff* as being "often filmed in static shots and left unmoved by the passing of characters"; therefore, he concludes, it "remains indifferent to human suffering and the futile scheme of Western colonization [and] [. . .] belies any hope of wealth and betterment in migrating west."[78] The relative absence of music, furthermore, allows the film to revel in the aural landscape's oppressive silence, only rarely broken by atmospheric foley sounds or an ominous, unmelodious soundtrack. This soundscape further underlines the landscape's "indifference" to the settler's efforts; indeed, the landscape seems to actively resist its exploitation as a stage for a national origin myth.

Secondly, *Meek's Cutoff* foregrounds a substantive view of landscape that goes against the scenic understanding favored by the classic Western. Thornham describes this as the "closed-in quality of the landscape."[79] She argues that the focus on everyday-activity as well as the film's visual style results in a landscape "which is immense but also claustrophobic and bewildering [. . .] This is not a landscape that the hero can ride over; it encloses, baffles, throws up obstacles. The film's female protagonists—cooking, mending, collecting firewood—live *in* it and with it."[80] Reichardt's film aligns itself with a perspective on landscape that transcends the visual and instead foregrounds the interactive quality of landscape. As Ingold argues, "the landscape is the world as it is known to those who

78 Mayer, "Neo Frontier Cinema," 7.

79 Thornham, *Spaces of Women's Cinema*, 25.

80 Ibid.

dwell therein, who inhabit its places and journey along the paths connecting them."[81] As the film makes clear, however, this does not include the white settlers who are hopelessly unfamiliar with the environment and its paths. This is illustrated in recurring landscape shots that seem to almost correspond to the landscape images of the classical Western which, as Tompkins argues, flatter "the human figure by making it seem dominant and unique."[82] However, by either entirely missing a central human figure or by blurring the shapes of the protagonists (see Fig. 4), these images in *Meek's Cutoff* refute an aesthetic of heroic landscape domination and instead foreground the futility of such an idea.

Fig. 4: *Meek's Cutoff* (Kelly Reichardt, 2010) The protagonists often appear as blurry shapes in the background and thereby refute an aesthetic of landscape domination.

This leads to the third aspect which is the film's foregrounding of subaltern, marginalized perspectives on the US rural landscape both in terms of gender and race. First of all, the narrative emerges from a distinctively female perspective

81 Ingold, *The Perception of the Environment*, 193.
82 Tompkins, *West of Everything*, 74.

which becomes most obvious in the scenes in which the camera stays with the women of the party even when what would be the plot of a more traditional Western is unfolding just off-screen. Thornham points out that "men dominate speech in this film, but the camera stays on the women; we see the men only in the distance as they discuss matters of importance, and, like the women, we have to strain to catch their words."[83] The film illustrates how "men impose their stories" upon the landscape, specifically in Meek's Manifest-Destiny-inspired ideas of dominating the terrain and finding riches which cast him as "a garrulous and self-conscious performer of the Western myth."[84] Moreover, the film denounces these nationalist narratives in the exposure of Meek as a con-artist who is lost in the very environment he claims to be so familiar with. At the film's climax, when Emily stops him at gunpoint from killing the Native man, the demystification of the male "Western hero" Meek and his proclaimed submission of the wilderness is complete.

Finally, the film draws attention to the racialized notion of landscape that is part of the Western myth. Referring back to Tompkins' concept of the Western landscape as "blank space," the film makes it clear throughout that the desert the protagonists are crossing is by no means an empty or uninhabited *space*, but a *place* in the sense that it is shaped by the bodily actions of a local Native community. Thornham points out that throughout, "we see traces of a culture that the pioneers simply cannot read, but whose off-screen presence we are made constantly aware: through the rock drawings, the pile of stones they pass, and the Native American's own words, signs, and gestures."[85] This reminds us that such examples of custom are central to Olwig's definition of *Landschaft*, the substantial understanding of landscape, in that they are "inscribed in the land through physical practice. The landscape [. . .] as a physical place was thus the manifestation of the polity's local custom and common law."[86] *Meek's Cutoff* illustrates how the white colonization of the West can be understood as the transformation of indigenous *Landschaften* into scenic landscape by highlighting the settlers' ignorance of the signs of local custom. The film itself, however, resists the uncritical adoption of the Western's landscape images that are inherently complicit in this transformation and instead reveals how this reactionary landscape vision can be visually countered. Thornham points out how in Reichardt's film, "the land itself invites, and frustrates, a reading; during the long shots in which we gaze at it, we, like

83 Thornham, *Spaces of Women's Cinema*, 26.

84 Ibid.

85 Ibid., 29.

86 Olwig, *Landscape, Nature, and the Body Politic*, 214.

the group, struggle to distinguish marker, direction, signs of water."[87] Thereby, the film makes visible that, in order to challenge scenic landscape images which, as Olwig notes, "parallel [. . .] the structure of nationalistic discourse," landscape must be reframed as the interactive place of community, as *Landschaft*.[88]

Therefore, *Meek's Cutof*, like Reichardt's recent Western *First Cow* (2019), emerges as a powerful link between the classic Western and current indie films set in contemporary rural America. With films like *Wendy and Lucy*, *Night Moves (2013)*, and *Certain Women (2016)*, Reichardt has made some significant contributions to the latter category herself. Katherine Fusco and Nicole Seymour comment in their study of Reichardt's works:

> [*Meek's Cutoff*] clarifies Reichardt's status as a chronicler of US failure. Even when telling perhaps the most triumphant story Americans can tell (the settling of the West and, thus, the development of the United States in its current form) she focuses on the losers.[89]

This dedication to those left behind by the supposed march of progress who are exposed to scarcity and marginalization as well as the film's focus on a substantive understanding of landscape connects its critical view of the United States' mythicized past with the New Rural Cinema's perspective on rural poverty in the neoliberal present.

3 Rural horror — Specters in the wasteland

The Western is the most prominent genre that centrally engages with the historical complexity of US rural landscape; however, other significant examples have been put forward. For example, in his study of working-class identity in 1970s Hollywood films, Derek Nystrom mentions the cycle of action films referred to as Southerns, which he reads as a relocation of the Western's themes to the industrial development of the Southern states; another common assertion is the road movie and its urtext *Easy Rider* (Dennis Hopper, 1969), often understood as an interrogation of the Western's ideology made visible in the protagonists' opposed trajectory from West to East.[90] This section focuses on the rural horror film, sometimes referred to as backwoods horror that in its current form is commonly thought to have originated in Herschell Gordon Lewis' low-budget exploitation

87 Thornham, *Spaces of Women's Cinema*, 29.

88 Olwig, *Landscape, Nature, and the Body Politic*, 225.

89 Katherine Fusco and Nicole Seymour, *Kelly Reichardt* (Chicago: University of Illinois Press, 2017), 49.

90 See: Nystrom, *Hard Hats, Rednecks, and Macho Men*, 56.

film *Two Thousand Maniacs!* (1964) and continues to be a vivid strain of US genre cinema to this day.

The subgenre is of particular interest to this book because it arguably represents the longest running cycle of US films that unflinchingly address rural poverty while usually lacking the conciliatory rhetoric of the Horatio Alger myth. Rural horror films such as *Two Thousand Maniacs!*, *Deliverance*, *The Texas Chainsaw Massacre* (Tobe Hooper, 1974), *The Hills Have Eyes* (Wes Craven, 1977), *Southern Comfort* (Walter Hill, 1981) as well as recent outings like the *Wrong Turn* (2003–present) franchise are commonly misread as exclusively demonizing and dehumanizing the (white) rural poor. They can alternatively be seen either as attempts to drastically exaggerate and thereby subvert traditional class-based stereotyping, or as the cultural return of a repressed US class system and urban/rural hostility that establishes an unambiguous way to address the violence inherent in capitalist exploitation. Eric Savoy has asserted that the "entire tradition of American gothic can be conceptualized as the attempt to invoke [. . .] the specter of Otherness that haunts the house of national narrative."[91] In that sense, one might read rural horror films as a recent cultural form of a US Gothic tradition that has continuously served to address issues of divergence in class, race, or gender from a supposed national norm.

Until recently, rural horror was an almost exclusively white sub-genre—it used to pit a white, urban, mobile middle class against a white, rural, immobile underclass. Considering that the US South, a common setting for these films, has been the region with the largest African American population for generations, the relative absence of Black and other non-white protagonists was a notable gap that has seen some tentative challenges in more recent genre entries. Carol Clover suggests that the employment of poor white antagonists in these films "suggests that anxieties no longer expressible in ethnic or racial terms have become projected onto a safe target—safe not only because it is (nominally) white, but because it is infinitely displaceable."[92] Nevertheless, racism and the legacy of slavery are certainly present in the subtexts of these films as they contribute to the notion of backwardness associated with the US South that these films play on. It should also be noted, however, that until very recently, the US horror genre *as a whole* displayed an overwhelmingly white racial homogeneity.

91 Eric Savoy, "The Face of the Tenant: A Theory of American Gothic," in *American Gothic: New Interventions in a National Narrative*, ed. Eric Savoy and Robert Martin (Iowa City: University of Iowa Press, 1998), 13–14.

92 Carol Clover, *Men, Women, and Chainsaws. Gender in the Modern Horror Film.* 2nd ed. (Oxford: Princeton UP, 2015), 135.

Rural horror forms an exceptionally important part in understanding the New Rural Cinema which at times directly borrows this confrontational subgenre's iconography—examples include the prominent use of a chainsaw at the end of *Winter's Bone,* the setting of a dilapidated pig farm in *Undertow,* the focus on cultish religiosity in *Them That Follow (*Britt Poulton, Dan Madison Savage, 2019) and others. More crucial than these direct references, however, is the popularization of certain landscapes images and tropes that demonstrate the interlinkage between rural horror and the films at hand. Firstly, the New Rural Cinema is in dialogue with the lasting cultural impact of the figure of "the hillbilly" and its conflation of class and race with which horror films like *Deliverance* have familiarized not just domestic, but global audiences. Secondly, films like *The Texas Chainsaw Massacre* and *The Hills Have Eyes* established an iconography of the American wasteland that equates rural America with a landscape of ruin and poverty, yet thereby also enables a landscape understanding that disrupts the pastoral scenery. Finally, these horror films are almost always concerned with notions of community—even if frequently presented as entirely perverse—in a way that is otherwise rare in US cinema. I will close this section with an analysis of *The Tall Man* (Pascal Laugier, 2012) which emerges as a hinge film between rural horror and the New Rural Cinema.

3.1 The hillbilly

In a recent study of rural horror films, Linnie Blake asserts that "the United States has a very long history of representing the inhabitants of its own isolated rural places or backwoods communities as monstrous, grotesque, diseased, and polluted."[93] It thus seems necessary to provide some historical background on the emergence of the "hillbilly" as a cultural figure that haunts contemporary depictions of white rural poverty, and therefore also films like *Winter's Bone* and *Leave No Trace.* The mostly derogatory, sometimes embraced figure of the "hillbilly"—alternatively called "redneck", "white trash" or, longer ago, the "lubber" or the "cracker"—is, as Anthony Harkins puts forward, an ambiguous social construct. He argues that it "served at times of national soul-searching and throughout the twentieth century as a continually negotiated mythic space through which modern Americans have attempted to define themselves and their national

93 Linnie Blake, *The Wounds of Nations. Horror Cinema, Historical Trauma and National Identity* (Manchester: Manchester UP, 2013), 128.

identity and to reconcile the past and the present."[94] "Hillbilly" refers most commonly to the inhabitants of Southern Appalachia and the Ozarks; "redneck" appears to relate to Southerners in general, including Texas and Florida.[95] However, the different derogatory terms have long been bleeding into each other as Archie Green demonstrates.[96] Therefore, the concrete geographic placement of the ideological construct of the "hillbilly" is not of central importance; as Harkins relates, it can be found "anywhere on the rough edges of the landscape and economy."[97] The recent emergence and success of long-running (Reality) TV shows such as *Moonshiners* (2011–present), *Duck Dynasty* (2012–2017), *Hillbilly Blood* (2013–present), and many others, all of which employ proudly self-described "hillbilly" protagonists, suggests that the negotiation Harkins mentions continues in the twenty-first century as well.

Contrarily, Isenberg sees the hillbilly as a much more sinister symbol of a deliberately hidden, naturalized US class system. In *White Trash*, her extensive study on stereotyping rural poverty in the United States, she positions the hillbilly as a symptom of the specifically US American conflation of class and race. In the United States, a country that considers social mobility and the absence of a traditional class system as some of its core principles, she puts forward, poverty must necessarily be considered to have a biological, genetic origin. Therefore, she argues that the unshakable belief in meritocracy helped to mask a "relentless class system evolved out of recurring agrarian notions regarding the character and potential of the land, the value of labor, and critical concepts of breeding."[98] Matt Wray and Annalee Newitz come to a similar conclusion:

> In a country so steeped in the myth of classlessness [. . .] the white trash stereotype serves as a useful way of blaming the poor for being poor. "White trash" is not just a classist slur—it's also a racial epithet that marks out certain whites as a dysgenic race unto themselves.[99]

Isenberg builds on this assumption when she argues that the foundation of such a class of "trash" lies in the earliest days of British colonialism in North America. The barren, undeveloped "wasteland" required a substantial work force of "waste people" that would turn the wild terrain into farmland. British promoters of coloniza-

94 Anthony Harkins, *Hillbilly: A Cultural History of an American Icon* (Oxford: Oxford UP, 2005), 4.

95 See: Harkins, *Hillbilly*, 5.

96 See: Archie Green, "Hillbilly Music: Source and Symbol," *The Journal of American Folklore* 78:209 (1965), 204.

97 Harkins, *Hillbilly*, 5.

98 Isenberg, *White Trash*, 5.

99 Annalee Newitz and Matt Wray, *White Trash: Race and Class in America* (London: Routledge, 1997), 1.

tion in the sixteenth century consequently suggested to use the North American colonies as a "waste firm" for the growing numbers of the homeless and the poor in the motherland. America, Isenberg summarizes, "would become a place where the surplus poor, the waste people of England, could be converted into economic assets. The land and the poor could be harvested together."[100] Often, these so-called indentured workers had no other choice but to set forth on their journey to the colonies.

Ibram X. Kendi puts forward a similar historical argument, but focusses on the Black perspective on white rural poverty:

> Some uncorroborated reports suggest that enslaved Blacks created the term. Blacks had seen poor Whites doing the master's dirty work [. . .] while clinging to the stinking fallacy that the lowest of them was still better than the highest Black person. [. . .] Black consumers of racist ideas had come to associate Whiteness with wealth and power, and education and slaveholding. Only through the "White trash" construction could ideas of superior Whiteness be maintained, as it made invisible the majority of White people, the millions in poverty, by saying they were not ordinary Whites.[101]

Yet another historical point of origin of the "hillbilly" can be found in the groups of settlers, primarily from the British Isles, who had found permanent residence in the mountains and woods of the South. As Bernice Murphy argues in her study of the rural Gothic in US culture, these settlers "even early on in the movement to the frontier [. . .] saw themselves (and were perceived) as being different from the dominant settler culture."[102] Etymologically, the term supposedly originates in Scottish dialect. It may be a combination of "hill-folk", on the one hand, describing "a rebel against Charles II [because] Scots hill-folk [. . .] in 1693 were noted for [. . .] prudence in seeking isolation away from their rejected monarch's rule"; and "billie", on the other hand, used in Scottish dialect as companion or mate. Murphy goes on to describe these groups of settlers: "they saw themselves as an essentially classless society, had a lack of respect for centralized authority, high levels of personal freedom and individualism, were dominated by [. . .] small kinship groups, [and] mixed with the Indians (both racially and culturally)."[103] This last suggestion leads back to a racial confusion surrounding the white rural poor and points towards a visual motif of representing them with stereotypical Native characteristics.

---

100 Isenberg, *White Trash*, 21.

101 Ibram X. Kendi, *Stamped from the Beginning: The Definitive History of Racist Ideas in America* (London: Bodley Head, 2017), 238.

102 Bernice Murphy, *The Rural Gothic in American Popular Culture: Backwoods Horror and Terror in the Wilderness* (London: Palgrave Macmillan, 2013), 134.

103 Green, "Hillbilly Music," 204; Murphy, *The Rural Gothic in American Popular Culture*, 134.

Throughout US history, Meredith McCarroll argues, the white rural poor have been presented as being "less than white" or "unwhite." Especially, as she points out, the association of poor whites with Native Americans serves to construct an inferior national subject through the conflation of race and class. In popular culture, she claims, both Native Americans and poor Appalachian whites are made to represent "not only the ambivalence around the quaint past that cannot survive the pending process of industrialism but also the inevitable violent brutality that emerges outside civilized reaches."[104] This chimes with Clover's analysis of *Deliverance* in which she argues that in rural horror films "both redneck and redskin [sic] are figured as indigenous peoples on the verge of being deprived of their lands [. . .] to the point that the rednecks of modern Horror even look and act like movie Indians."[105] This powerful conflation of class and race, McCarroll summarizes, "functions to preserve whiteness while maintaining an ambivalence about the clearly inferior racial other."[106] She specifically identifies rural horror films in perpetrating "the caricature of the isolated mountaineer who turns to (sexual) violence and grotesque torture of outsiders and intruders" and, like Clover, traces these images back to the success of *Deliverance*.[107] While *Deliverance* is not always read as a clear-cut horror film, I will consider it as part of the 1970s rural horror cycle as it proved extremely influential in the development of the sub-genre's central themes and iconography. It differs from *The Texas Chainsaw Massacre, The Hills Have Eyes* and others insofar as its more realistic, slightly less monstrous portrayal of "hillbillies" has made many critics believe that its intentions are indeed to imply that the murderous, sexually perverted "traits are inbred in some hillbilly communities in the South," as Larry Langman and David Ebner claim, for example.[108]

Furthermore, McCarroll explicitly establishes a link between rural horror films like *Deliverance,* on the one hand, and *Winter's Bone* on the other, relating to their common focus on isolated landscapes. She acknowledges that, in comparison to horror films dealing with isolated rural communities, *Winter's Bone* "resist[s] the clear victim-perpetrator dichotomy and instead demonstrates the difficulty for Ree to ever leave her mountainous home. In these and other films the isolation is

---

104 Meredith McCarroll, *Unwhite: Appalachia, Race, and Film* (Athens, GA: University of Georgia Press, 2018), 22.

105 Clover, *Men, Women and Chainsaws, 136.*

106 McCarroll, *Unwhite*, 38.

107 Ibid., 23.

108 Larry Langman and David Ebner, *Hollywood's Image of the South: A Century of Southern Films* (Westport, CT: Greenwood, 2001), 112.

at least partly to blame for the evils of the community."[109] I disagree with McCarroll insofar as both many rural horror films as well *Winter's Bone* situate the causes of the "evils" she describes within the context of capitalist society—such as the spatial restructuring of the means of production from the rural to the urban and the economic devastation it causes—not within the communities themselves. Regarding *Deliverance* in particular, I agree with Nystrom's extensive analysis of the film which posits that the concrete class dimension the film draws up has mostly been ignored in favor of condemning the film for its grisly (sexual) violence.

The film, based on James Dickey's novel, follows a group of four middle-aged, middle-class white men on a canoe trip on the Cahulawassee River, which is soon going to be damned up and turned into a lake. After being consistently condescending to the local, impoverished inhabitants, the group is suddenly attacked by two or more "mountain men." One of the protagonists, Bobby (Ned Beatty), is violently raped, two others are murdered. The mild-mannered Ed (Jon Voight) is able to outsmart and kill their pursuers. A final coda suggests, however, that his encounter with the "other America" has severely traumatized him. Nystrom argues that "many critics aligned the hill people with nature [. . .] thus the violence visited upon the middle-class vacationers by the mountain men is described as an expression of nature."[110] The emphasis on ecological destruction and structural poverty that the film displays from its very first images, however, strongly suggests that readings such as Nystrom's are more productive. Nystrom interprets the film as an articulation of the conflict of integration of the old "Vanishing South" into the narrative of the "Sunbelt—the South as a booming economic region in the 1970s. The film asks its audience to consider what has been violently repressed and effaced to secure the [. . .] [middle-class] sovereignty over this transformed landscape."[111] As we will see, such socio-economic subtexts of rural horror are often ignored.

The extreme geographical isolation McCarroll mentions, leads to another aspect of the stereotypes surrounding poor rural communities: incest and intermarriage. These notions have long been cited as evidence for a measurable, racial inferiority of white rural communities in general and isolated mountain communities in particular. In the late eighteenth and early nineteenth century, for example, the research institute Eugenics Records Office (ERO) undertook supposedly scientific studies which set out to prove that large numbers of the rural whites were "genetic defectives" due to wide-spread incest. The consequences of studies

109 McCarroll, *Unwhite*, 23.

110 Nystrom, *Hard Hats, Rednecks and Macho Men*, 68.

111 Ibid., 77.

like these went as far as open calls for sterilization.[112] Murphy argues that while this sort of eugenic practice was discredited in the 1940s for its obvious links to fascism, their influence lingers in US culture until today, particularly in the rural horror genre. She claims that "part of the reason why these stereotypes were so resonant was because the 'Poor White Trash' category medicalized by the ERO drew upon [. . .] pre-existing categories of the rural white."[113] She then goes on to argue that "the backwoods horror sub-genre [. . .] draws upon [this] powerful strain of eugenic thinking."[114] She references 1970s films like *Deliverance* and *The Hills Have Eyes* as well as current examples of rural horror films such as *Albino Farm* (Joe Anderson, 2009) for their ongoing engagement with notions of genetic defectiveness and implicitly suggests fascist undertones in these films.

Further highlighting the problematic nature of this kind of stereotyping, Murphy claims that "it is rare to see an American Horror film in which those who live in rural poverty are depicted with any degree of sensitivity or complexity."[115] She follows this argument by comparing films like *Wrong Turn* and *The Texas Chainsaw Massacre* to the, from her perspective, more positive example of *Winter's Bone*:

> [*Winter's Bone*] depicts the rural poor with a striking degree of sympathy and sensitivity. [. . .] *Winter's Bone* certainly isn't a backwoods horror film and nor does it aspire to be despite containing characters who, in a slightly different context, certainly would fit in. Here, the brutal pragmatism so often twisted into callousness and cruelty in backwoods horror becomes a signifier of the stoicism and resilience necessary to survive in an environment in which both the family and nature have little nourishment to offer.[116]

Murphy's comparison is warranted in the context of her study of rural gothic narrative elements yet seems baffling from a genre perspective inasmuch as it completely ignores both the specificity and complexity of the horror genre as well as any notion of class within these films. Rural horror's employment of the "hillbilly" is, as Blake notes in relation to *Wrong Turn*, "a knowing illustration as to how the monstrous other may be deployed to serve dominant ideologies of class and nationhood."[117] While making a similar point about the invisibility of class as *Winter's Bone*, rural horror films arguably *have to* do away with a certain degree

112 Newitz and Wray, *White Trash*, 2; see: Harkins, *Hillbilly*, 111.
113 Murphy, *The Rural Gothic in American Popular Culture*, 144–145.
114 Ibid., 176.
115 Ibid., 173.
116 Ibid., 175.
117 Blake, *The Wounds of Nations*, 143.

of sensitivity and complexity in order to be recognizable as an entry into the larger context of the horror genre. The violence perpetrated by its "hillbilly" antagonists demonstrates not necessarily, or exclusively a reactionary, classist tendency as suggested by Murphy, yet may offer a possibility to draw attention to inequality and poverty. This is achieved by the drastic on-screen violence and, as Robin Wood points out in his influential study of 1970s horror, the presence of "the Other as it operates within our culture, of its relation to repression and oppression, and of how it is characteristically dealt with."[118]

To accuse these horror films of a lack of sensitivity is to miss their point; their aim is not to foster understanding for the rural poor but to conjure up, to come back to Savoy's claim, "the specter of Otherness that haunts the house of national narrative" by means of exaggeration and interrogation of preconceived stereotypes.[119] Rural horror films drastically highlight regional economic inequality within the US and the degradation the victims of extreme poverty experience. This act of making poverty visible is in itself a progressive project, specifically if placed within decaying landscapes and infrastructure suggesting systemic failures rather than individual incapability. As the author and political activist Michael Harrington writes in *The Other America* (1962), his influential study of poverty in the US: "That the poor are invisible is one of the most important things about them. They are not simply neglected and forgotten [. . .] what is much worse, they are not seen."[120] Rural horror is perhaps the most consistent and the most popular US cinematic project countering this invisibility of poverty. Because it does so within the sometimes-problematic tropes and limitations of its generic conventions, however, which are often unpalatable to both mainstream cinemagoers and critics, these interventions tend to be ignored.[121]

---

118 Robin Wood, *Hollywood from Vietnam to Reagan* (New York/Chichester: Columbia UP, 1986), 73.

119 Savoy, "The Face of the Tenant," 13–14.

120 Michael Harrington, *The Other America: Poverty in the United States*. 2nd ed. (New York: Simon & Schuster, 1997), 7.

121 The situation might have changed in recent years with a wave of US Horror films that address social justice issues surrounding race and gender, rely on high production values, and have at times even been graced with Academy-Award-nominations. However, there still exists an undercurrent of direct-to-DVD/direct-to-streaming horror releases that confirm to Robin Wood's assessment of the genre. Wood asserted in 1986 that, despite being immensely popular, Horror films "are dismissed with contempt by the majority of reviewer-critics, or simply ignored" (Wood, *Hollywood from Vietnam to Reagan*, 77). While he notices a certain upswing in respectability conferred on the genre by Alfred Hitchcock's *Psycho* (1960), he asserts that "the disdain still largely continues" (ibid.).

Furthermore, critics of rural horror often assume a straight-forward viewer identification with the urban protagonist group and a repulsed reaction to the "hillbillies." Clover, for example, argues that the rural horror film follows the maxim that "people from the city are people like us [the spectators]. People from the country [. . .] are people not like us."[122] After she lists certain negative features generally attributed to the rural antagonists—unwashed, inarticulate, sexually perverse—she concludes: "Finally, and above all, country people are poor—if not utterly impoverished, at least considerably poorer than their city visitors."[123] She then concedes that the films almost always place these protagonists within the context of "their dilapidated houses [which] are surrounded by rusting cars," a landscape that clearly signposts systemic inequality.[124] She concludes that rural horror's narratives illustrate "the confrontation between haves and have-nots, or even more directly, between exploiters and their victims."[125] Paradoxically, however, she continues to assume throughout the chapter, that "the film's 'we' [is] city people" and that it is them that the audience is supposed to sympathize with and thereby encouraged to overcome their own "economic guilt" towards rural devastation they (as urban people) have implicitly caused.[126]

Clover's reading does, however, not take into account the verifiable, substantial proportion of rural viewers of the 1970s rural horror cycle. Jacqueline Pinkowitz makes a convincing claim that many rural horror exploitation films of the sixties and seventies reached marginalized rural audiences through their exhibition in cheap drive-in cinemas.[127] In his Marxist reading of the splatter subgenre—an extremely violent variety of horror to which many of the rural horror films appertain—Mark Steven extends this perspective when he asserts that the genre's position on the disreputable margins of the film industry is mirrored in its interest in marginal antagonists and, therefore, in its appeal to marginalized audiences. His argument is worth quoting at some length here:

> Splatter films are popular, but they are simultaneously marginalized. Traditionally sustained by grindhouse theatres and cheaply produced videos, even since becoming more accessible splatter holds an outsider status, inassimilable into the mainstream. These films seem to recognize their status not only as commodities but also as an aggressive reaction

122 Clover, *Men, Women and Chainsaws*, 124.
123 Ibid., 126.
124 Ibid.
125 Ibid.
126 Ibid., 131; ibid., 134.
127 See: Jacqueline Pinkowitz, "Down South: Regional Exploitation Films, Southern Audiences, and Hillbilly Horror in Herschell Gordon Lewis's *Two Thousand Maniacs!*" *Journal of Popular Film and Television* 44:2 (2016), 115.

> against the marketization of particular images. [. . .] Reflecting this situation at the level of narrative, where those contextual matters and production issues can be expressed unambiguously, splatter films regularly concern themselves with violence enacted by the economically disenfranchised and the socially marginalized, and regularly against the beneficiaries of that system which ensures their status as underclass. If mutilation is indeed the message, here that message is delivered by [. . .] unemployed abattoir workers [. . .] [or] by the hillbilly opponents of a long-secured federation. Splatter's antagonist subjectivity belongs to those whose exclusion from the commodity is at its uttermost brutal. The true heroes of splatter are the victims of capital.[128]

The use of the word "heroes" is certainly a provocation here considering that rural horror's underclass characters habitually engage in torture, murder, and rape. It is accurate, however, that it is indeed usually the antagonists who become the recognizable focus of these often long-running horror franchises such as Leatherface in *The Texas Chainsaw Massacre* and its many sequels and prequels, or the monstrous clan surrounding Three Finger and Saw Tooth in the original *Wrong Turn* series. The urban protagonists remain more or less anonymous and are only rarely granted a backstory. Pinkowitz comes to a similar conclusion in her exploration of rural horror's first entry *Two Thousand Maniacs!* when she argues that "it is possible that *Maniacs'* marginalized audiences (and filmmaker) found some type of solidarity with the hillbillies' non-mainstream positionality and their maligned culture."[129] Kjetil Rødje puts forward the following, adjacent argument in his study of splatter films:

> When considering the composition of the original audience for these movies, it seems plausible that the films' victims do not share the same demographic profile as the typical audience members. Hence, audiences are not invited to identify and sympathize with the victims slaughtered on-screen. Rather, the films feed into already existing biases, connecting with possible feelings of resentment directed towards more privileged social groups. [. . .] The portrayals confirm stereotypes and reinforce perceptions about social groups economically and culturally distant from the audience members.[130]

While this fatalistic, cynical celebration of ultra-violent, often misogynist class conflict may be ethically problematic and far removed from the New Rural Cinema's more measured, broadly neo-realist approach to rural poverty, both are connected by their desire to critically engage with the figure of the hillbilly and its ongoing significance for maligned, poor country people more generally. Both cycles emerge from an urgency to address the unspoken rupture in the suppos-

---

128 Mark Steven, *Splatter Capital*. London: Repeater Books, 2017, 15.

129 Pinkowitz, "Down South," 117.

130 Kjetil Rødje, *Images of Blood in American Cinema: The Tingler to The Wild Bunch* (London: Routledge, 2015), 64.

edly homogenous national image that attempts to naturalize its class-based discrimination. The rural horror films willfully and gleefully escalate the stereotypes and eugenic notions of genetic inferiority associated with the rural poor and thereby raise the "hillbillies" from the mere inane to the downright monstrous in their imagined class confrontations—and thus grant them a caustic anti-capitalist agency.

The films of the New Rural Cinema, on the other hand, seek to counter these stereotypes by emphasizing more realistically the isolated landscapes their characters' dwell in and generally avoid focusing on confrontations between urban and rural protagonists. The films staunchly assume a rural subjectivity and attempt to dissolve the harmful notion of the hillbilly altogether. The following section will shift the focus from the inhabitants on to the environments rural horror generates and establish a connection between these sometimes hellish wastelands and the landscapes designated by the infrastructural decline of neoliberal austerity politics.

3.2 The wasteland

The emergence of the initial cycle of rural horror films in the 1970s is often associated with a simultaneous economic recession in the United States. Mark Steven argues:

> In the early 1970s economic expansion was met by stagflation when accumulation was driven downward by the decline of industrial manufacture's rate of profit [. . .] this signal crisis was displaced by a shift from manufacture into finance, [. . .] [nevertheless] that very shift led to the further extirpation of industrial labor, primarily through foreclosures, offshoring, and mass redundancy.[131]

These economic conditions directly inspired the narratives and environments of the first wave of rural horror, as in the case of *The Texas Chainsaw Massacre*: Tobe Hooper's much-discussed debut, Steven claims, "presents its horrors as indexical to the circumstances faced by the industrial labor force in the early 1970s. Here a slaughterhouse foreclosure and a petrol shortage combine to generate the conditions of possibility for gore."[132] Furthermore, *The Texas Chainsaw Massacre* remains a powerful example of the cinematic construction of rural landscapes because it combines a realist iconography of rural decline with gothic imagery of "haunted" mansions, human and animal remains, graveyards, and secret attics.

---

131 Steven, *Splatter Capital*, 73.
132 Ibid.

While *Deliverance* in its opening and closing scenes only hinted at a similar notion—its ending portrays, as Clover describes, "a community in the process of literal dismemberment" as a small rural town is deconstructed before its planned flooding—*The Texas Chainsaw Massacre* fully envisions the rural South as a desolated, otherworldly place.[133] Its setting, as Christopher Sharrett argues, is "a deserted wasteland of dissolution [. . .] yards of dying cattle, abandoned gasoline stations, defiled graveyards, crumbling mansions, and a ramshackle farmhouse of psychotic killers. *The Texas Chainsaw Massacre* [is] [. . .] recognizable as a statement about the endtime of American experience."[134] David Bell makes a similar point when he describes the film's wasteland as a spatial manifestation of "an inevitable, entropic implosion [. . .] of frontierist expansionism."[135] The wasteland here is not only indicative of regional economic devastation but of a rural-urban rift so fundamental that it heralds a cataclysmic ending of the consolidating myths of the frontier and Manifest Destiny.

A similar argument can be made for *The Hills Have Eyes*, which director Wes Craven himself has described as a "fairy tale[. . .] for the apocalypse," even if compared to *The Texas Chainsaw Massacre*, the film is clearly more inspired by the iconography of the Western than by gothic fiction.[136] The opening credits are displayed over images of a desert mountain range in the twilight of the approaching dawn. Only Don Peake's ominous synth-score dispels the notion that the film might be a clear-cut Western in these first moments, and instead firmly positions the images within a horror tradition. In an instant, the interplay between landscape imagery and music thus establishes the setting as existing on "the fringes of the US frontier, now portrayed as wasteland."[137] This is reinforced directly after the credits, when the film's setting switches to the nearby dilapidated petrol station owned by Fred (John Steadman). The grizzled owner, as will gradually emerge, is in constant, but reluctant contact with the "family" of mutant cannibals living in the surrounding hills and is indeed their leader Jupiter's biological father. His petrol station is located near the ruins of a burned-down house—the fire, we later learn, was set by his mutant son—as well as all kinds of rusted de-

133 Clover, *Men, Women and Chainsaws*, 128.

134 Christopher Sharrett, "The Idea of Apocalypse in *The Texas Chainsaw Massacre,*" in *Planks of Reason: Essays on the Horror Film*, ed. Christopher Sharrett and Barry Keith Grant (Lanham, MD: Scarecrow Press, 2004), 318.

135 David Bell, "Anti-Idyll: Rural Horror," in *Contested Countryside Cultures: Rurality and Socio-Cultural Marginalisation*, ed. Paul Cloke and Jo Little, London: Routledge, 1997, 105.

136 Wes Craven, "'Fairy Tales for the Apocalypse': Wes Craven on the Horror Film," Interview by Christopher Sharrett. *Literature/Film Quarterly*, 13:3 (1985), 142.

137 Sharrett, "The Idea of the Apocalypse," 139.

bris and waste. In an ironic employment of a visual cliché featured in countless Westerns, a tumbleweed is blown across the dusty road, signaling abandonment and encroaching wilderness. The surrounding desert seems vast, impenetrable, and hostile which indeed chimes with the film's title: the suggestion that the "hills have eyes" clearly casts the wasteland itself as an antagonistic force against the unsuspecting urban Carter family on their way to California.[138] Furthermore, the cannibals are depicted throughout as extensions of nature, both through their position in the frame—hidden between rocks or shrubbery, blending into the darkness of the desert—as well as through their costumes which feature bones, feathers, and sticks.

This clearly casts them as parallel to Native Americans in the film's central, Western-inspired conflict between a "civilized" and a "savage" family unit. While I agree with McCarroll that this taps into a potentially racist discourse surrounding the stereotypical Indians' "savagery or spirituality [which] hinges on white performance of white imagining of Native American culture to preserve and improve white society," I am interested in its significance for the film's landscape here.[139] What I think is crucial in *The Hills Have Eyes*, is the notion that the rural landscape is alive, inhabited, and not reducible to easily traversable, *mappable*, scenic space. In a key scene, the map which Bob Carter has brought literally causes him to crash the family truck and RV. After Bob has diverged from the highway, mother and daughter struggle over the map in order to figure out their way out of this stretch of desert. When a fighter jet passes just above the car—there is a military base nearby—the map almost seems to develop a life of its own as it flies into Bob's face.[140] He loses control over the car and crashes it, leaving the family stranded in the isolated landscape inhabited by the cannibals. The conflict between the Carters and the cannibals is, therefore, also one between a scenic understanding of landscape as map associated with the urban winners of capitalism, and an interactive notion of *Landschaft*. That the latter is associated with the murderous clan of mutants, sarcastically references both the historic violence used in conquering and consolidating the land as well as the present-day suffering hidden away in the unseemly corners of the US countryside.

Thus, taking into consideration rural horror's focus on confrontations between urban tourists and rural inhabitants, it becomes clear that these films de-

138 It remains unclear where exactly the film is supposed to take place. As the Carter family is on their way to California, one might assume Arizona, Nevada, or Utah. It was shot in the desert surrounding San Berdino, California.

139 McCarroll, *Unwhite*, 25.

140 See also the concept of the "crisis of the map" to describe the geographies of "the weird and the fantastic" developed by Greve and Zappe (2019), which I will elaborate on in Chapter Five.

liberately attempt to attack the notion of a scenic countryside—both in the sense of a pastoral aesthetic and of Olwig's notion of scenic space. By foregrounding the iconography of the wasteland—or the "anti-idyll," to use Bell's term—they uncover the economic realities hidden underneath the veneer of the scenic landscape.[141] The construction of landscape in the 1970s rural horror cycle as "anti-idyll" can be read as a deliberate formal disruption, or unmasking, of pastoral beauty in order to foreground the existence of rural poverty. This disruption violently shifts the perspective from an urban tourist's view to a rural inhabitant's more substantive sense of place, and thus, from scenic landscape to *Landschaft*. In a sense, films like *The Hills Have Eyes* explore the horrifying dialectic of Ingold's claim that "through living in it, the landscape becomes part of us, just as we are part of it," as the interaction with the wasteland here clearly breeds mental illness, sadism, and violence.[142]

The more recent cycle of rural horror—beginning in 2002/2003 with the original *Wrong Turn* (Rob Schmidt, 2003), *Cabin Fever* (Eli Roth, 2002), *House of 1000 Corpses* (Rob Zombie, 2003), and the big-budget-remake of *The Texas Chainsaw Massacre* (Marcus Nispel, 2003)—is different in so far as it knowingly references the original cycle to a degree of pastiche; crucially, these more recent films mostly elide political contextualization of the rural wasteland by increasing the amount of gore and sadistic violence to an extreme degree that interrupts both the narrative and the cinematic engagement with the wasteland. The remade *The Texas Chainsaw Massacre*, for example, expands a scene of the original in which a victim is hung up on a meat cleaver by having the killer Leatherface rub salt into the screaming man's wounds; at the same time, however, the economic background of mass unemployment and industrial decline is almost entirely absent here, at least explicitly. On the one hand, it may therefore seem as if rural wastelands in these twenty-first-century-iterations emerge much less from a genuine urgent interest in the implications of rural marginalization and more from a strictly commercial approach.

On the other hand, if we understand the 1970s cycle as a response to a specific economic downturn, as Steven suggests, the early-2000s reappearance of rural horror can be read as an expression of a cynical acceptance that thirty years on, things had generally not changed for the better in rural America. As argued before, under neoliberalism and its economic "turn to more cutthroat free-market policies in the 1980s, American capitalism has systematically under-

141 Bell, "Anti-Idyll," 105.

142 Ingold, *The Perception of the Environment*, 191.

developed rural and small-town regions of the United States."[143] 2002, the year that many of the films of this new cycle were released, marked the beginning of a rise in rural child poverty rates in the US that would increase dramatically until 2012. Already sparse infrastructure in rural areas was further diminished by the slashing of government funding. The distinctive reappearance of this particular kind of genre film at this particular time is thus not entirely without political relevance.

Strikingly, the new rural horror cycle also coincides with the emergence of early outliers of the New Rural Cinema cycle like *Undertow* and Debra Granik's debut film *Down to the Bone* (2004). One might argue therefore that the rural wasteland as a significant setting in US cinema that allows for the investigation of economic inequality and rural-urban divisions in the US has spread from the realm of the horror genre to other film cycles such as, but not limited to, the New Rural Cinema.[144] The New Rural Cinema utilizes images of rural landscapes as wastelands to comment on rural poverty, yet they exchange the aggressive, fatalistic tone of rural horror for more ambiguous approaches. This tendency is also reflected in the representation of marginalized rural communities.

3.3 Community / *Landschaft*

In the rural horror film *Southern Comfort*, a squad of Louisiana Army National Guard soldiers on a weekend maneuver becomes lost in the bayou, a labyrinthine swamp landscape that is impossible to navigate for the mostly urban men.[145] From the very beginning, the film introduces the nine members of the squad as a disparate, cantankerous group of individualists, following their own credos and philosophies. When one member of the squad shoots a round of blank ammunition at a group of Cajun hunter-trappers, the Cajuns begin to hunt down and kill the soldiers in the impenetrable woods and swamps of the bayou. The attackers remain almost completely invisible and are only fully revealed in the film's climax. In this "showdown," the two remaining soldiers reach a Cajun village deep in the bayou where a communal festivity is being held. The contrast between the

143 Edelman, "How Capitalism Underdeveloped Rural America."

144 Another example is the recent cycle of violent post-apocalyptic science fiction films such as *The Road* (2009) and *Book Of Eli* (2010).

145 As with *Deliverance*, one may disagree with my assessment of *Southern Comfort* as a horror film here. Both films certainly refrain from stylised Gothic elements and create a much more realistic view of the rural landscape and its inhabitants. However, the film follows a narrative structure that sits comfortably within the conventions of the rural horror genre.

two rival sets of protagonists now becomes glaring: whereas the Cajuns are presented as one homogenous community living in close connection to their environment, the soldiers as representatives of State power do not share a unified enough group identity to counter their attackers. Even though the two soldiers are eventually rescued, the film's sympathy seems to rest on the side of the Cajuns and their embodiment of community and custom.

While the film has commonly been read as an allegory for the Vietnam War and described by its director Walter Hill as a "displaced Western," it is relevant in this context for its cinematic construction of a solidary rural community that calls to mind Olwig's notion of the *Landschaft*.[146] Olwig argues that "custom, upon which the common law of the land was based, was inscribed in the land through physical practice. The landscape [. . .] as a physical place was thus the manifestation of the polity's local custom and common law."[147] The notion of custom as a unifying feature is strongly underlined in the final scenes taking place in the Cajun village, where a raucous festivity is being held, including traditional cooking, singing of folk songs, and dancing. While there is no explicit focus on the political organization of the Cajun community in *Southern Comfort*, its collective group identity in itself is political. This holds especially true if one does indeed read the film as a comment on the Vietnam War and its historic implications of defeated US imperialism in the face of a socialist alliance of adversaries, which is mirrored here in the soldiers' pointless and violent invasion of the Cajun community's landscape.

This points to a frequently recurring tendency in the rural horror sub-genre: the rural antagonists are mostly part of a homogeneous collective visualized as intrinsically connected to their landscape and often presented, as discussed before, as incestuous kinship networks. By contrast, the urban protagonists are commonly depicted as a weak heterogeneous group. This weakness is illustrated among other things in the pervasive narrative motive—commonly perceived by reviewers as clunky story-telling—which has the members of the urban group voluntarily or involuntarily split up and then in turn be individually dismembered by the rural aggressors. A central trait of the stereotypical "hillbilly"—going back as far as the above mentioned "hill-folk" in Scotland and their disobedience to the monarch—is his or her rejection of central authority which displays a striking similarity to Olwig's notions of Renaissance rural polities and their political autonomy.

---

146 Donnar, Glen. "'Ah, You Lose You in There': Gothic Masculinities, Specters of Vietnam and Becoming Monstrous in Southern Comfort," in *War Gothic in Literature and Culture*, ed. Agnieszka Soltysik Monnet and Steffen Hantke (London: Routledge, 2015), 137.

147 Olwig, *Landscape, Nature and the Body Politic, 214.*

This alignment of collectivism with superiority is a notable exception in US cinema. US genre cinema in particular is known for its propagation and positive identification of individualism as freedom, a central feature of US national ideology that, as Robert Watkins puts it, "has only grown with the extension of the market to more and more facets of cultural life"—i.e., the proliferation of neoliberalism as hegemonic ideology.[148] As established by Robert Bellah and colleagues in their study *Habits of the Heart: Individualism and Commitment in American Life* (1985), one should distinguish between two kinds of individualism here. Firstly, they mention utilitarian individualism, the idea that "an individual can get ahead on his [sic] own initiative"[149] and, therefore, that everyone is responsible for her or his own economic well-being or failure. Secondly, there is an "expressive individualism" which "holds that each person has a unique core of feeling and intuition that should unfold or be expressed if individuality is to be realized."[150]

Bryan Warnick and his colleagues have applied Bellah's model to US cinema and write in their introduction: "The American middle class reveres both types of individualism [. . .] The middle class takes these values as socially normative and it expects them to be reflected in entertainment products."[151] However, these two types of individualism are disrupted in many rural horror films. The utilitarian approach is constrained by the films' focus on the wasteland which suggests more complex socio-economic factors as causes for rural poverty than just supposed unwillingness to work. The so-called "culture of poverty" theory that, as established in Chapter One, blames the victims of poverty for their own misery is negated by the visual evidence of closed factories, destroyed nature, extreme isolation, and absent infrastructure. Expressive individualism is presented as ineffective in so far as any potential urban hero or heroine separated from the urban group is usually murdered within minutes. Often, the films actively stress underlying conflicts within the urban group that eventually lead to its disintegration and subsequent death of its members. When there are urban survivors at the end of the narrative, it is often implicitly suggested—as, for example, in *Deliverance, The Hills Have Eyes*, and *The Texas Chainsaw Massacre*—that they are irrevocably

148 Robert Watkins, *Freedom and Vengeance on Film: Precarious Lives and the Politics of Subjectivity* (London/New York: I.B. Tauris, 2016), 1.

149 Robert Bellah, William M. Sullivan, Richard Madsen, Ann Swidler, and Steven Tipton, *Habits of the Heart: Individualism and Commitment in American Life* (Berkely: University of California Press, 1985), 33.

150 Ibid., 333–334.

151 Bryan Warnick, Heather Dawson, D. Spencer Smith and Bethany Vosburg-Bluem, "Student Communities and Individualism in American Cinema," *Educational Studies* 46 (2010), 170.

traumatized by their experiences. This is because they often had to become killers themselves in order to survive their ordeal, or simply because they have peered into a terrifying abyss within the supposedly homogenous and benign US landscape. Thus, even the core individualist myth of the legitimacy of vengeance is flawed here. Watkins argues that freedom and vengeance underpin a large part of US cinema "finding near continual validation and reinforcement in the cultural mainstream with movie after movie."[152] As we see in most rural horror films, there is usually some degree of violent vengeance enacted by the survivors of the urban group. However, again, they often leave the survivors traumatized and terrified and thereby deny their viewers the pleasurable catharsis of vengeance.

For a number of reasons, such the almost exclusive whiteness of rural horror's communities of the disenfranchised, rural horror films cannot, and do not intend to, assume any kind of utopian potential, however. Obviously, these communities are usually presented as entirely perverse, pathological, and repugnant, with *Southern Comfort* being an unusual outlier, and, as highlighted before, not as political entities or polities. It seems unlikely that the sadistic cannibals of *The Texas Chainsaw Massacre*, for example, could emerge as an example of a rural polity in Olwig's definition. Even the Cajun community in *Southern Comfort*—certainly a less caricatured group of antagonists than most rural horror films have to offer and, notably, an existing minority group—is tainted by their unquestioning readiness for violence. While rural horror arguably overall engages with collectivism and notions of *Landschaft* more intensely than many other US film genres and cycles, their progressive potential is limited. Undoubtedly, they draw a connecting line between (urban) individualism and economic devastation in the rural parts of the country in an extremely effective manner. In terms of resistance, however, they do not offer much more than the potentially empowering glee of seeing the members of the white, urban, privileged class chopped up and sometimes devoured by the otherwise invisible rural poor.

The New Rural Cinema certainly engages with notions of collectivism and individualism in more complex, less binary ways than rural horror. Undoubtedly, the collectivism/individualism dynamic is a central concern of the four case studies discussed here. *Ballast*, for example, interrogates the concept of the nuclear family as a potential site of resistance in absence of any social infrastructure; *Beasts of the Southern Wild* features a close-knit, rebellious rural community that describes itself as "beast-like" and, while not monstrous in any way, do attempt to chase away unwanted rural invaders associated with the State. Therefore, these films do reverberate with the notion of collectivism on the margins suggested and

152 Watkins, *Freedom and Vengeance on Film*, 2.

familiarized by the tight-knit communities of rural horror. *The Tall Man*, while not a US-American film but a French-Canadian co-production, serves to demonstrate the ongoing dialogue which exists between the horror genre's tropes of rurality and indie films focused on US rural poverty and marginality.

The Tall Man (2012)

The Tall Man begins with a voice-over monologue spoken by a young girl still unknown to the viewer at this point; it is accompanied by images of a derelict small mining town in Washington State (shot in British Columbia, Canada) that adhere to the iconography of the wasteland common to both rural horror and the New Rural Cinema: abandoned cars, rusty metal waste, stray dogs (see Fig. 5). The voice-over then explicitly attributes these conditions of possibility to the effects of deindustrialization: "Our town has been dead for six years. At first, we blamed the closing of the mine. The lack of jobs. The lack of money. The lack of everything. But then we had much worse to blame, for something had come to Cold Rock. Something bad that was destroying our town even more." Thereby, the very first minutes of the film already connect the economic downfall of the town with a vaguely eerie, possibly supernatural story element.

Fig. 5: Abandoned cars, rusty metal waste, and a stray dog: iconography of the wasteland in *The Tall Man* (Pascal Laugier, 2012).

The film's protagonist—though, crucially, not its narrator—is revealed a few moments later: Julia (Jessica Biel, known for her role in the remake of *The Texas Chainsaw Massacre*) is a nurse and the only remaining medical worker in the poverty-stricken town after her husband Robert, Cold Rock's only doctor, supposedly passed away. Her medical practice, set-up in the abandoned school building, provides one of the last social structures still existent in the impoverished area.

In the following scene, she delivers the child of a teenager living with her abusive mother and tries to convince the family to give the baby up for adoption which they decline. Subsequently, the voice-over informs the viewers: "Something had come to Cold Rock that was taking the children. Something so menacing, so terrifying, that the people finally gave it a name." This mysterious entity which has been seen kidnapping the children of the town is known as the Tall Man.

After the first act of the film focusses on a tense confrontation between Julia and the hooded Tall Man who invades her home and ostensibly kidnaps her young son, the film introduces a major "plot twist" about halfway through its running time: Julia's husband Robert is revealed to be still alive and the person behind the Tall Man. Moreover, it becomes apparent that she is his accomplice in the kidnappings. The couple have kidnapped the town's young, neglected children in order to give them up for adoption to wealthy (or at least wealthier) urban adoptive parents. They perceive their criminal endeavor as a charitable mission to lift these children from poverty and domestic violence and have invented the myth of the Tall Man as a cover story for their operation. The film's narrator is later revealed to be Jenny, the Tall Man's last "victim," the younger sister of the teenage mother from the opening scene, who convinces Julia's husband to take her away voluntarily from her abusive family. The film closes with Julia in prison—suspected of murdering the missing children—and Jenny visiting a liberal arts college in an unnamed city, leading a free, independent life.

Because of its ambiguous position between horror, psychological thriller, and rural drama, *The Tall Man* proved itself difficult to market for the film's producers. Reviews on genre-related websites were generally lukewarm, as most reviewers had expected a typical rural horror film, while more mainstream publications dismissed the film outright for the story's implausibility and its uneven tone. One of a few positive exceptions is Jeanette Catsoulis' review in *The New York Times* which highlights how "ultimately [. . .] [the] story draws more energy from class than from criminality: awash in sludgy browns and rotting greens—the colors of poverty and decomposition—this unpredictable oddity is a little bonkers but a lot original."[153] This generally bewildered reaction reflects the film's attempt to connect themes of rural poverty and class mobility with the tropes of the horror genre; while it certainly goes about this endeavor very differently—and much less violently—than the 1970s rural horror films, it is indebted to their focus on the rural wasteland and violent class conflict.

153 Jeanette Catsoulis, "A Small-Town Buzz About the Missing," *The New York Times* (August 30, 2012), https://www.nytimes.com/2012/08/31/movies/the-tall-man-a-thriller-directed-by-pascal-laugier.html?ref=movies.

On the one hand, *The Tall Man* is decidedly not a rural horror film in the tradition of *Deliverance* or *The Texas Chainsaw Massacre*. Even though the rural poor are certainly not portrayed without stereotypes, there are no overly caricatured "hillbilly monsters" to be found here, and the film relies more on suspense than gore. On the other hand, the film plays with its audience's knowledge of rural horror's tropes, particularly before the reveal of the narrative twist, and plants a possible conspiracy of the townspeople against Julia as a narrative red herring.[154] Furthermore, its ending cynically exposes class conflict in a way that is familiar to viewers of rural horror: the central crime is perpetrated by the community's only educated, middle-class couple who are stealing the locals' children. A casual line by Julia's husband near the end finally suggests that there are other "Tall Men" operating in other impoverished communities around the US. Notably, however, the film remains relatively ambiguous about the kidnappings: a final line of voice-over has Jenny wondering: "Whether she [Julia] was a good person or not, I'm still not sure."

Apart from its engagement with the horror genre, *The Tall Man* deviates from the New Rural Cinema insofar as it is essentially a film about the problems and prospects of rural-to-urban class mobility. While the rusted cars in Cold Rock signify immobility, escape is possible through the dark, ghostly figure of the Tall Man, who contributes to the demise of the town by taking its children but enables them to have a brighter future. The film's final images show Jenny on a sunny, brightly lit campus and imagine a possible alternative to rural poverty solely in the form of a radical rupture with rural life. The ending can be read as a reaffirmation of individual sovereignty, thus falling back into line with the "American myth of individualism" and its inherent "practice (or even just the desire) of casting off the past and starting a new life from scratch."[155] Nevertheless, the film's engagement with rural decay, absence of social structures, and the weakness of the law connects the underlying themes of the New Rural Cinema with rural horror's drastic caricatures.

---

154 In addition, the kidnapper's nickname, the Tall Man, refers to the recurring villain of the highly successful franchise following the low-budget, small-town-set horror film *Phantasm* (1980).

155 Watkins, *Freedom and Vengeance on Film*, 2.

4 'Psychological ruins': African American perspectives

Seen through the lens of African American culture and, more specifically, African American cinema, the US countryside is inextricably connected to the historical trauma of slavery. Broadly speaking, however, African American Cinema of roughly the last fifty years has favored urban settings and has concerned itself largely with the contemporary experience of racism, violence, and inequality in US cities. As Paula J. Massood relates: "During the last half of the twentieth century, African American film was increasingly identified as city film in the public imagination. Its narratives were commonly assigned to specific urban settings" such as Brooklyn on the East Coast and Compton on the West Coast.[156] Rural settings, on the other hand, mostly appear in historical films that are directly concerned with either slavery and the Civil War or the civil rights movement of the 1960s. Prominent recent examples include *12 Years a Slave* (Steve McQueen, 2013), *The Birth of a Nation* (Nate Parker, 2016), *Mudbound* (Dee Rees, 2017), and *Harriet* (Kasi Lemmons, 2019). This association of rural landscapes with the collective traumatic past might explain why contemporary Black rural experiences arguably are a neglected topic in US cinema. Jacqueline Najuma Stewart argues:

> African American film culture and Black urban migration emerged from a shared set of conditions and desires. For many migrants, the promise of "the North" and "the city" contained the dream of being liberated from the abuses and restrictions that characterized life in the South.[157]

The overall focus on urban life in African American cinema could thus be understood as a reverberation of the "Great Migration" of the early twentieth century which led thousands of Black families to the urban North. This historic internal mass migration was mostly caused by economic hardship and the repressive Jim Crow laws in the South.

This section will therefore mainly investigate the relative absence of images of contemporary Black rural life in US cinema. When such images *do* appear—in recent films such as *Dayveon* and *Hale County This Morning, This Evening* (RaMell Moss, 2018)—they fall in line with similar concerns of landscape and neoliberalism designating the films discussed in this book. Again, it is central to mention that due to limited space, this chapter cannot possibly do justice to the scope of this diverse topic—or, for that matter, engage in detail with the fundamental challenges the cat-

---

156 Paula J. Massood, *Black City Cinema: African American Urban Experiences in Film* (Philadelphia: Temple UP, 2003), 1.

157 Jacqueline Najuma Stewart, *Migrating to the Movies: Cinema and Black Urban Modernity* (Berkeley: University of California Press, 2005), xvii.

egory African American cinema itself poses in terms of authorship, nationality, spectatorship, etc. In his introduction to African American Cinema, Arthur Knight points out some of these conceptual challenges. For example, he raises the fundamental question of national belonging: "African American cinema is often thought of as part of American cinema, while at the same time, African American cinema is also often thought of as part of a global Black diasporic cinema."[158] Furthermore, he stresses the difficulty of a cohesive definition: Can we ever consider mainstream Hollywood cinema as part of such a category, or must there be a focus on indie productions? Is African American cinema necessarily a cinema of social activism? Is African American cinema made by, of, or for African Americans or a combination of the three? A focus on the "by" would favor an auteurist approach, a focus on "of" would consider the historic construction of Blackness on screen, and a foregrounding of "for" would have to look at distribution, popular genres and cycles. Nevertheless, it seems vital to explicitly incorporate this marginalized perspective on US rurality in order to contest the "normalizing claim to whiteness" and structural racism that haunts the United States' past and present, particularly with regards to rural poverty.[159]

The relative absence of cinematic representation of rural African Americans may at first glance be a reflection of population statistics: according to the Economic Research Service of the US Department of Agriculture, only about eight per cent of the current (2018) rural population is Black. As Joyce Allen-Smith points out, however, these statistics hide, "the heavy concentration of rural Blacks in specified areas, notably the Mississippi Delta and the Black Belt" stretching from Virginia to Texas.[160] This concentration, she continues, "has its roots in plantation agriculture and the systems of slavery and sharecropping [. . .] For decades, many counties in these areas have been among the poorest in the country."[161] Nevertheless, African American popular culture at large, and cinema in particular, are now so closely associated with urban America that the word "urban" itself has gradually become a problematic euphemism. As Stewart relates, this linguistic conflation "while supporting a host of troubling stereotypes about African Americans' taste and the translatability of Black identity, functions to designate story lines and markets [. . .] that have proved to be extremely profitable."[162] A possible film-historic

158 Arthur Knight, "African American Cinema," *Oxford Bibliographies* (October 27, 2016), https://www.oxfordbibliographies.com/view/document/obo-9780199791286/obo-9780199791286-0213.xml.

159 Singh, *Black is a Country*, 20.

160 Allen-Smith, Joyce E., "Blacks in Rural America: Socioeconomic Status and Policies to Enhance Economic Well-Being," *The Review of Black Political Economy* 22:4 (1994), 9.

161 Ibid.

162 Stewart, *Migrating to the Movies*, 249.

point of origin for the popular brand of urbanity African American Cinema came to embody, might be Melvin Van Peebles' early Los-Angeles-set film *Sweet Sweetback's Baadasssss Song* (1971).

Massood traces this association of Blackness and urbanity further back to its origin in the "Great Migration" which "radically redefined the nation's African American population, nearly reversing the ratio of urban and rural residents and removing some 40 percent of Black residents from the Old South."[163] The scope of this population movement can hardly be overstated: "Between 1910 and 1930, an estimated 1.2 million African American migrants moved to the North, increasing the population in northern urban centers by 300 percent."[164] Furthermore, Massood demonstrates the influence this internal mass migration had on popular cinema. While African American art and literature at the time engaged with the complex, conflicting experiences of urbanity—both a "promised land" that offered an escape from racial oppression in the South as well as a dystopia of urban neglect—"Hollywood films from 1929 to 1943 utterly failed to recognize the socio-political changes in the American landscape."[165] This failure, in her opinion, is especially apparent in the Black-cast musicals of the time which, instead of incorporating the new Black urban experience, positioned its African American characters in "variations of a pastoral, southern setting [. . .] a seemingly static rural space—the antebellum idyll—in which an indeterminate yet bygone past is signified through iconography of a rural, preindustrial southern agricultural economy."[166] If urban spaces appear at all in films like *Hallelujah* (King Vidor, 1929) and *Green Pastures* (Marc Connelly and William Keighley, 1936), they are presented as hubs of crime, sexuality, and sin. In the end, the protagonists mostly return to their anachronistic rural Southern homes.

Massood convincingly argues that these narratives were "ignoring discourses of progress and change, which were so central to African American life between the two World Wars."[167] The effect of these Hollywood musicals was thus to "reconfirm ideology that removed African Americans [. . .] from a 'civilized' world that was urban and therefore modern."[168] This reductive legacy of Black representation, Massood puts forward, determined a backlash in the following decades of African American cinema, visible in its fascination with modern urbanity: early gangster films like *Dark Manhattan* (Harry Fraser, 1937), the Blaxploitation cycle of the

163 Massood, *Black City Cinema, 12.*

164 Ibid.

165 Ibid., 14.

166 Ibid.

167 Ibid., 16.

168 Ibid.

1970s, the neo-realist films of the so-called LA Rebellion, and the Hood Films of the 1990s demonstrate Black film culture's consistent "strong identification with urban experience, in terms of both content and audience."[169] Films such as the small-town-set *Nothing but a Man* (Michael Roemer, 1964) remained exceptions.

This historical perspective might explain the reluctance of Black film-makers to engage with contemporary rural modes of living. At times, this reluctance is even spelled out in most drastic terms: the satirical horror film *Get Out* (2017) by director Jordan Peele, for example, follows a young Black man from New York City on his trip to meet his white girlfriend's parents in rural Upstate New York. The plot gradually confirms the protagonist's worst fears: the white family is "enslaving" Black people by supernaturally taking possession of their bodies. Even though *Get Out* does not technically feature a Southern setting—while the film is shot in Alabama, the narrative takes place in Upstate New York—the association of rural America with slavery is all too clear here. *Get Out* even manages to include a central reference to cotton (as the filling of an armchair, a prop crucial to the narrative), thus raising connotations of slave plantations without ever showing a single cotton field.

Nevertheless, the rural past does shine through in African American cinema, if to vastly different degrees and from different perspectives. In the 1990s, for example, sociologists noted a wave of "reverse migration" of African Americans moving from northern cities back to their ancestors' rural homes in the South due to "enhanced economic opportunities in sun-belt communities [. . .] and an increased desire to move away from inner-city problems such as youth crime."[170] Massood finds this movement echoed in films like *Down in the Delta* (Maya Angelou, 1998), in which a woman takes her troubled children from Chicago's inner-city back to her family's home in rural Mississippi. *Down in the Delta* takes a critical, rather one-dimensional view towards Black urban life as demonstrated in its "oversimplified assertion that the city is solely aligned with gangsta [sic] culture."[171] Nevertheless, Massood concedes, the film suggests:

> [A] Reconsideration of the South as a site that is dynamic and filled with possibility rather than a space that is static and unchanging. [. . .] In *Down in the Delta* the South, a primary symbolic site of the past, is refigured for the future. How realistic this South will be and how much African American and American films might register the negative as well as imaginatively celebrated aspects of slavery's legacy remains to be seen.[172]

169 Stewart, *Migrating to the Movies*, 248.
170 Massood, *Black City Cinema*, 216.
171 Ibid., 218.
172 Ibid.

Massood's contemplation of a prospective Black rural cinema that refigures the South as a site "filled with possibility" has largely failed to materialize. Recent African American films set in the contemporary South approach their rural settings in a way that falls into line with the New Rural Cinema: in films like *Ballast, Dayveon,* and *Burning Cane* (Phillip Youmans, 2019), the South is presented as a deserted, ruinous wasteland and its impoverished Black communities as devoid of hope and perspective. Crime, drug use, alcoholism, and violence are rampant. The city has disappeared entirely as a potential point of escape, democratic institutions and communitarian structures are almost entirely absent or corrupted. *Beasts of the Southern Wild* offers, as we shall see, some exceptions to this generally pessimistic tone but appertains to a similar iconography of ruin and waste.

Slavery's legacy goes mostly unmentioned in these new rural films, but it is omnipresent nevertheless—the cinematic landscapes are haunted by their histories of atrocities against Black bodies. In *Burning Cane*, for example, one of the main characters, a priest suffering from alcoholism and depression, is involved in a drunken traffic accident and crashes his car nearby the site of former slave quarters. The fields of sugar cane constantly in the background are a similar reminder of the slave plantation system. Farah Jasmine Griffin summarizes this haunted quality of African American renditions of the South in her study of African American migration narratives when she writes: "Southern earth is fertilized with the blood of Black people. [. . .] On the surface it is a land of great physical beauty and charm, but beneath it lay Black blood and decayed Black bodies. Beneath the charm lay the horror."[173] *Ballast, Burning Cane,* and other films show how this buried horror seeps back onto the surface. They shroud their landscapes in a persistent feeling of anxiety and hopelessness and thereby inscribe a history of injustice and degradation onto the land. In that sense, they are also indebted to the tropes of Southern Gothic fiction.

The connection of the rural with the past in US cinema is thus especially pronounced, and especially traumatic, in African American cinema focusing on rurality. In her article on what she terms African American Migration Films—for example *To Sleep with Anger* (Charles Burnett, *1990), Daughters of the Dust* (Julie Dash, 1991)—Jeannine King writes on the symbolic charging of Northern and Southern landscapes:

> While the South is ostensibly static, its symbolic presence controls the inner life of migrants in the North. The movies offer a distinctive resolution to the haunting traces of the Southern

173 Farah Jasmine Griffin, *"Who set you Flowin'?": The African-American Migration Narrative* (New York/Oxford: Oxford UP, 1995), 16.

> past: the narrative and artistic expression not of continuity but of brokenness. The *psychological ruins* of an abandoned South become the site of delayed confrontation and mourning.[174]

Her term "psychological ruins" serves well to describe current cinematic incarnations of African American rural experiences. *Dayveon,* for example, follows the eponymous young boy in an impoverished stretch of rural Arkansas. Mourning the gang-related murder of his brother, he joins the same local crime gang, and ends up brutally robbing his own stepfather. The film is a fitting example of King's focus on violent confrontation and trauma playing out in the haunted landscapes of the South. In a key scene, Dayveon is attacked by a swarm of bees nesting in a tree nearby his house, underlining the hostility of the environment surrounding him. The pointed difference between what King terms migration films and contemporary rural Black cinema, however, is that even the memories of "movement and freedom" of the Great Migration seem to have vanished in the current films and given way to a view of the South as "an inherently constrictive space" that arises not solely from the legacy of slavery but from an intersectional understanding of class and race under neoliberalism.[175]

Therefore, no matter if African American cinema is understood as part of a US national cinema or as belonging to a global diasporic cinema, these rural-set films demonstrate how "the fundamental systemic inequalities created by four hundred years of imperial and colonial economic and political domination [. . .] [are] exacerbated by neoliberalism."[176] Rural poverty and isolation affect Black communities more intensely because, as Allen-Smith notes, "their plight is inevitably linked to the unique history and development"[177] of the US South. Furthermore, as Singh points out, neoliberal ideology, while eschewing overt racism based on "racial inferiority," enables its proponents to base their "resistance to Black calls for social justice on a defense of market individualism."[178] Assuming a "color-blind" market, "a form of antiracism that is seen as equivalent to American nationalism has been the rationale for overturning policies and programs once deemed essential to fulfilling an antiracist national agenda."[179] Neoliberalism's exacerbation of racism does not come in the form of new Jim Crow laws but in shape of the rollback of programs designed to achieve equality, "filtered through a logic of neoliberal discipline that vehemently opposes government intervention

174 Jeannine King, "Memory and the Phantom South in African American Migration Film," *The Mississippi Quarterly* 63:3 (2010), 478. Emphasis added.

175 King, "Memory and the Phantom South," 477.

176 Braedley and Luxton, "Competing Philosophies," 16–17.

177 Allen-Smith, "Blacks in Rural America," 9.

178 Singh, *Black is a Country*, 10.

179 Ibid.

into the 'natural' workings of the marketplace."[180] This is reflected in the new Black rural films' implicit treatment of racism: overt racist conflict is largely absent in the films' narratives, however, the effects of the systemic exclusions shape the constrictive landscapes and conditions of possibility the films' Black protagonists are inhabiting.

In that sense, current rural African American cinema is a challenge to Olwig's understanding of landscape as a social concept, as community and polity. Especially his claim that "the United States has [. . .] not been characterized by the rigid, hierarchical class structure of Britain, nor has it experienced Britain's massive landscaping by a powerful class of landowners" is contested in the way African American films use landscape images to evoke the past horrors of slavery and its integral relation to the Southern landscape.[181] Considering Olwig's focus on how the propagation of a scenic understanding of landscape in the US "helped naturalize a colonial imperialism that simultaneously required the removal, and even extermination, of the previous native population, often deemed to be racially inferior," it is notable that he all but ignores a similar imperialistic employment of scenic landscape in the naturalization of African slavery.[182] The vast fields of cotton and cane permeating the landscape, for example, which feature prominently in some of the films, are a constant reminder of past atrocities. A diasporic, historically disenfranchised community living on the land built on the murdered bodies of their ancestors will undoubtedly form a very specific engagement with, as Olwig puts it, the "landscape as shaped by ideas of law and justice, and as entangled with nature and the environment."[183] Their dwelling will have to come to terms with an environment that is "pregnant with the past" of custom and tradition, on the one hand, as well as with oppression and dehumanization, on the other hand.[184]

In order to illuminate this unique perspective of African American rural films, I will close this section with an analysis of the experimental documentary *Hale County This Morning, This Evening*. The film endorses an understanding of landscape resting on the "knowledge born of immediate experience, by privileging the understandings that people derive from their lived, everyday involvement in the world," chiming therefore with Tim Ingold's concept of the dwelling perspective.[185] Furthermore, the film, as its director RaMell Moss relates in an inter-

180 Ibid., 11.
181 Olwig, *The Meanings of Landscape*, 45.
182 Ibid., 12.
183 Ibid., 1.
184 Ingold, *The Perception of the Environment*, 189.
185 Ibid.

view, sets out to counter and "to reflect a history of sinister framing" of African Americans in general and of the rural "Black Belt" communities in particular.[186]

Hale County This Morning, This Evening (2018)

Hale County This Morning, This Evening loosely follows two young men living in the eponymous Southern county in rural Alabama through their everyday lives: Daniel Collins and Quincy Bryant are shown playing basketball, interacting with their families, and talking about their expectations for the future. Crucially, however, the film also offers a kaleidoscopic view of its setting, focusing in equal amount on local customs (church services, a funeral, a fair, children at play, etc.) as well as on the natural surroundings (fields, animals, the sky) and ultimately makes a point about the interconnectedness of the two.

In combination with the film's focus on illustrating the passage of time—for example, by including long static shots sped up with time lapse technology—this approach calls to mind Tim Ingold's concept of the dwelling perspective. Ingold understands the creation of landscape as constant interactivity between inhabitants and their surroundings over time: "through living in it, the landscape becomes a part of us, just as we are part of it."[187] Landscape in this sense represents a form of embodiment, "a movement wherein forms themselves are generated"[188]—an eternal becoming rather than an inscription into a medium. Nevertheless, past interactions remain visible: Ingold describes landscape as "an enduring record of—and testimony to—the lives and works of past generations who have dwelt within it."[189] Implicitly referring to the specific, traumatic history of Southern Black communities, *Hale County* encapsulates the complex questions surrounding rural Black dwelling in the US today. One of the intertitles irregularly interrupting the flow of images throughout the film seems to summarize these issues in a provocative question: "What happens when all the cotton is picked?" This clearly refers to the legacy of plantation slavery and queries how its long-lasting influence impacts upon Black rural lives today.

Indeed, a long scene shot from a car driving along a sprawling field of cotton provides one of the most memorable images of the film. It is accompanied by the asynchronous foley sounds of children at a basketball game as well as with a sub-

186 RaMell Moss, "Filming the Black Belt: An Interview with RaMell Moss," Interview by Max Fraser. *Dissent Magazine* (Fall 2019), https://www.dissentmagazine.org/article/filming-the-black-belt-an-interview-with-ramell-ross.

187 Ingold, *The Perception of the Environment*, 193.

188 Ibid.

189 Ibid., 189.

tly disharmonious, monotone score. On the visual level, the cotton field represents, to use Ingold's words, an example of "landscape [. . .] as the taskscape in its embodied form: a pattern of activities 'collapsed' into an array of features" in a particularly traumatic sense: it is the permanent, physical record of the legacy of slavery.[190] The aural dimension of disembodied children's voices calls to mind the idea of a landscape haunted by its past put forward by Jeannine King: it underlines the ghost-like coexistence of the traumatic past—the countless, nameless dead underneath the fields—and the present, everyday life for African Americans in the South.

It should be stressed, however, that the film distances itself from any possible Gothic undertones in this scene and instead constructs a highly ambivalent aural and visual landscape. The children's voices are cheerful, chanting in celebration of the basketball match, meaning that there is no exaggerated air of dread, rather a slightly alienated everyday matter-of-factness. Yet it would be just as one-sided to read the scene as a "victory" of the aural representation of joy over the traumatic memories present on the visual level; both have to be seen in interaction here. Ingold argues:

> The landscape seems to be what we see around us, whereas the taskscape is what we hear. [. . .] While both the landscape and the taskscape presuppose the presence of an agent who watches and listens, the taskscape must be populated with beings who are themselves agents, who reciprocally "act back" in the process of their own dwelling.[191]

The asynchronous montage of sound and image in this scene draws attention, to use Ingold's term, to the emergence of a new layer of dwelling. The visible landscape (the cotton field) as a "collapsed" testimony of the (traumatic) past is being constantly altered by its inhabitants—an interactive process audible in the children's voices and visualized in the velocity of the tracking shot. The legacy of slavery cannot be erased, yet with the passing of time every new generation of inhabitants is inevitably part of its continuation and transformation.

A similar notion is expressed in the film's repeated focus on circular motions which indicate both a constant progression of life cycles as well as repetition and stasis. A prominent scene, for example, shows Quincy's toddler Kyrie running in a circle around the family's cramped living room. The scene's long, uninterrupted shot creates an almost hypnotic watching experience and is increasingly charged with ambivalent meaning. On the one hand, as Simran Hans writes in her review of the film, there is an undeniable joy in the boy's untiring game, "exhausted but

190 Ibid., 162.
191 Ibid.

defiant and entirely unaware of the limitations of his small body."[192] On the other hand, as the scene goes on and on, it also carries a notion of futility and pointlessness and, in the historical context, could suggest that there is no way out of the cycle of repression and racism for the community. The presence of racism is only hinted at in *Hale County* but is prominent nevertheless: numerous scenes show the film's protagonists and, at one point, even the filmmaker himself being stopped and interrogated by police patrols. Without ever explicitly foregrounding these events, the film therefore hints at the pervasive problem of police brutality and systemic racism against African Americans. It is in these scenes, that Moss' intention "to reflect a history of sinister framing" becomes most prominent and most explicitly political.[193]

The film's repeated use of circular movements also points towards its understanding of landscape, however, and cannot solely be understood as a visualization of the "vicious cycle" of racial oppression and violence. Kylie's circular movement around the living room is, for example, mirrored in a brief shot depicting wheeling birds as well as in a scene focusing on a single bee crawling in circles; the repeated images of the rising and setting sun and moon similarly point towards much larger, astronomical rotations. Coming back to Ingold's argument that embodiment is "movement wherein forms themselves are generated," these images take on a new significance.[194] Ingold asks:

> Is it possible to identify a corresponding cycle, or rather a series of interlocking cycles, which build themselves into the forms of the landscape, and of which the landscape may accordingly be regarded as an embodiment?[195]

Hale County depicts Black rural life as precisely that, as a series of interlocking cycles which are constantly in the progress of constructing landscape through lived experience and interactivity. Therefore, while following a more experimental structure and a non-fictional mode, the film's concept of landscape is closely related to that of the New Rural Cinema. It points, however, more explicitly than the other films of this study which focus on rural Black communities, towards the difficulty of landscape as "a nexus of community, justice, nature, and environmental equity" in the context of the historical trauma of slavery and ongoing racial repression.[196]

---

192 Simran Hans, "Hale County, This Morning, This Evening review — poetic and profound," *The Guardian* (January 20, 2019), https://www.theguardian.com/film/2019/jan/20/hale-county-this-morning-this-evening-review.

193 Moss, "Filming the Black Belt," Interview by Max Fraser.

194 Ingold, *The Perception of the Environment*, 157.

195 Ibid.

196 Olwig, *The Meanings of Landscape*, 16.

Chapter Four
Disrupted Geography and the Criminal Margins – *Winter's Bone* (2010)

Debra Granik's filmography retains a coherent line of thematic concerns across at least three of her films. *Winter's Bone*, Granik's sophomore feature film, takes place in an isolated mountain community in which deep poverty and drug-related violence have destroyed almost all traces of communal solidarity. The film focuses on 17-year-old Ree (Jennifer Lawrence) who needs to find her father Jessup in order to stop the bank from repossessing her home. In her direct follow-up film, the documentary *Stray Dog* (2014), Granik follows one of *Winter's Bone's* central non-professional actors: Ron "Stray Dog" Hall. Hall played the role of drug-boss Thump Milton in the previous film and is shown here in his real-life capacity, as the promotional tagline would have it, "biker, Vietnam vet, and lover of small dogs." *Stray Dog* is concerned with, on the one hand, Hall's commitment to the social welfare of war veterans and his own struggles with post-traumatic stress. On the other hand, the film also foregrounds its setting, the trailer park Hall owns and operates in an impoverished region of Southern Missouri. The trailer park, a recurrent negative symbol for US poverty, emerges here as a positive communal place characterized by cooperation and multi-ethnic coexistence under conditions of economic hardship.

This real-life setting may well have served Granik as an inspiration to adapt Peter Rock's novel *My Abandonment* (2009) for the screen. The novel also focuses on the extreme post-traumatic disorders of a veteran and a defiant trailer park community. In *Leave No Trace*, her adaption of Rock's novel, the communal trailer park in the forest represents an alternative to the relentless individualism central to US ideology, and to the bureaucracy of neoliberal state welfare. *Leave No Trace* and *Winter's Bone* prominently engage with the nexus of rural landscape, community, and poverty in US society that is the focus of this book. They refute a scenic understanding of landscape and instead demonstrate how an embodied vision of US rurality as polity contains the possibility of countering neoliberal mechanisms of marginalization through collectivism and solidarity. *Leave No Trace* will be discussed in detail in the following chapter.

The very first image of *Winter's Bone* calls to mind a passage from *Landscapes of Fear* (1979), in which human geographer Yi-Fu Tuan examines the social construction of the US countryside. He writes:

> Rural people are exposed to the rough as well as the gentle sides of nature. The harshness of nature is seldom depicted in geographical sketches of the country scene, except where the topic is frontier settlement. Too often we are presented with the warm palettes of spring and sum-

https://doi.org/10.1515/9783110779417-005

> mer, or the poetic hues of autumn, rather than the bleak, discomforting greys of winter. [. . .] To isolated communities in the mountains of Appalachia, winter is a state of siege.[1]

The phrase "bleak, discomforting greys of winter" is a fitting description of the first impression of the isolated mountain community in the Ozarks the film provides. It opens on a dreary, wintry landscape: leafless branches framed against a grey sky, a barren field in the foreground, a few abandoned cars and a small house huddled in the background. Even further back, the dark grey mountains are towering above the scene (see Fig. 6). Tuan's notion of a "state of siege" seems to be visualized in this opening image: Winter has taken command of this land—no human being is visible, the landscape emanates a sense of desolation, abandonment, and coldness.

Fig. 6: The film opens on a dreary, wintry landscape: opening shot of *Winter's Bone* (Debra Granik, 2010).

Granik shot her film on location in the Ozarks as described in the source novel by author Daniel Woodrell and produced it in close collaboration with local inhabitants, many of whom appear as non-professional actors in supporting roles. In an interview for *Sight & Sound*, Granik explained her approach:

1 Yi-Fu Tuan, *Landscapes of Fear* (New York: Pantheon, 1979), 140.

> The novel describes a specific set of coordinates for a reason. The region is Woodrell's muse. He spent all this time making these observations and fitting together strands of history and culture, and the dialogue is very specific. Ultimately, we had to make it there.[2]

The notion of regional custom that resonates with the director's phrase "strands of history and culture" already hints towards the concept of the polity as based on a shared customs and culture that Olwig puts forward. In this section, I will analyze how *Winter's Bone* frames a specific relation between landscape and community within the context of neoliberal marginalization, individualism, and patriarchy.

The section will firstly look at how *Winter's Bone* constructs its characters' perspective in a world permeated by extreme poverty: how does the film's landscape reflect their conditions of possibility, how does it illustrate "what is possible, what must be overcome, what is to be struggled for and against?"[3] Whilst many readings of the film focus on its dialogue with the Western's frontier narratives and its folk tale inspired symbolism, the spatial dimensions of class, and of neoliberal marginalization, remain largely unmentioned. Secondly, I will analyze the film's engagement with what Lorimer has termed "embodied acts of landscaping," an enmeshed relation between the characters and their surroundings that, at times, seems to dissolve the boundaries between landscape and its inhabitants.[4] It is in these moments that the film suggests a cooperative agency in the fictional rural community. Finally, I will investigate how the film positions itself towards the possibility of communal cooperation in the face of economic hardship and a patriarchal social structure: does *Winter's Bone* conceive a "living land of people" and thus a potential site of a radical democratic alternative to neoliberalism's economic rationality?[5] Or does it show how such "democratic imaginaries" are thwarted by neoliberal regimes?[6]

1 Disrupted geography: Poverty, genre, landscape

As the film revolves around the notion of deep rural poverty, it seems important to evaluate how *Winter's Bone* visually and narratively conveys its characters struggle with poverty, and how this struggle is reflected in the construction of the

2 Debra Granik. "Meth and the Maiden," Interview by James Bell. *Sight & Sound* 20:10 (2010), 29–30.

3 Mitchell, "Landscape," 51.

4 Lorimer, "Cultural Geography," 85.

5 Olwig, *Landscape, Nature, and the Body Politic*, 220.

6 Brown, *Undoing the Demos*, 17.

filmic landscape. What limitations, physical and ideological, does the landscape impose on its characters? The very first images of the film already convey extensive information about Ree and her family's dire living situation without resorting to dramatic exposition informed by squalor or suffering. I want to focus here on the film's opening minutes which function as an introduction into the mountain community and its conditions of possibility. After the initial image, a melancholic acapella rendition of the folk song "Missouri Waltz," the state's official song, begins to play on the soundtrack. Ree can be seen hanging out the laundry, while her two siblings are bouncing up and down on an old trampoline that is placed in the family's backyard. In the background, we can see their home, a small wooden cabin that is surrounded by a variety of objects strewn around its perimeter: old tires, buckets, furniture, toys—items possibly not discarded or without value but simply positioned there for lack of storage space.

The trampoline as a prop especially lends itself to interpretation: a different film dealing with rural poverty might have avoided showing this object at all. After all, a trampoline of this size is certainly not cheap and might even be considered a (modest) luxury item. It seems strangely out of place in the grey, inhospitable environment of the scene. The film not only passingly shows the trampoline but prominently features it in the first shot of its main protagonist's home—a decision that gives insight into the film's perspective on its characters' poverty. While the following narrative certainly does not shy away from the Dolly family's hardship, the central inclusion of the trampoline suggests a complex backstory that defies expectations. It might have been found somewhere, it might have been a gift or, as seems most likely, a remainder of a time before Jessup Dolly's disappearance, when he still earned enough money with his illegal drug business. Whichever may be the case, its central inclusion speaks for a measured view on poverty that does not have to exclude moments of ease or other seeming contradictions to get its point across.

After the film's title has been displayed over a stark image of leafless branches against a grey sky, the next part of this opening passage takes place inside the Dollys' cabin. Ree is shown in a mid-shot in the cabin's small kitchen area washing her hands and face. Around her, various pots and pitchers can be seen. There are bottles of detergents next to the sink. In the background, we can make out a fridge covered in magnets, postcards, and drawings. It is an early example of a visual technique used throughout the film that Granik herself has described as creating spaces "layered with objects," a look achieved by shooting the film on location in lived-in houses.[7] Without resorting to an overstated focus on, for example, decay or dirt, this mise-en-scène visually conveys poverty through one of the central "lacks" of the Dollys' living situation: confinement, a lack of space. The viewer immediately gets a sense of the confined, crowded space this family of four—and, not too long ago, five—has to get by with. It is emphatically not a space of neglect and dilapidation—the colorful images pinned to the fridge as well as the warm red of the curtains immediately attest to that—yet there is hardly any doubt that this is an intensely limited place for the amount of people living here.

In the next shot, Ree's two siblings Sonny and Ashlee can be seen sleeping fully clothed on two sofas, covered in various blankets. Again, the film eschews dramatic signifiers of coldness such as shivering or blue lips yet there is no doubt it is not warm in the house. In the source novel—to which the script adheres closely here—author Daniel Woodrell describes the corresponding scene: "The house was cool in the brighter spots and chill in the shadows."[8] The lack of heating alluded to here harks back to Tuan's notion of winter as a metaphoric "enemy" that is often eschewed in depictions of rural poverty in favor of more pastoral images. Hunger, another palpable, bodily aspect of the Dollys' experience of deep poverty, comes into focus in the following sequence. The film uses two short but telling close-ups in this scene. First, we see a meagre amount of butter or lard being dropped in a hot pan. Its whitish color and grainy consistency look unappealing. Next, there is a close-up of Ree chopping a potato directly into the buttered pan. Crucially, she is not peeling it but just slicing it as is, quite possibly in order not to waste any of it. These two shots suggest that the Dollys' poverty is dramatic indeed. Without careful rationing and usage of all possible resources, Ree might not be able to feed her family. The end of this sequence even intensifies this notion by showing that there is another mouth to be fed: the guard dog. Ree takes out a plastic bowl of the fridge, opens the lid, sniffs the contents and deems them just about still good enough to be fed to the dog.

The opening minutes of *Winter's Bone* also introduce the character of Ree's mother who is suffering from severe mental health problems. In contrast to the source novel, she does not speak for the entirety of the narrative as she has completely withdrawn from the world around her. The film first starts to make the viewer notice her condition when Ree is seen casually washing her hair. Without explicitly referencing it, the film already hints at her poor mental health by briefly showing her and Ree as reflections in the cracked bathroom mirror. The camera positions the long crack directly over the two characters before quickly

7 Debra Granik, "Telling a Backwoods Tale with Chilling Accuracy," Interview by Erin Trahan. Boston.com (June 13, 2010) www.archive.boston.com/ae/movies/articles/2010/06/13/winters_bone_director_strived_for_authenticity_in_cast_script_set.

8 Daniel Woodrell, *Winter's Bone* (London: Sceptre, 2016), 7.

panning to a close-up of Ree's face "outside" of the mirror image. This sequence gestures towards the proven connection of poverty and mental health issues and an acute crisis in medical assistance in rural parts of the United States. According to a 2015 study conducted by the US National Center for Health Statistics (NHCS), there is a strong causal relation between poverty and mental health. It finds that "a total of 8.7% of adults with income below the federal poverty level had serious psychological distress, compared with 1.2% of adults with incomes at or above 400% of the poverty level." It concludes that "as income increased, the age-adjusted percentage with serious psychological distress decreased."[9] Furthermore, the scene adds to the growing list of daily domestic tasks and caregiving that Ree must perform by herself.

The final part of the opening passage begins with Ree walking Sonny and Ashlee to school. Ree is providing some form of education herself by asking her siblings to spell words and solve simple math problems on their walk. After showing the three siblings and their dogs walking along a non-asphalted backroad through a grey, wintry landscape, the film quite abruptly cuts to Ashlee in a classroom, working on an arts project. This transition is stunning because it employs an elliptic editing technique the film will use throughout: we are not shown how the characters approach a certain place, they are simply and suddenly there. This style makes for what I call a *disrupted geography* of the film's spaces that from the very beginning portrays the mountain community as an isolated, dispersed locale, impossible to map or structure. The film denies its viewers mastery over the geography by eschewing totalizing views of the landscape and instead emphasizing and emulating the embodied vision of its characters (see Fig. 7). We find a very similar visual technique in other films of the New Rural Cinema, notably *Ballast* and *Frozen River*, two films with which *Winter's Bone* also shares its focus on coldness and isolation.

What follows are three short segments in which the film focuses on Ree's reaction to different scenes she witnesses while inside the school. These are faintly reminiscent of the Kuleshov effect and its experimental montage of visual stimuli and expressionless faces. First, the film cuts to a close-up of Ree watching her little sister interact in class. Ree seems content her siblings can escape their deprived home environment for a while and prepare themselves for an undoubtedly challenging future. At the same time, viewers are also invited to assume that Ree herself had to leave school to care for her siblings and her mother full time. Her look is not only caring but also seems to wish for a simpler past that circumstances have denied

9 Judith Weissman, Laura Pratt, Eric Miller, and Jennifer Parker, "Serious Psychological Distress Among Adults: United States, 2009—2013," *NCHS Data Brief* 203 (2015), 2; ibid., 1.

Fig. 7: Eschewing totalizing views of the landscape and instead emphasizing and emulating the embodied vision of its characters: Ree (Jennifer Lawrence) in *Winter's Bone* (Debra Granik, 2010).

her. The sacrifices Ree has to make in order to provide for her family become strikingly clear. The next shot takes us into a different room in which embarrassed teenagers are taught to properly hold and handle baby dolls during a sex education lesson. Ree's bemused reaction visible through the small window in the door—which is mirrored in a later scene in which she reservedly reacts to a friend's newborn baby—is almost comical in its blank astonishment. It also directly interacts with the prior shot of Ashlee in the other room. The viewer and Ree realize in unison that school here seems to prepare its students first and foremost for their inevitable later roles as parents—thereby, the film already hints towards the ideological and systemic limitations on its characters' development and education.

The final section of this triptych of reaction shots begins with a group of students holding rifles who pass Ree in the hallway, one of them even greeting her by name. They walk into a gymnasium and take part in a military drill of the ROTC (Reserve Officers' Training Corps). For the third time in a row, the film cuts to a close-up of Ree's face watching through a window, this time with a deeply impressed, almost longing expression. As will become clear later in the film when Ree actively tries to join the military, the army seems like a possible, logical escape: steady pay, an opportunity to leave her oppressive surroundings behind, and, as the uniform marching of the recruits suggests, a possibility to shed the crushing individual responsibilities she carries and merge with a group. Nevertheless, this casual presence of heavy weaponry in a school context certainly also adds to a certain iconography generally associated with the championing of guns as expressions of freedom in rural America. In these first minutes, the film familiarizes the viewers with the landscape's conditions of possibility by carefully hinting at the dramatic extent of its characters' poverty and contextualizing it within a specific regional culture. However, it also defies certain expectations and clichés about the rural poor. *Winter's Bone* uses a variety of cinematic means to make the Dollys' class status abundantly clear. Without a doubt, they belong to the United States' underclass, inhabiting a landscape that is characterized first and foremost by its inhospitality and infrastructural deficiencies.

The means by which the film depicts this landscape—disrupted geography, interior spaces "layered with objects", use of non-professional actors, etc.—have been described by Linda Badley in her chapter on contemporary indie films made by female directors as "neo-neorealistic," alluding to their origins in Italian neorealism.[10] More specifically, she describes *Winter's Bone* as "representational, low key, and concerned with the day-to-day routines of ordinary life" and as adopting an "austere aesthetic."[11] This can be linked to what Baron and Tzioumakis describe as the "neo-naturalistic aesthetic" of early regional independent films, which confirms *Winter's Bones*' position within the tradition and historic trajectory of US indie cinema.[12] Indeed, one of the earliest definitions by Annette Insdorf, quoted by Baron and Tzioumakis, reveals just how firmly the film is positioned within this much debated category. Insdorf argues that independent cinema's difference from Hollywood is the result of:

> A combination of such elements as casting, pace, cinematic style, and social and moral vision. Countering big stars with fresh faces, big deals with intimate canvasses and big studios with regional authenticity, these filmmakers treat inherently American concerns with a primarily European style.[13]

This naturalist style, which Insdorf considers "European," Baron and Tzioumakis argue, has often been used to "critique dominant social structures that privilege isolated human agency and disregard the integral relationships among human behavior, history, and the environment."[14]

At the same time, however, Badley points out that the "neo-neorealist" women's indie films she analyzes "often transmit their political 'messages' through a nuanced

10 Linda Badley, "Down to the Bone: Neoliberalism and Genre in Contemporary Women's Indies," in *Indie Reframed: Women's Filmmaking and Contemporary American Independent Cinema*, ed. L. Badley, C. Perkins, and M. Schreiber (Edinburgh: Edinburgh University Press, 2016), 122.

11 Ibid.

12 Baron and Tzioumakis, *Acting Indie, 149.*

13 Annette Insdorf. "Ordinary People, European Style: How to Spot an Independent Feature," *American Film* 6:10 (1981), 58.

14 Baron and Tzioumakis, *Acting Indie*, 137.

use of melodrama and Hollywood genre tropes."[15] It is perhaps not surprising, therefore, that a major part of the writing on *Winter's Bone* has approached the film from a genre perspective, aligning it with the classical Western, the "Post Western," the Gothic, and film noir respectively.[16] I want to focus on comparisons with the Western, since *Winter's Bone* directly invites such comparisons by citing the iconography and narrative structure of the classical Western in various ways. Nevertheless, these genre analyses of the film often seem to ignore or merely touch upon the real-life inequalities of class and gender that visibly drive the film's narrative and visual structure and which implicitly turn it into a comment on rural poverty under neoliberalism. To subsume the film's concerns with marginality, extreme poverty, and landscape under such genre-centered approaches thus seems ultimately limiting.

Pasquale Cicchetti's text in particular is revealing in this respect as the author does indeed engage with notions of space and community in *Winter's Bone* yet comes to some rather jarring conclusions that demonstrate the problems of reading the film without reference to its socio-political context and its treatment of class. In drawing up his comparison to the classic Western, Cicchetti reads the film's setting (which he calls a "village") as "hardly civilized land,"[17] a distorted mirror image of the Western's frontier town. He argues:

> *Winter's Bone* reverses the cultural values associated with the borderland community. Whereas the traditional frontier trope is used to imply generally a pattern of expansion, this film seems to express a profound impasse in the social and political dynamics of the borderland; the rhetoric which imbued the image of the frontier as one of progression and discovery is replaced by an image of isolation and seclusion.[18]

This inverted spatial parallelism between *Winter's Bone* and the Western is a convincing observation. It does beg the question, however, *why* the film employs such an inversion. If one might already flinch at his description of an impoverished, underdeveloped community as "hardly civilized," Cicchetti's following descriptions of the Ozark community are even more problematic. The author argues that "far

15 Badley, "Down to the Bone: Neoliberalism and Genre in Contemporary Women's Indies," 122.

16 Pasquale Cicchetti, "'I Ain't Going Nowhere.' The House, the Mobile Hero and the Frontier in *Winter's Bone,"* in *Spaces of (Dis)Location*, ed. Rachael Hamilton, Alison Macleod, and Jenny Munro (Newcastle upon Tyne: Cambridge Scholars, 2013), 73–90; Jesús Ángel González, "New Frontiers for Post-Western Cinema: Frozen River, Sin Nombre, Winter's Bone," *Western American Literature* 50:1 (2015), 51–76; John Berra, "Rural Crimewave: Reconfiguring Regional Spaces through Genre in US Indie Cinema," in *A Companion to American Indie Film*, ed. Geoff King (Oxford: Wiley-Blackwell, 2017), 325–347; David Denby, "Thrills and Chills," *New Yorker* (May 7, 2010), https://www.newyorker.com/magazine/2010/07/05/thrills-and-chills.

17 Pasquale Cicchetti, "'I Ain't Going Nowhere'," 75.

18 Ibid.

from expressing any kind of Utopian ideal, the community at the core of the narrative is depicted as a self-ruling criminal enclave beyond the reach of the law."[19] Not taking into account the narrow view of the potential interpretations of a Utopian community in the text here, it becomes obvious that Cicchetti does not contextualize the mountain community within the conditions of possibility created by existential rural poverty. Being beyond the reach of the law, one might argue, has indeed been the prerequisite for many Utopian communities throughout history and therefore, criminality is a very ambiguous term in this context. Cicchetti does not offer a description here that would preclude the film's community from being a Utopian community which, for reasons explored further below, it definitely is not.

Instead, he goes on to claim that *Winter's Bone* is an inherently regressive text because it sets up the "space of domesticity [as a] [. . .] eulogized space, a space of intimate affection, to be defended against external encroaching."[20] In his opinion, this external aggression is not, however, the forces of neoliberal capitalism—specifically in the form of a private bail bond company—that threaten a 17-year-old girl with the loss of her home but the "crime-based enclave" surrounding her.[21] By refusing to consider the brutal economic circumstances the film exists in, Cicchetti's text falls in line with the victim-blaming of the "culture of poverty" theory omnipresent in US culture which fosters the "image of the idle, irresponsible poor."[22] By extension, such a notion suggests that it is poor people's inadequate values or attitudes that keep them in poverty over generations and prompts them to commit crimes, and not a logical outcome of a capitalist class system.

This approach finds its pinnacle in Cicchetti's understanding of Ree's absent father Jessup, whose disappearance causes the prospective loss of the Dollys' homestead to begin with. Jessup is murdered because of his intention to cooperate with the Sherriff to expose the community's drug operation, probably to lighten his own sentence. A long-standing producer of methamphetamine born into the tight-knit community and absent throughout the entire film, Jessup is hardly an unequivocally positive figure. However, Cicchetti claims:

> [Jessup] can be understood effectively as the shadow of the old frontier hero: the lone rider type, who would set out to cross the border, thus channeling the expansive push of the frontier community [. . .] By making his move across the sealed border of the Ozark community, Jessup could possibly have reopened the communal space. [. . .] it has the potential for paving the way for a deep renovation of the world-image of the film and re-connecting the borderland society to a broader national narrative; for example, to a different, more "optimistic" or

19 Ibid.

20 Cicchetti, "'I Ain't Going Nowhere'," *75.*

21 Ibid., 77.

22 Standing, *The Precariat*, 53.

> even Utopian model of representation. Yet, the community of *Winter's Bone* does not desire to be part of any kind of broader narrative.[23]

Jessup's association with the Western hero is indeed hinted at in the film. For example, in a central scene, Ree looks at old photographs, one of which shows her father and her uncle Teardrop (John Hawkes) as children dressed in cowboy costumes. Nevertheless, Cicchetti's reading of "lone rider" individualism is completely at odds with the film's positioning of community. To be sure, *Winter's Bone* depicts an isolated, deeply paranoid, and ultimately failed community that cannot serve as a functioning social model such as Olwig's notion of the polity. The reason for this disintegration is, however, not the culture of the "crime-based enclave" but exactly the ideology that both Jessup and Teardrop exemplify: a violent, patriarchal individualism that is both inherent to the Western genre and at the core of neoliberal ideology. Indeed, there is a quantifiable connection to be made between neoliberal policies such as a reduction of government-supported social institutions, the deepening of inequality, and a parallel rise in homicide. A study by Craig McLean and colleagues concludes:

> We suggest that neoliberalism indicators associated with diminished government size, lower government spending, and "tax cuts" tend to also be justified based on the value of economic efficiency and growth. Such policies [. . .] lead to conditions of poverty and inequality that have long been associated with homicide. Importantly, these neoliberal policies that tend to reduce government size and spending also serve to shrink many of the government-supported social institutions and programs that may prevent violence.[24]

To understand the "self-ruling criminal enclave" merely as a genre trope clearly misses this point.

Cicchetti's argument that the community needs to open itself to a "broader narrative" is therefore self-defeating. That broader narrative *is* neoliberalism and has clearly already pushed the community to the margins and forced its members to subsist mainly on drug trafficking. Ignoring this context consequentially leads Cicchetti to understanding Ree's final, if possibly only temporary, reclaiming of her homestead as "opting for the safety of nostalgia" instead of considering her very real fear of homelessness.[25] Furthermore, while *Winter's Bone* hardly offers a positive, Utopian vision for the future, it does position communal collaboration as the only way to counter the forces of marginalization—even if it is eventually doomed to fail.

---

23 Cicchetti, "'I Ain't Going Nowhere'," 76.

24 Craig McLean, Michael Long, Paul Stretesky, Michael Lynch and Steve Hall, "Exploring the Relationship between Neoliberalism and Homicide: A Cross-National Perspective," *International Journal of Sociology*, 49:1 (2019), 53.

25 Cicchetti, "'I Ain't Going Nowhere'," 86.

2 "Ancient and a Creepy Sort of Sacred" — Custom and embodied vision

Writing on *Winter's Bone* has mainly approached the film from a genre perspective. When there are references to a wider social context in these genre-centered texts, they often, if not always, remain vague. For example, John Berra writes in his article on what he calls the "rural crime wave" that *Winter's Bone, Frozen River,* and similar films "serve to update cinematic representations of [. . .] increasingly uncertain US economic conditions."[26] Watkins argues that Ree's struggles may be "extreme, [but] they are also increasingly common in today's unequal economy."[27] Perkins is slightly more specific when she describes the film's settings as spaces "in which neoliberal capitalism has permeated every aspect of life" but does not further expand on this idea.[28] However, Linda Badley's chapter on *Winter's Bone* and related films convincingly brings together questions of genre, film style, and "social-historic context."[29] Titled "Neo-Neorealism and Genre in Contemporary Woman's Indies," her chapter investigates films that feature "middle and lower-class female protagonists who find a limited agency within a meticulously rendered web of intersectional circumstances in which they are embedded."[30] She argues that through their use of realist stylistic devices, films like *Winter's Bone* "situate melodrama and genre within a meticulously depicted social reality."[31] This, in turn, enables "the articulation of their female-oriented social and political commentary as to their critical success and popular appeal."[32] In relation to Granik's film, she specifically mentions "stylistic austerity, bleak and isolated winter setting and class concerns" in this context.[33]

Ortner delivers a similar reading of the film's social and political context in her book on US independent cinema under neoliberalism. She argues that films like *Frozen River* and *Winter's Bone* "can be read as telling stories about the implications of the contemporary neoliberal economy not only for poor women but for many middle-class women who face the specter of downward mobility for

---

26 Berra, "Rural Crimewave," 329.

27 Watkins, *Freedom and Vengeance on Film*, 166.

28 Claire Perkins, "Life During Wartime: Emotionalism, Capitalist Realism, and Middle-Class Indie Identity," in *A Companion to American Indie Film*, ed. Geoff King (Oxford: Wiley-Blackwell, 2017), 351.

29 Badley, "Down to the Bone," 122.

30 Ibid., 121.

31 Ibid., 133.

32 Ibid., 127.

33 Ibid., 124.

themselves and their children."[34] She goes on to deliver a brief, but fitting description of the film's visual and spatial portrayal of rural poverty:

> We see the poverty of Ree and her family, living in shacks in the backwoods of the Ozarks, running out of food, hunting squirrels for dinner, being helped just before the point of desperation by a kindly neighbor. Here too it is winter, and despite the green of the forests, the film has a cold and hungry look. [. . .] the physicality (and ugliness) of poverty is powerfully realized.[35]

She then reiterates her argument that films "about poor/lower-class women can be read as allegories of the potential fate of any woman in the new social order, in which neoliberal policies [. . .] and various patriarchal biases combine to render women particularly vulnerable to downward mobility."[36]

A possible reason for why such explicitly socio-political readings of the film remain the exception might be that *Winter's Bone* does not include many outright references to concrete socio-political contexts that go beyond the limited, enclosed space it envisions. Moreover, as argued before, since the effects of neoliberalism are commonly associated with cities and, particularly, their spaces and modes of work, one might not necessarily assume that *Winter's Bone* is intent or able to comment on experiences of marginalization under neoliberal capitalism. In fact, it is even difficult to judge if the film takes place in the present—meaning the year of its production, 2010—or in the past. Its setting is, as Thornham suggests, "cut off from the world of history" and appears as removed from the modern world.[37] Certainly, cars, clothing, and furniture all hint towards the twenty-first century but references to contemporary events or real-life persons remain largely absent—the only glaring exception is the central role methamphetamine plays in the narrative. This drug has been a factor of rural life in America since at least the 1980s, but its spread started to accelerate significantly in the early 2000s.[38]

Winter's Bone depicts a geographical place that, while representing contemporary rurality, is above all steeped in tradition. It is characterized, as Thornham puts it, as "the unseen Other of American modernity."[39] James Bell connects this sense of oldness to the film's landscape aesthetic when he writes that "the grey skies, the bleached colours, the wooden houses with their yards strewn with old furniture, cars, and junk—all are deeply expressive of a community with a dis-

34 Ortner, *Not Hollywood*, 190.

35 Ibid., 195.

36 Ibid., 197–198.

37 Thornham, *Spaces of Women's Cinema*, 43.

38 See: Rachel Gonzales, Larissa Mooney, and Richard Rawson, "The Methamphetamine Problem in the United States," *Annual Review of Public Health* 31:1 (2010), 386.

39 Thornham, *Spaces of Women's Cinema*, 42.

tinct sense of its own ancestry, for better or worse."[40] Debra Granik adds in the interview that her main character Ree "feels that she comes from old people, which is rare for Americans—the idea that she has an ancestry tied to the landscape."[41] The idea of an ancient land with old customs is also already present in the source novel, in which Woodrell describes a part of Ree's environment like this: "The new part of Hawkfall was old to most folks, but the old part of Hawkfall seemed ancient and a creepy sort of sacred."[42] These notions of traditions, customs, and ancestry which are, in Granik's words, "tied to the landscape" are expressed in the film through a focus on bodily practices and everyday tasks.

It is in the film's focus on landscape as a "milieu of involvement," that the political engagement with neoliberal capitalism takes shape and is channeled into a claim for landscape as a social, communal concept.[43] In line with Ingold's argument that "it is through being inhabited that the world becomes a meaningful environment," the film presents its viewers with customs and activities that transform the rural cinematic landscape from mere setting into a "meaningful environment."[44] Thornham argues that "Granik's film [. . .] has reversed the practices of the Western genre it references, overturning its relentless linear drive and substituting a sense of space as at once immense and intensely, and tactily, *lived.*"[45] Such tactile practices include, for example, the Dolly family's hunt for squirrels, the communal scene of music-making and singing of folk songs as well as Ree's final, intense immersion into the lake containing her father's bones.

All these moments of involved activity and custom serve to illustrate how enmeshed the marginalized characters are within their surrounding landscape. Tim Ingold describes this intertwined relation when he writes that "through living in it, the landscape becomes a part of us, just as we are part of it," and that "the world emerges with its properties alongside the emergence of the perceiver as person."[46] This is also illustrated in the main character's ability to "read" her physical surroundings. When her neighbor and distant cousin Blond Milton (William White) attempts to trick Ree into believing her father accidentally burned to death while producing methamphetamine, she is able to recognize the deception. By "reading" the ruins of the burned-down hut and the plants that have started to overgrow it, she recognizes that the drug lab was destroyed long before her fa-

40 James Bell, "Meth and the Maiden," *Sight & Sound* 20:10 (2010), 28.

41 Debra Granik, "Meth and the Maiden," Interview by James Bell. *Sight & Sound* 20:10 (2010), 28.

42 Woodrell, *Winter's Bone*, 49.

43 Wylie, *Landscape*, 161.

44 Ingold, *The Perception of the Environment*, 173.

45 Thornham, *Spaces of Women's Cinema*, 46.

46 Ingold, *The Perception of the Environment*, 191; ibid., 168.

ther's disappearance. One is reminded of Maurice Merleau-Ponty's observation "who sees cannot possess the visible unless he [sic] is possessed by it, unless he *is of it*."[47] Ree is undoubtedly "of it," of this stretch of land, and can navigate her way through the inhospitable landscape and its potential deceptions. Her "embodied vision"—"the interconnectivity of eye, body, and land"—her emotions and perceptions are central in the film's construction of landscape.[48] The way in which *Winter's Bone* favors an "embodied vision," rather than a "masterful perspective" is crucial to understanding the film's politics, especially its ethics of representing a vulnerable community.[49]

As we view the world of the Ozarks through Ree's eyes and follow her on hidden paths through the landscape, we grasp her connection to this stretch of land and come to an understanding of landscapes, as Christopher Tilley has defined, as "perceived and embodied sets of relationships between places, a structure of human feeling, emotion, dwelling, movement and practical activity."[50] What is striking about the "embodied acts of landscaping" the film envisions, is precisely their communal, cooperative quality and the fluidity with which they unfold in a place that seems largely "ungoverned." It is here that the film's focus on collaboration as a form of resistance against an economized, increasingly unequal world becomes visible. Through its foregrounding of the interaction between inhabitants and landscape, *Winter's Bone* visualizes the connectedness of the Ozark community to their surroundings and to each other. By stressing its longevity—what Thornham calls "cut off from the world of history" and Olwig terms "time out of mind"[51]—the film falls into line with Olwig's definition of the *Landschaft* and the central role custom plays in its formation: "Custom, upon which the common law of the land was based, was inscribed in the land through physical practice. The landscape [. . .] as a physical place was thus the manifestation of the polity's local custom and common law."[52] Again, this holds true for both the "everyday" activities Ree, her family, and neighbors are shown performing throughout the film as well as the more extraordinary merging of bodies and landscape in the climactic scene of the film—both are the result of cooperation and interactivity.

---

47 Maurice Merleau-Ponty, *The Visible and the Invisible*. Evanston: Northwestern UP, 1968, 134. Emphasis added.

48 Wylie, *Landscape*, 177.

49 Ibid., 178.

50 Christopher Tilley, *The Materiality of Stone — Explorations in Landscape Phenomenology* (Oxford: Berg Publishers, 2004), 25.

51 Thornham, *Spaces of Women's Cinema*, 43; Olwig, *The Meanings of Landscape*, 26.

52 Olwig, *Landscape, Nature, and the Body Politic*, 214.

Simultaneously, the weakness or absence of governmental "natural" law as portrayed in the film, for example, in the helplessness of the Sheriff, chimes with the notion of governance as a description of decentralized power under neoliberalism. Brown defines governance as "a transformation from governing through hierarchically organized command and control [. . .] to governing that is networked, integrated, cooperative, partnered, disseminated, and at least partly self-organized."[53] There is no sense of centralized democratic structures in the isolated Ozark community—the Sheriff's inability or refusal to effectively intervene in the criminal activity points to a receding influence of "hierarchically organized command and control." However, the lawlessness of the place also offers potential for resistance: in this liminal space, forms of cooperation can emerge and establish networks of community that is independent of hierarchical control. If, for example, we understand the film's climax, the retrieval of Jessup's bones, as both an act of radical cooperation and (female) solidarity, as well as an extraordinary instance of embodied landscaping practice, it becomes clear how the film envisions a resistant if unfulfilled potential of "embodied practice and performance" in the fluidity of ungoverned space.[54]

Finally, a short dream sequence encapsulates the film's juxtaposition of landscape, embodiment, and marginalization. It comes just after Ree has painfully experienced the mistrust and paranoia that has disintegrated the community: when she attempts to ask drug boss Thump Milton (Ron Hall) for his support for a second time, his wife Merab (Dale Dickey) and her sisters violently assault her, assuming she wants to avenge her father's death. Back at home, severely injured and under the influence of strong painkillers, Ree falls asleep. The film then inserts a visually striking sequence shot on black-and-white eight-millimeter film. A squirrel, quite possibly Ree's dream avatar, jumps frightened from branch to branch whilst the threatening sounds of a chainsaw as well as falling trees can be heard on the soundtrack. The sequence ends with the image of a flock of ravens and a column of smoke rising from the woodlands.

The sequence is remarkable for several reasons. It stands out, firstly, because of its stylistic divergence from the rest of the film and, secondly, because of its foreshadowing of the climatic scene's employment of a chainsaw. Furthermore, the sequence suggests an encroaching industrialized world which is almost entirely absent from the rest of the film and can be understood as a subtle, poetic foray into eco-cinema. Generally, *Winter's Bone* does not invite ecopolitical readings as much as other films of the New Rural Cinema such as *Beasts of the Southern Wild*, *Leave*

53 Brown, *Undoing the Demos*, 123.

54 Wylie, *Landscape*, 166.

No Trace, or *First Cow*. However, Ree's intimate identification with the vulnerable animals whose habitat is supposedly threatened in this scene, demonstrates the relevance of the film's embodied vision for wider political concerns that form the bases for both ecocritical approaches as well as for the notion of landscape as polity. Taking into account Sean Cubitt's suggestion that "the central tenet of ecological thought [. . .] [is] the mutual mediation of matter and energy [. . .] through complex and evolving relations," it becomes obvious that the relational, interactive concept of landscape *Winter's Bone* foregrounds through its focus on embodied acts of landscaping is indeed the key to its political significance.[55]

Thornham writes of the sequence: "When Ree dreams that the timberland is being destroyed by machines, it is with the animals [. . .] of the forest she identifies. Contact with the world outside is troubled, characterized by wariness, distrust, and secrecy."[56] As such, the oneiric identification with the squirrel can be understood as more than just a metaphor for Ree's fear of losing her own "habitat" as a result of the potential repossession of her home. It underlines Ree's intense physical and affective connection to her precarious surroundings as the film makes the coalescence with the Ozark landscape strikingly visible. In juxtaposing her experiences with images of a frightened animal, the dream sequence conveys both the sense of entanglement as well as that of constant threat that is so central to the film's treatment of its marginal landscape. Furthermore, as Ree arguably adopts the squirrel's subjectivity, the film makes a point for the potential equality of human and non-human inhabitants in their creating of a landscape as well as their shared experience of vulnerability and displacement as living bodies in space.

3 "The world becomes uninhabitable" — Ree and the struggle for landscape

In their investigation of "neoliberalism and everyday life," Braedley and Luxton undertake analyses of the "benefits and losses on the basis of gender, race, and class" that neoliberal policies have determined in the past decades.[57] In relation to questions of gender, the authors write: "One of the central distinguishing features of neoliberalism is the gender regime that anchors it."[58] They go on to ana-

55 Sean Cubitt, "Ecopolitics of Cinema," in *The Routledge Companion to Cinema and Politics*, ed. Yannis Tzioumakis, Claire Molloy (London: Routledge, 2016), 40.

56 Thornham, *Spaces of Women's Cinema*, 44.

57 Braedley and Luxton, "Competing Philosophies," 12.

58 Ibid.

lyze the challenges that women face in neoliberal capitalism, especially in the context of its biopolitics. They claim:

> The leading proponents of neoliberalism are men. They have built into its theory and implementation a specific commitment to maintaining their male privilege. At its core is their insistence that individuals and their families are responsible for social reproduction, and their refusal to acknowledge collective responsibility for the well-being of the population.[59]

Winter's Bone places its critique of neoliberal marginalization at precisely this juncture of patriarchy, individualism, and the marketization of society. The film's elements of communal cooperation are almost always marked as female whereas the overwhelming sense of threat, violence, and paranoia is clearly marked as male. This final section on the film argues that, firstly, *Winter's Bone* suggests an enduring relationship between landscape, customary law, and community that falls into line with Olwig's concept of landscape as polity. Secondly, it will go on to show how this relationship is compromised by, as Brown writes, "the neoliberal triumph" of marketization which, ultimately, "is extinguishing [. . .] the domains through which democracy [. . .] materializes."[60] The domain in question here is the film's landscape.

As shown in the previous section, *Winter's Bone* puts great emphasis on the rural communities' bodily practices—in music, food, movement—and the way custom, as Olwig describes it, is "inscribed in the land through physical practice."[61] It is worth looking at the concrete acts that Olwig names as defining customs for the Renaissance communities he writes about: do they apply to the film's Ozark community and the "relationships between place, space, body, and polity in the making of [its] political landscape?"[62] The central aspect of the polity was "the meeting place of its representative legal body."[63] This council was called a *Ting* or *Thing* and was held on a main place (German: *Platz*) and, from the Middle Ages, "at the village green, urban square, or marketplace [. . .] It was here where *things* were ordered and put into place. The things at issue at the *thing* were legal matters, in accordance with the earliest meaning of the word."[64] In these public meetings, customary law was interpreted according to the matter at hand and relying on precedent.

The members of the council were respected people from the community and as such "a person's place in society was thus manifested by his or her place in the

59 Ibid., 15.

60 Brown, *Undoing the Demos*, 79.

61 Olwig, *Landscape, Nature, and the Body Politic*, 214.

62 Ibid.

63 Ibid.

64 Ibid.

physical place at the symbolic heart of the landscape/country."[65] Is there an equivalent to such a council to be found in the community *Winter's Bone* depicts? First, it must be noted how the film's community is, from a spatial perspective, the opposite of a village or town organized around a village green or town square, what Olwig calls the "symbolic heart of the landscape." This is why Cicchetti's identification of the film's setting as a "village" seems somewhat misjudged. Instead, the film depicts its setting as a loose cluster of dispersed cabins and plots, connected by winding roads and hidden paths but lacking a center. As Thornham notes, "it is a wilderness that is full of boundaries and fences and crisscrossed by paths and electricity pylons."[66] By refraining from the use of master shots, aerial shots, or other means of depicting a large part of its setting at once, the film constructs a disrupted geography that, on the one hand, falls into line with the above mentioned "embodied vision" of its main character. On the other hand, it also serves as a visual manifestation of a community in dissolution. A striking example is Ree's journey to the final resting place of her father. As Merab and her sisters drive her to Jessup's watery grave, they blindfold her in order to keep her from remembering the way to the scene of the crime. The absent images of the journey both draw attention to Ree's subjectivity as well as the community's disconnectedness.

If there is an instance of council in *Winter's Bone*, it would be the meeting under the conduct of Merab and Thump Milton assembled after the attack on Ree. It is here that Ree's destiny is discussed and decided upon, yet the circumstances are hardly those of a functioning democratic community. After Merab and her sisters have brutally beaten Ree, she awakes under the cold neon lights of the Miltons' stable. The shot of the automatic door slowly closing behind Ree as well as the close-ups of chains and hooks inside reference the iconography of rural horror and its notions of deeply disturbed clannishness and thus signal from the very beginning that we cannot expect a fair, democratic process. Two blurry, shaky shots from Ree's lowered perspective make clear that a group of people are gathered around her looking down on her beaten body. "You was warned nice and you wouldn't listen," says Merab as Ree spits out a dislocated tooth. Another subjective pan around the assembled council reveals some familiar faces, both male and female, that Ree has met throughout her journey. Merab's plaid, blue-grey shirt sticks out and seems to visually align her with Ree who wears a similar piece of clothing, suggesting her eventual decision to help Ree find her father's remains. The next lines of dialogue underline the gravity of the meeting. Megan (Casey MacLaren), Thump's granddaughter, asks Ree menacingly: "What are we ever going to do with

65 Ibid., 215.

66 Thornham, *Spaces of Women's Cinema*, 41.

you, baby girl?" "Kill me, I guess," is Ree's resigned response, causing some intense glances between Meghan, Merab, and the assembled men. "That idea has been said already," replies Meghan. "Got any others?" "Help me. Ain't nobody said that idea yet, have they," Ree glibly answers. Finally, Thump Milton enters the room and listens to Ree's plea for help, which he denies.

On the one hand, we might see this meeting as a rather fitting example of Olwig's central claim that "the polity of the landscape/country was thus built on law, not blood. A most vital function of this law, in fact, was to mediate between the differing blood relations inhabiting the landscape and thereby to preserve the peace."[67] After all, this is an example of two families—or possibly two branches of the same family—attempting to solve a critical issue through customary law rather than through governmental legal proceedings. Megan's question "Got any others?" also suggest that there exists an overall interest to "preserve the peace." There is, thus, undoubtedly a sort of communal law in place that regulates conflict.

However, it is obviously impossible to interpret this violent, secretive meeting as a positive example of communal justice and the film certainly does not imply so. Ree's extremely vulnerable position at the mercy of the drug-kingpin and his associates and the extreme imbalance of power make this more a case of mob law than justice. It is worth noting here, again, that Olwig links his concept of landscape as polity founded on communal law to the gradual and targeted usurpation of this understanding. In Renaissance Northern Europe, an imperial reinterpretation of landscape as a scenic category that served to consolidate the power of the monarch and the state finally squashed the power of the independent *Landschaften*: "The monarchy [. . .] saw their law as natural but their sense of natural law was very different from the law conceived by the champions of customary law. They regarded the natural law of the monarchy as universal and opposed to the particularity of convention."[68] These imperial claims were reflected both in perspectival landscape art and in the controlled act of landscaping the environment itself, for example in the form of extensive, representative landscape gardens. What we witness in this scene in *Winter's Bone* can be understood as the remnants of a formerly functioning council that has been gradually corrupted and ousted to the criminal margins. Here, however, the spatial context is not that of the landscape garden symbolizing centralized power, but the disrupted geography formed by neoliberal governance.

67 Olwig, *Landscape, Nature and the Body Politic*, 214.

68 Olwig, *The Meanings of Landscape*, 35.

As touched on above, the nameless Ozark community (the novel names it Hawkfall, Granik and Anne Rosellini's adaption however strikingly omits any mention of a name) lacks a center, square, or any other place that would serve to facilitate "deliberate constructions of existence through democratic discussion, law, policy."[69] Official congregation seems unthinkable in this inhospitable, disconnected landscape. At the same time, the state has almost entirely receded from the public sphere: all governmental institutions the film introduces—the Sheriff as personified universal law, the school, the military, and, by extension, the privately employed bondsmen—are presented as useless, helpless, or even as complicit with the faceless forces of marginalization and injustice. There is a US flag hanging from the Dollys' porch, but there seems to be hardly a tangible connection to the organizational structure of the state left in this environment. It is impossible, therefore, to understand the film's landscape images without taking into account neoliberal governance in terms of both a "transformation from governing through hierarchically organized command and control [. . .] to governing that is networked, integrated [. . .] and at least partly self-organized" and of the larger context of neoliberal austerity politics "that has dismantled public institutions and political spaces [. . .] [and] alters the principle of 'inclusion for all'."[70] As Brown argues "governance has become neoliberalism's primary administrative form, the political modality through which it *creates environments*, structures constraints and incentives, and hence conducts subjects."[71] The landscape of the Ozark community is the outcome of this creation of unjust environments.

Furthermore, *Winter's Bone* clearly genders this injustice by underlining the cooperation between women throughout and contrasting it with male individualism. Thornham reads the film's narrative as a modern-day folk tale and interprets its gender politics in this context:

> Ree, like the hero of myth and folktale, is both guided and opposed by a series of mirrored character pairs, with each encounter occasioning both a gift (a drink, money, a "doobie") and a warning. Woman after woman first opposes and then helps and guides Ree, and man after man is characterized by unpredictability and threat.[72]

Teardrop, Thump Milton, Little Arthur, and most of all Ree's father Jessup himself, represent a selfish individualism and paranoid anti-statism that, crucially, is shown to play a major part in neoliberalism's dismantling of democracy through its upholding of male privilege. Brown makes out different national varieties of

69 Brown, *Undoing the Demos*, 221–222.

70 Ibid., 123; ibid., 72.

71 Ibid., 122. Emphasis added.

72 Thornham, *Spaces of Women's Cinema*, 42.

neoliberal politics which, in the United States, intersect with "a strange brew of long-established antistatism" that is arguably particularly pronounced in rural America. Ree's own individual quest "to discover the truth and save her home, *should* be a masculine one" and therefore causes hostile reactions in the male protagonists from the very beginning: her own uncle tries to violently dissuade her from pursuing her goal, her friend Gail's boyfriend refuses to lend her his car, and Thump Milton denies even her most desperate plea for help.[73] Thornham rightfully argues: "What Ree encounters on her quest is patriarchal power."[74] Even Merab, who finally ends up guiding her towards her father's grave, asks her on their first encounter: "Ain't you got no man to do this?"

Ree's vulnerable position as a woman pursuing an inherently male quest is gradually recognized by the women around her. As Jesús Ángel González summarizes, "if there is hope in this abandoned frontier community, it is in the women's hands and in female solidarity."[75] The acts of female communal cooperation throughout lead to the film's climax, the excavation of her father's hands from a lake which, visually, can be understood as the film's most intense instance of the blurring of boundaries between inhabitants and landscape. When Ree reaches into the dark water and finds her father's hands, Ingold's claim that "the landscape becomes a part of us, just as we are part of it" regains a sinister, new prominence.[76] The proof of death that the hands provide enables Ree to keep her home and even to partake in her father's bail money. This seemingly happy ending, however, cannot conceal the fact that hardly anything has changed for Ree: "the world order that she re-enters is patriarchal, and largely unchanged."[77] The very last scene as well as the post-credit-snippets while certainly applying a slightly less bleak imagery, ultimately suggest a futility of the female acts of communal cooperation that only serve to uphold the patriarchal, neoliberal world order. As Brown relates:

> There are only two possibilities for those positioned as women in the sexual division of labor that neoliberal orders continue to depend upon and reproduce. Either women align their own conduct with this truth [. . .] in which case the world becomes uninhabitable, or women's activities and bearing [. . .] remain the unavowed glue for a world whose governing principle cannot hold it together, in which case women occupy their old place as unacknowledged props and supplements to masculinist liberal subjects. As provisioners of care for others in households [. . .] women disproportionately remain the invisible infrastructure for all developing, mature, and worn-out human capital.[78]

73 Brown, *Undoing the Demos*, 20; Thornham, *Spaces of Women's Cinema*, 43.

74 Ibid., 45.

75 Jesús Ángel González, "New Frontiers," 71.

76 Ingold, *The Perception of the Environment*, 191.

77 Thornham, *Spaces of Women's Cinema*, 45.

78 Brown, *Undoing the Demos*, 104–105.

What Cicchetti reads as the film's supposedly conservative reaffirmation of domestic "eugolized space [. . .] to be defended against external encroaching" is Ree inevitably yielding to the logic of neoliberal biopolitics. If she does not return to her role as "provisioner of care," the film's world will literally become uninhabitable for Ree, her siblings, and her mother.[79]

This ambivalence becomes especially apparent in Uncle Teardrop's final appearance and the short inserts accompanying the film's end credits. Whereas the film's opening scene is based around the Dollys' trampoline as a prop, the final scene is held together by the banjo that Ree finds in her closet. A noticeably long close-up of the musical instrument seems to point to this significance from the beginning—it is a signifier of US folk and country music, and thus a considerable element of regional custom. Not least, it also inevitably calls to mind a central scene in one of the most well-known cinematic explorations of rural backwardness, *Deliverance*. When Teardrop arrives in Ree's backyard, he gives Sonny and Ashlee two chicks to raise up. Right after that, the interaction with the bondsman occurs, officially confirming that Ree is out of immediate peril. Both events seem to signal a happy ending in that they confirm narrative closure and hope for the Dollys' future. A brief close-up of Ree's mother smiling even seems to hint at a potential improvement of her mental condition. Teardrop plays a few chords on the banjo at the request of his niece and nephew, and, for a moment, Cicchetti's "space of intimate affection" seems indeed to come into existence.

However, the film immediately complicates, or even negates, Teardrop's contribution to a sense of safety and community that is hinted at by his playing of the banjo which used to belong to his brother. As he drops the instrument, muttering "I was never good like your daddy was," he looks at Ree and implies to her that he has become aware of the identity of Jessup's murderer. Earlier in the film, he had asked Ree to never tell him if she ever found out who killed Jessup because he would seek vengeance and probably be killed himself in the process. His implicit announcement that he is aware of the identity of his brother's killer confirms that further violent conflict is inevitable. As he gets up to leave, the visibly shocked Ree offers him the banjo which now more clearly than before becomes a symbolic promise of, as Brown describes it, "the unavowed glue for a world whose governing principle cannot hold it together" which, throughout the film, it has fallen on the female characters to provide for.[80] Unsurprisingly, Teardrop rejects the instrument and responds: "Why don't you keep it here for me?" Thereby,

---

79 Cicchetti, "'I Ain't Going Nowhere'," 75.

80 Brown, *Undoing the Demos*, 104.

he both underlines his unbroken sense of blind individualism—pursuing vengeance with no regards for the potential consequences for his family and larger community—and at the same time consigns Ree to her former role as "unacknowledged prop [. . .] and supplement [. . .] to masculinist liberal subjects."[81] It is no coincidence, then, that young Ashlee picks up the banjo, suggesting her own future role within the gender hierarchy. The film's ambivalent ending therefore suggests two different interpretations.

If one reads, as both Cicchetti and González do, the final scene as a "semi-happy ending typical of post-Westerns," the focus lies on Ree's reclamation of her home, as Cicchetti calls it, her "retreat into the protective shell of domestic time-space."[82] Ree's final declamation to her younger siblings—"I ain't going anywhere"—would have to be understood as a "renunciation as much as an accomplishment" in that she gives up her previous attempt of leaving the community and is content in having secured her homestead.[83] Again, the banjo as a prop is crucial in this way of reading the scene. Cicchetti claims:

> Whether Jessup's death will be avenged or not is now beyond the scope of Ree's re-established world. She has won her place back. As a result, however, the remnants of the frontier and the time of history are now ultimately separate: the symbolic legacy of the past (the banjo) and the historic responsibility of the loss [. . .] remain on two distinct planes. The latter pertains to a domain which is now definitely cut off from the domestic time-space [. . .]. Teardrop's double rejection of the banjo certifies the break.[84]

If the film would indeed offer this conclusion as a celebration of familialism, one would have to agree with Cicchetti that its outlook is ultimately regressive. Again, however, it seems rather one-sided to divorce the ending's undoubtedly hopeful tone from its social context as well as, crucially, its focus on landscape. For what is "happy" about this ending is not Ree's reintegration into the role of "provisioner of care" but the tangible, successful result of cooperation and solidarity. Calling to mind Mitchell's reading of Olwig that "there is a struggle for landscape, and it is at the same time a struggle for justice," Ree's temporary victory over the forces of oppression shows how such a struggle for spatial justice can only be won cooperatively and in a space in which governmental law has almost wholly receded.[85] This more positive understanding of the ending is underlined by the stills and short clips that accompany the film's end-credit-sequence. The stills show the Ozark landscape in a way that is absent from the film itself: shots of

81 Ibid., 105.

82 González, "New Frontiers," 71; Cicchetti, "'I Ain't Going Nowhere'," 88.

83 Ibid.

84 Ibid.

85 Mitchell, "Cultural Landscapes," 788.

blossoming trees suggesting the coming of Spring and apparently historical photos of actual inhabitants of the Ozarks suggest that change is possible through the interplay of environment and community. A final, post-credits clip of Ashlee running through the snow suggests the agency of a younger generation in reclaiming their intimate connection to the surrounding landscape not only as history and tradition but as a potentially utopian outlook of democratic cooperation as well.

On the other hand, *Winter's Bone's* final scene might be understood as visualizing the impossibility of such democratic imaginaries. The intensification of marginalization in neoliberal capitalism through "the shrinking, privatization, and/or dismantling of infrastructure supporting families, children, and retirees" returns the responsibility of care to women.[86] Brown continues:

> Privatizing public goods uniquely penalizes women to the extent that they remain disproportionately responsible for those who cannot be responsible for themselves. In this respect, familialism is an essential requirement, rather than an incidental feature of the neoliberal privatization of public goods.[87]

Landscape understood as place is, of course, one of these public goods. Therefore, the film demonstrates how, in its marginal, rural context, an alliance of male individualism and neoliberal anti-socialism thwarts any attempts to expand the existent acts of female solidarity beyond a personal, secretive level of cooperation.

It is notable that several films of the New Rural Cinema employ female protagonists to make similar points about neoliberalism's inherent male privilege and demonstrate how "neoliberal policies [. . .] and various patriarchal biases combine to render women particularly vulnerable to downward mobility."[88] *Frozen River*, for example, resembles *Winter's Bone* in its narrative focus on a woman in an impoverished region who is forced into crime in order to provide a home for her family. In Courtney Hunt's film, Ray (Melissa Leo), a single mother in wintry Upstate New York, takes up smuggling immigrants over the Canadian border after her husband, a compulsive gambler, has left with the savings intended for a double-wide mobile home for the family. Ray, like Ree, relies on female solidarity in the end: her partner-in-crime is Lila (Misty Upham), a Mohawk woman who, after initial hostilities, ends up providing care for Ray's family. *Ballast*, as we will see, also foregrounds a single mother's struggle with poverty and care work. Finally, *Nomadland* suggests a slightly more upbeat perspective on the theme: its protagonist Fern (Frances McDormand) finds a certain freedom from

---

86 Brown, *Undoing the Demos*, 105.
87 Ibid.
88 Ortner, *Not Hollywood*, 197–198.

her role as “provisioner of care” after her husband’s death and begins a new, adventurous life as a van-dwelling “nomad” in precarious, short-term employment.

Whereas *Nomadland* follows the conventions of the road movie and its exploration of freedom and self-discovery on the open road, the existent political landscape in *Winter’s Bone* confines its female inhabitants to their domestic realm and, by invoking the supposedly natural role of women, becomes, as Mitchell argues, a “vehicle for all manner of exclusionary, alienating, expropriating and often [. . .] patriarchal social practices.”[89] Only if we think of landscape, “as polity and place, and [of] nature as a complex, historically constituted concept imbued with social values” will landscape “cease[. . .] to be a vehicle for environmental determinism and nature fanaticism identified with race and gender.”[90] As Teardrop’s rejection of the banjo at the end of the film demonstrates, however, there seems to be no possibility for radical ways of rethinking the relation of community and landscape in the context of neoliberal patriarchy.

89 Mitchell, “Landscape,” 54.

90 Olwig, *Landscape, Nature, and the Body Politic*, 226.

Chapter Five
The Wilderness Illusion – *Leave No Trace* (2018)

In an interview with trade publication *Screen Daily* promoting the release of *Leave No Trace*, Debra Granik explains her motivation in directing yet another film centered around marginalized rural protagonists: "There's been a war against poor people for the last 25 years; it's been ugly and hostile and cruel. [. . .] So you've got to find some scrappy survivors, use some humor so it's not dreary, and get to work on another social realist [film]."[1] Her association of the topic of poverty with social realism is striking in this quote. It confirms Badley's categorization of Granik's work within "a widespread post-postmodern return to realism in world cinema."[2] Asserting her indie credentials, Granik describes social realism as "micro-niche counter programming" in that films like hers are both relatively cheap to make (around a $5 million budget for *Leave No Trace*) and offer textual variance from US mainstream films. Indeed, like the films Badley analyses, *Leave No Trace* "forces spectators to immerse themselves in the monotony, oppression, and hazard experienced by ordinary [. . .] women in *specific environments.*"[3] It is these environments that Granik's third feature film highlights in a unique, distinctive manner.

Leave No Trace visually tells its protagonists' story through the various rural landscapes they are inhabiting and traversing throughout the narrative: the park, the "tamed" countryside, and, finally, the trailer park in the forest. The first section will therefore offer a close analysis of these landscapes and suggest their relevance for the characters' conditions of possibility and, thus, for a political reading of the film. The film in turn evaluates these environments' potentials for the forms of social coexistence they allow and their relevance to the US concept of wilderness. The second section is dedicated to the film's approach to an embodied understanding of landscape, specifically in its central employment of performances of custom such as beekeeping. The final section evaluates the film's political landscape, specifically with regards to race, and its implications for alternative modes of living on the margins.

1 Debra Granik, "*Leave No Trace* director Debra Granik on carving her own niche in social-realism," Interview by John Hazelton. *Screen Daily* (1 December, 2018), https://www.screendaily.com/features/leave-no-trace-director-debra-granik-on-carving-her-own-niche-in-social-realism/5134942.article.

2 Badley, "Down to the Bone," 123.

3 Ibid.

https://doi.org/10.1515/9783110779417-006

1 "How near to good is what is wild!"

The opening landscape images in *Leave No Trace* are strikingly different from those of *Winter's Bone*. Whereas the previous film's icy color palette is dominated by blue and grey, *Leave No Trace* positively overwhelms its viewers with the saturated, radiant shades of green of a sunlit forest thicket. This is a lush vegetation, a seemingly veritable wilderness only inhabited by the film's main protagonists. Even before their intention to hide is made explicit by the narrative, the two main characters, the 13-year-old Tom (Thomasin McKenzie) and her father Will (Ben Foster), are visually blending in with their surroundings. Their dark green clothes as well as their positioning in the frame communicates both their familiarity with the terrain as well as their desperate reliance on the forest's ability to disguise them from the outside world.

As the film gradually reveals, Will is a widowed veteran of an unspecified war —though his age would suggest the wars in Iraq or Afghanistan—suffering from severe PTSD which causes him to reject life within the confines of society. Driven by the codes of military life, he has been living off the grid with his daughter for an unspecified amount of time. As he is constantly living in fear of being discovered, he has taught Tom techniques of camouflage and survival which determine their daily routine. They are presented in the opening minutes of the film: making a fire, gathering rainwater, foraging mushrooms, and, particularly, leaving no trace of their presence and practicing for the emergency of sudden discovery. Father and daughter sleep in a small tent together and have constructed a primitive shelter to store their belongings in. The narrative of both the novel and the film is inspired by the real-life story of a father and daughter living in Oregon's municipal Forest Park for four years. They were discovered in 2004 and their story was made public in a much-noticed article by journalist Maxine Bernstein.[4]

The film begins in medias res, giving no context initially about the specific geographic location of the setting. A combination of long shots underlining the forest's vastness and visually pleasing close-ups of plants, soil, and insects as well as the soundtrack of "densely-textured ambient sounds" bestow the terrain with an enchanted quality.[5] Its natural beauty and lush, fertile vegetation make it appear as a hospitable living environment, far removed from the barren wasteland of the Ozarks in *Winter's Bone*. This is underlined by the ease and confidence with which Tom navigates through the forest. She visibly feels at home and can find shelter

4 Bernstein, Maxine. "OUT OF THE WOODS. POLICE RESCUE FATHER, GIRL WHO SAY FOREST PARK WAS THEIR HOME FOR FOUR YEARS," *The Oregonian* (May 20, 2004) section A1, 1–6.

5 Hannah Paveck, "Care at the Margins: Debra Granik's *Leave No Trace*," *Another Gaze* (May 19, 2018), https://www.anothergaze.com/care-margins-debra-graniks-leave-no-trace-2018.

and nourishment thanks to her father's survival lessons. The film mainly takes on her subjectivity here, as does the original novel which is entirely written from her perspective. Low-angle shots of trees suggest a childlike perspective that align the viewer with Tom's perspective and frame the narrative from the very beginning as a coming-of-age story. The forest emerges as an exciting and beautiful natural playground—or even as a mythical kingdom over which Tom and her father rule as its only inhabitants. Undoubtedly, Tom is aware of her father's severe mental-health condition as, so the film suggests in a nocturnal scene in the tent, he regularly wakes in panic from trauma-induced nightmares. As the soundtrack of helicopter noises indicate an aural memory of war echoed in the nightmare, this scene indicates that the film does occasionally shift to Will's interiority. Tom eagerly takes part in his routines and security drills without complaining, providing stability for her traumatized father. Nevertheless, the overall atmosphere of these opening moments is hardly one of threat or upheaval. Father and daughter have achieved a kind of harmony in their surroundings (see Fig. 8).

Fig. 8: Father and daughter have achieved a kind of harmony in their surroundings: Tom (Thomasin Mc Kenzie) and Will (Ben Foster) in *Leave No Trace* (Debra Granik, 2018).

A small first disturbance of this elusive tranquility comes when Tom discovers a group of prisoners in orange uniforms picking up litter under the surveillance of a police marshal. Not only does the bright color of their uniforms stand in stark contrast to the green color palette of the surrounding terrain, the group's presence also already points to the fact that the seemingly secluded forest is not as far removed from civilization, or from the grasp of the state, as it might seem at first. This notion is soon confirmed when Will suggests a trip to "the town" to buy new clothes for his daughter and stock up on food. As they leave the forest, it becomes clear that it is a municipal park close to a large city, later revealed to be Portland, Oregon—vast, but hardly a secluded wilderness. The proximity to the city enables Will to access amenities such as supermarkets as well as to have his prescription of, presumably, opioids filled which, however, he does not take himself but sells to other veterans suffering from addiction.[6]

The national or municipal park is a space of great importance in US national identity as it reflects "conflicting American attitudes towards landscape and country."[7] Hence, its prominent use as the film's opening setting already gestures towards a larger political context. The national park movement's origin harks back to nineteenth century transcendentalists such as Henry David Thoreau and Ralph Waldo Emerson who saw America's "wild" nature as the key to the young nation's development. As Thoreau wrote in his famous essay "Walking" (1862): "How near to good is what is wild!"[8] Paradoxically, the exponential economic development increasingly threatened the United States' natural spaces. Thoreau in particular had a "truly visionary solution to the problem of the transient glory of America: to preserve the elixir of wildness by emparking some of it as a place where the nation could re-create its natural potentiality."[9] These ideas in turn influenced landscape architects such as Frederick Olmsted who "realized, in practice, the landscape visions of men like Thoreau and Emerson."[10] Olmsted was impressed with the concept of the British landscape garden and its spatial shaping of the terrain according to national values but dismayed by the fact that they were owned by "a very few, very rich people."[11] In an influential report (1865) on his plans to turn Yosemite into the first national park, he suggested "rigidly enforced" laws that "prevent an unjust use by individuals, of that which is not individual but public property."[12] This call for a rigid use of force inevitably calls to mind Tom and Will's later removal from the park grounds by police, and sets the scene for the film's overall contrasting of a supposed national community and the solidarity between its marginalized members. The choice of Forest Park as the film's setting, apart from its

---

6 The ongoing opioid addiction crisis affecting (not only) the rural United States is not extensively reflected in either the films or the New Rural Cinema at large. Only a few narrative films have yet tackled the subject, for example *Ben is Back* (2018) and *Crisis* (2021).

7 Olwig, *Landscape, Nature, and the Body Politic, 212.*

8 Henry David Thoreau, *Walking* (Thomaston, ME: Tilbury House, 2019), 63.

9 Olwig, *Landscape, Nature, and the Body Politic,* 188.

10 Ibid., 192.

11 Olmsted, Frederick Law, "Preliminary Report upon the Yosemite and Big Tree Grove," [1865] in *The Papers of Frederick Law Olmsted: The California Frontier, 1863– 1865*, ed. Victoria Post Ranney, Charles Capen McLaughlin, Charles E. Beveridge, 488– 516 (Baltimore: Johns Hopkins University Press, 1990), 504.

12 Olmsted, "Preliminary Report," 505.

obvious connection to the real-life story, seems especially significant in this context: Olmsted's landscape architecture firm was hired by the Municipal Park Commission of Portland in 1903 to study the existing terrain and published an extensive report recommending a park system for the city.[13]

In its opening passage, the film seems to ponder the radical potential of the idea at the core of the national park movement: a "natural commons for the country, conceived as a legal and social community."[14] When Tom and Will are later evicted from the park, on the legal grounds that residence in the park is not permitted, however, the paradox behind the concept "to link park preservation for the masses with the progress of the nation" is gradually revealed.[15] Granik has alluded to these "brutal vicissitudes of capital" herself when she noted in an interview with *Sight & Sound* that "an unprecedented number of Americans [are] living on federal land, some for very gnarly reasons to do with drugs and alcohol but others ousted on an economic level."[16] Will and Tom's forceful removal lays bare the inherent problem that the preservation of a "natural commons" for the nation results in its strict policing: "the only way of preserving the wild elixir of the American nation is to preserve the wild *from* the American people, not to empark it *for* the American people."[17] This notion was made explicit by another influential landscape architect, the founder of the American wilderness preservation movement John Muir who writes in a report from 1895: "one soldier in the woods, armed with authority and a gun, would be more effective in forest preservation than millions of forbidding policies."[18] By this logic, "the need to use force to protect nature from the common people advocated by Muir gives the park the same exclusive status as that of the British landscape parks" and therefore thwarts any possibility of creating a truly common place for the nation as community.[19]

Moreover, Tom and Will's removal also calls to mind the historical background of the creation of America's national parks which is inevitably connected to colonial conquest and exclusion. The conquest of Western landscapes like Yosemite in particular "was more than the conquest of space; it was also the conquest of peoples and the place of their polities."[20] The removal of both white

13 Olmsted, John Charles, "Report of the Park Board, Portland, Oregon," [1903] *Wikisource*, https://en.wikisource.org/wiki/Olmsted_report_on_Portland,_Oregon_parks.

14 Olwig, *Landscape, Nature, and the Body Politic*, 212.

15 Ibid., 202.

16 Debra Granik, "Vanishing Point," Interview by Ryan Gilbey. *Sight & Sound* 28:7 (2018), 48.

17 Olwig, *Landscape, Nature, and the Body Politic*, 203.

18 John Muir, *The Yosemite*. [1914] (San Francisco: Sierra Club, 1988), quoted in Olwig, *Landscape, Nature, and the Body Politic*, 205.

19 Olwig, *Landscape, Nature, and the Body Politic*, 205.

20 Ibid., 201.

European settlers and especially Native Americans was thus a necessity for these landscapes to become symbolic reservoirs of the American spirit. Olmsted cynically justified this purge by referring to "uncivilized" people's inability to aesthetically appreciate nature:

> The power of scenery to affect men is in a large way, proportionate to the degree of their civilization and to the degree in which their taste has been cultivated. [. . .] Among a thousand savages there will be a much smaller number who will show the least sign of being so affected than among a thousand persons taken from a civilized community.[21]

The disenfranchisement of the Native Americans was not enough, however, to create spaces of national significance. The fact that Yosemite and other landscapes did not conform to the idea of untouched wilderness, but were cultural landscapes shaped by centuries of human interaction before the arrival of European settlers had to be disavowed: "the landscapes in the park were seen to be the creation of Nature."[22] The opening passage of *Leave No Trace* visually traces this movement from the idea of the national park as an Edenic open space (from Tom's perspective) to a heavily policed ideological site, thereby acknowledging a central flaw in America's conception of rurality. Its supposedly free and natural state is an artificial construct, or as Mitchell puts it "the result and reflection of the cultural imperatives of those who make and represent the landscape" upheld by brute force which is most acutely felt by vulnerable people like Will and Tom.[23]

By extension, their expulsion from the supposed "natural commons" of the nation can be read as a metaphor for the constraints of liberal democracy in neoliberal capitalism which, as Brown argues, is "rife with internal exclusions and subordinations."[24] There is no room in this ideologically charged space for marginalized people whose very existence contradicts liberal democracy's "promise of inclusive and shared political equality, freedom, and popular sovereignty."[25] The film makes this larger context explicit by linking its protagonists' eviction from the park to the fate of its other vulnerable inhabitants: the wild camp of homeless veterans where Will sells his prescription drugs is disbanded as a result of their discovery as well. The focus on veterans as the victims of marginalization chimes with the film's demystification of the national park as a symbol of US potentiality. The overrepresentation of veterans in the homeless population casts a

---

21 Olmsted, "Preliminary Report," 503.

22 Olwig, *Landscape, Nature, and the Body Politic*, 206.

23 Mitchell, "Landscape," 49.

24 Brown, *Undoing the Demos*, 44.

25 Ibid.

similarly damning light on notions of US exceptionalism and on a national identity strongly linked to militarism.[26]

It is worth mentioning here, however, how strongly the film contrasts the idyllic opening images of the park with the short segment taking place in Portland. The city is portrayed as a futuristic conglomerate of steel and glass "captured in angular shots and blue-grey tones, all vertical lines and reflective surfaces."[27] The mise-en-scène emphasizes the cold and mechanical world of the city, as exemplified by the short scene aboard an aerial tram. In addition to the vehicle's futuristic levitation, the film specifically "isolates the computerized voice-over of the aerial tram's speaker-system which directs passengers to disembark—a quotidian form of the societal instruction Will and Tom typically manage to evade."[28] Furthermore, their birds-eye-view on the city is far removed from their enmeshed perspective within the forest thicket as illustrated by the opening low-angle shots. These strong contrasts between the depiction of an emparked rural landscape and the encroaching city seem to suggest an ecocritical argument that is, however, never explicitly formulated. Therefore, the scene seems to be more productively read as a further visualization of Will's trauma-induced fear of (urban) society. Indeed, a helicopter flying over the city causes Will to stop in his tracks, the sound undoubtedly triggering a traumatic memory. In contrast to Ree's sealed-off world in *Winter's Bone*, Will and Tom's living environment is thus not hermetic: there exists an outside to the deceptive calm of the national park and it is depicted as inherently threatening.

Nevertheless, *Leave No Trace* cannot be accused of romanticizing the rural, an otherwise common narrative trait in US cinema in which "the countryside takes on almost sacred qualities."[29] As Mills writes on the complex relation of US Americans to their country's rural environments: "More is involved than simply contrasting the supposedly unspoiled natural world with the over-mechanized and brutalizing world of violent and overcrowded cities."[30] The apparent wildness of the national park is debunked by both its permeability of urban elements (joggers, prisoners, police, a necklace Tom finds on the wayside) as well as by its strict prohibitive policies. However, the next stage in Tom and Will's journey takes them to a version of rurality in which the natural environment, plants, and

26 On the overrepresentation of veterans in the US homeless population see: Jamison Fargo, Vincent Kane, Dennis Culhane, Ellen Munley, George Sheldon, Elizabeth Ann Montgomery, and Stephen Metraux, "Prevalence and Risk of Homelessness Among US Veterans," *Preventing Chronic Disease*, 9: E45, 2012, https://www.ncbi.nlm.nih.gov/pmc/articles/PMC3337850.

27 Paveck, "Care at the Margins."

28 Ibid.

29 Mills, *The American Landscape*, 51.

30 Ibid.

animals are subjected to relentless shaping, and which is even further removed from the United States' wilderness ideal.

Directly after their arrest, Tom and Will are brought to a social care home—an intermediate stop on their journey—in which both are separately subjected to questioning by social workers Jean (Dana Millican) and James (Michael J. Prosser). Similar to the scenes in the city, the color palette here is dominated by bleak greys, browns, and blues—the only pointed exceptions are potted plants and large posters, in one case even a whole wallpaper that depict lush forest sceneries. These landscape images, on a narrative level, point towards what is to come, namely the mannered, tamed nature of Will and Tom's new countryside home. On the other hand, these decorative representations call to mind Olwig's understanding of the "mindscaping" effect of landscape art: their central perspective reflects the alienation and expropriation of any truly social practice and understanding of landscape which, as Mitchell summarizes, "in the process [. . .] instill a new relationship between land, law and justice" that is suited to exercise centralized power.[31]

Even though the representatives of this central authority, the social workers, are presented in a relatively positive light here the film depicts their automatized methods of psychologically categorizing Will and Tom as almost violent acts of re-education. Again, we are reminded of Olwig's notion of "mindscaping": the landscapes' fixation within their frames mirrors Tom and Will's forced computerized assessment. The scene in which Will is subjected to the relentless personal questions of a computerized psychological test until he breaks down—recalling the robotic voice-over in the earlier scene on the aerial tram—is particularly striking. It forms the film's most direct, biting critique of neoliberal practice in the context of a completely impersonal approach to mental health that situates mental illness as a problem firmly within the individual, not in its social surrounding.

Tom and Will are eventually rehoused nearby the national park on the grounds of a Christmas tree farm. The scene detailing Will's first workday on the farm pursues the theme of tamed nature which initially is presented in an extremely negative light. After the two protagonists have moved into their new home and met the farmer Mr. Walters (Jeff Kober), the film abruptly cuts to a noisy tree-netting conveyor belt. Compared with the tactile, peaceful close-ups of plants in the film's opening, this mechanized netting process is presented as an environmental violation. Nature, here, is first and foremost a commodity that is handled and processed. The theme is continued when Will's new boss describes how the trees need to be pruned to appeal to the company's customers. What in other circumstances might have seemed like a perfectly normal description of

---

31 Mitchell, "Cultural Landscapes," 788.

tasks takes on a sinister tone here: seen from Will's perspective, the trees' processing and packing becomes and all-too-fitting metaphor for his own relocation from the supposed freedom of Forest Park's wilderness to his new agricultural home. Later, Will watches a horse in a stable through prison-like iron bars. Not only does he clearly identify with the domesticated animal, but the moment also directly precedes his abrupt decision to escape against his daughter's will.

It is striking, however, to compare Will's negative experiences on the tree farm to Tom's perspective which is more ambiguous, caught between her father's obsession with the freedom of wilderness and the potential of belonging to a community of equals in her "transition to adulthood."[32] The film employs these diverging perspectives as part of Tom's coming-of-age experience: possibly for the first time in her life, she experiences a world in which her father does not control her either directly or inadvertently through his mental health issues. I want to particularly foreground the scene in which Tom participates in a Future Farmers workshop, "an agricultural education program which teaches high school students how to raise rabbits."[33] Firstly, Tom's brief encounter with a local teenage boy who takes part in the workshop hints towards the possibility of a relationship, friendly or romantic, which has been denied to her so far due to her father's lifestyle. On an even more fundamental level, it is simply the social interaction with unfamiliar people—who also happen to take an interest in nature and animals—that has evidently been missing from Tom's life. For a moment, as Karen Wells points out, it seems like the film is set to venture into the territory of the "classic teen film [which] centers the story of a girl and her transition to adulthood as she negotiates romantic and sexual relationships with boys and her new place in her own family."[34] This possibility is thwarted, however, by Will's clandestine decision to leave.

Secondly, I want to point out the role humor plays in this scene. The rabbit show takes a similar function as the gentle mocking of the church dance troupe earlier in the narrative but with a clearer focus on the nature/culture divide the film centers on: it subverts Will's fraught perspective on "civilized" community by showing a gentler, slightly silly side to it. Tom's apparent curiosity stands in contrast to her father's adverse point of view. The domesticated rabbits are treated with utmost respect and care in the scene, so much so that it becomes endearingly comical. As will become clear later in the film, the rejection of society which Will represents is called into question, if not yet presented with a suitable alternative at this point in the narrative. The film's central argument, however,

32 Karen Wells, *The Visual Cultures of Childhood: Film and Television from The Magic Lantern to Teen Vloggers* (London: Rowman & Littlefield, 2020), 126.

33 Paveck, "Care at the Margins."

34 Wells, *The Visual Cultures of Childhood*, 126.

begins to emerge in this scene: landscape is necessarily interaction—between humans, animals, and the environment—and leaving no trace might be neither possible nor desirable.

This notion is enforced by the circumstances of the protagonists' hasty, aimless escape from the farm. Their journey first leads them back to Forest Park—an Eden both they and the other veterans have been irrevocably cast out off—and then to a forest in Washington State, the closest to actual wilderness they will reach throughout the film. Crucially, this environment is presented very differently from the lush vegetation in the park: here, any sense of adventure has disappeared and increasingly, the pair is confronted with the actual challenge of survival. This very real sense of danger is visually enhanced by the relentless rain and the visible breath due to coldness which contribute to the inhospitable atmosphere of this environment. In contrast to the deep greens of the opening setting, this forest is portrayed in a greyish tone. Living in this wild terrain seems utterly impossible. Soon, Tom's boots are leaking water and she starts to shiver violently from coldness. In their makeshift camp at night, she even mentions the possibility of freezing to death in their sleep. The compulsive nature of Will's desire to escape society becomes horribly tangible here. Fleeing the safety and comfort of the farm without any plan or goal, he is endangering both his own and his daughter's life. The effects of these self-destructive tendencies are made explicit when, on the next day, Will falls and breaks his leg on his way to buy supplies. Luckily, Tom manages to find her unconscious father and alert hunters who drive them to the trailer park run by Dale (Dale Dickey), the film's final and most ideologically complex environment.

The trailer or RV (recreational vehicle) has a fraught, ambiguous history in the United States that clearly feeds into the film's central tension between individualism and community. As Isenberg writes in her cultural history of white poverty, the trailer "occupies an important, if uncertain, place in the American cultural imagination. Representing on the one hand a symbol of untethered freedom, the mobile home simultaneously acquired its reputation as a 'tin can,' a small cheap, confined way of life."[35] Moreover, ever since a housing shortage during World War II caused the US government to supply cheap housing to soldiers and manufacturers, trailer parks acquired their negative association with low class status. With trailer parks appearing in impoverished rural and suburban areas all over the country after the war, "'trailer trash' became a generic term, no longer regionally specific" to the particularly neglected rural South.[36] Over time,

35 Isenberg, *White Trash*, 241.
36 Ibid., 243.

RV manufacturers and advertisers tried to rid the trailer and the trailer park of their notoriety as hotbeds of crime, prostitution, and decay. This proved to be difficult, however, as for a long time after the war "trailer parks were exiled to the least desirable lots, a sorry distance from the nicer, better-protected residential areas."[37] Inevitably, "'trailer park' became a dirty word."[38] Arguably, this notion still prevails today, making it a prime example of how landscape images "sustain mystification" of economic relations under capitalism.[39]

The symbolic position between untethered freedom and a confined way of life the trailer occupies becomes the stage on which the final conflict between Tom's desire of belonging and Will's escapism plays out. The trailer park in *Leave No Trace* seems to represent the perfect synthesis between their desires. Situated deep in the woods and almost blending into the forest environment, the RV park is clearly situated on the margins of society, but immediately emanates a sense of community, hospitality, and solidarity. Dale, the proprietor, offers an empty trailer to Tom and Will to recuperate and even outright refuses rent payment at first. The trailer park emerges here as a viable place of community that offers self-organized shelter to marginalized people while circumventing the normative profiling of neoliberal state welfare. Several scenes show the inhabitants engaged in friendly social interaction: playing music, drinking beer, cooking, etc. (see Fig. 9). Hilaria Loyo describes it as:

> A [chosen] family of [. . .] "economic fugitives" bound together by a common sense of abandonment [. . .] and rejection of the constraining neoliberal securitarian nation. This is a community governed by an unwritten rule of mutual support and collective solidarity, rather than the rule of blood, as key governing tools that go beyond survival.[40]

Therefore, it subverts the prevalent cultural images outlined by Isenberg that identify the RV park with neglect and confinement.

Nevertheless, Will is unable to remain in the community: in the film's climatic scene father and daughter finally separate, as Tom finds a new home in the trailer park and Will goes back into the wild. In terms of the coming-of-age narrative, Tom has emancipated herself from her loving but controlling father and has, as Wells summarizes, "found some kind of community in this clearing, populated by people with their own traumas and held together by a woman [Dale] who is

---

37 Ibid., 244.

38 Ibid., 245.

39 Cosgrove, "Prospect," 58.

40 Hilaria Loyo, "Resignifiying the National Home. Gendered Domopolitics and Neoliberal Geographies of Exclusion in Debra Granik's Cinema," in *Screening the Crisis: US Cinema and Social Change in the Wake of the 2008 Crash*, ed. Juan A. Tarancón and Hilaria Loyo (New York: Bloomsbury, 2022), 177.

Fig. 9: Inhabitants of the RV park engaged in social interaction. *Leave No Trace* (Debra Granik, 2018).

motherly towards Tom."[41] Crucially, however, the film follows this emotional separation with a significant coda. As Dale mentioned earlier in the film, the community even takes care of outsiders like Will by providing them with groceries and supplies. The final scene shows Tom placing a bag of groceries in an arranged place and clicking her tongue as a signal to her father. The film's ending is also its most drastic divergence from the original novel. In Rock's novel, the father dies a violent death.

Granik emphasizes the radical openness of the community that enables Will to pursue his extreme lifestyle while also providing a sense of belonging to Tom. The film's ending attempts to construct a counter argument to the relentless liberalism of US dominant ideology which fuels the glorification of the wilderness ideal and is represented in Will's continuous urge to escape social contexts. Indeed, the final scenes call to mind the film *Into the Wild* (Sean Penn, 2007) which circles around a character that similarly rejects even loose, non-traditional forms of communal living. In fact, the protagonist Chris (Emile Hirsch) also passes through various forms of cohabitation, the last of which is a trailer park not unlike the one seen in *Leave No Trace*. At the end of *Into the Wild*, Chris dies alone in the Alaskan wild.

The differences between the two films are more important than their similarities here, however. Whereas *Leave No Trace* empathically depicts Will's antisocial compulsion as benevolent but ultimately as too extreme to serve as a positive example for his daughter, the heavily romanticized *Into the Wild*, as Watkins

41 Wells, *The Visual Cultures of Childhood*, 123.

argues “offers a seductively compelling vision of ‘freedom from’—freedom from government, from coercion, from society, from others” and is ultimately not interested in presenting viable alternatives.[42] Watkins continues his analysis of *Into the Wild* with regards to anti-capitalist discourse under neoliberalism: “the difficult task for political theory, political practice, and popular culture is to offer a less liberal and more democratic vision of ‘freedom with’ (freedom with others) and ‘freedom within’ (within power, unchosen conditions) [. . .] without wishing away our subjectivity.”[43] The trailer park in *Leave No Trace* certainly approaches these criteria; it remains to be seen how the film goes about this task structurally and conceptually.

2 The warmth of the hive

In her analysis of *Leave No Trace*, Hannah Paveck acknowledges the film’s “broadly humanist ethics” yet heavily criticizes its lack of ecologic consciousness. She argues:

> Given our current environmental context, the film’s depiction of the forest—and later use of animals—as *backdrop* for human concerns is troubling. Today, addressing the ethics of retreat goes beyond the question of responsibility (or lack thereof) for other humans, encompassing, and often prioritizing, responsibility towards non-human animals and environment.[44]

Questions regarding the film’s engagement with eco-cinema are warranted. Not only does the film’s title invoke the seven so-called “Leave No Trace” principles of outdoor living—dispose of waste, minimize campfire impacts, etc.—advocated from the 1960s onwards by wilderness conservation institutions such as the National Park Service in the US. Especially the film’s first half also seems to hint towards ecological concerns by focusing on the threatened forest and the commodification of nature on the tree farm. Ultimately, this expectation is a misunderstanding the film actively invites. Its concerns are not traditionally ecological, yet deeply humanist in that it concerns itself with (rural) landscape as polity, not as nature. It actively disavows politicized imaginations of an untouched, scenic landscape and instead invites reflections on landscape as a product of human interaction with the environment. These themes are certainly in dialogue with eco-cinema’s concerns yet ultimately, *Leave No Trace* does not

42 Watkins, *Freedom and Vengeance on Film*, 88.

43 Ibid., 89.

44 Paveck, “Care at the Margins.” Emphasis added.

advocate for ecological preservation, but for landscape as a social concept and a vehicle to counter neoliberal marginalization.

Paveck's criticism of the film goes further than just accusing it of an indifference towards ecological concerns, however. She goes on to suggest that *Leave No Trace* actively eschews ecocriticism in favor of broader audience appeal:

> The film's critique seems specifically calibrated to appeal to a polarized America: its targets of veteran care and social institutions over community are palatable across the political spectrum [. . .] By ultimately sidelining ecological questions, *Leave No Trace* may have secured broad appeal; but in doing so, the film misses the mark—ethically and politically—in presenting a contemporary narrative of retreat.[45]

I agree with Paveck insofar as *Leave No Trace* does not explicitly promote ecological themes. The trailer park is not presented as especially eco-friendly—in contrast to, for example, the organic farm in Kelly Reichardt's *Night Moves* (2013)—and even the tree farm is not characterized as excessively "anti-ecological" in the strict sense, more as a symbolic threat to Will's urge to individual freedom. Nevertheless, I find her argument problematic insofar as it demonstrates a perhaps too rigorous view of ecological, and political, cinema per se. As Sean Cubitt writes in his introduction to eco-cinema, "ecocriticism has to aim beyond celebrations of green themes and condemnation of anti-ecological motives towards a global understanding of the ecological aspects of all forms of film and every kind of cinematic practice."[46] The film's focus lies on the disenfranchised protagonists and their ability to find shelter and community, what Paveck calls "questions of care." Therefore, *Leave No Trace* is predominantly a film about class which, however, also touches on some aspects of eco-cinema.

The central question here is if *Leave No Trace* indeed, as Paveck claims, uses animals and the natural environment as a mere "*backdrop* for human concerns."[47] The term "backdrop" indicates a separation directly opposed to, for example, Ingold's interactive understanding of landscape. According to Ingold's "dwelling perspective" landscape emerges "with its properties alongside the emergence of the perceiver as person, against the backdrop of involved activity."[48] The film indeed favors such an involved understanding from its very beginning. Therefore, it is highly relevant for the relation of bodies and their surroundings that, ultimately, is at the heart of ecological thinking.

45 Ibid.

46 Cubitt, "Ecopolitics of Cinema," 42.

47 Paveck, "Care at the Margins." Emphasis added.

48 Ingold, *The Perception of the Environment*, 168.

The initial setting, Forest Park, at first appears as an idyllic environment which father and daughter have made their home by engaging in "embodied acts of landscaping."[49] Their everyday tasks shape their surroundings and, vice versa, their behavior is influenced by the forest surrounding them. They have, for example, installed a makeshift shower in a tree, stashed their important documents in a trapdoor hidden in the ground, and arranged tree trunks to form a kind of "living room." Will especially is accustomed to the environment and presumably due to his military training, is able to "read" and utilize the landscape for his aim of concealment. Therefore, the film suggests, by utilizing the afore mentioned techniques of tactile close-ups and low-angle shots, that the pair have built an affective relationship with this landscape, and made it a *place* through their bodily interaction with the environment. A place, we are reminded, "owes its character to the experiences it affords to those who spend time there" and derives its meaning from "the kind of activities in which its inhabitants engage."[50]

Their expulsion from the park denies the possibility of transforming this particular space into place, however. As a physical, symbolic, and legal manifestation of both US nationalism and the wilderness ideal, the park resists such an affective engagement and instead makes visible the hegemonic "power to define what a landscape is, what it means, who belongs to it and who belongs in it."[51] Before Will and Tom are forcefully evicted, the briefly glimpsed presence of the prisoners forced to clean up the park calls to mind that the landscape idea under capitalism is marked by alienation and expropriation. It "both establishes the geography of production and works to naturalize that geography, to make it seem inevitable that those who build the landscape are not the same as those who own the landscape."[52] The prisoners are used to rid the park of its evidence of human interference, to sustain the illusion of wilderness. From the very beginning, the film thereby rejects the dissociative notion of landscape as passive "backdrop" that Paveck identifies. It understands landscape as the result of constant interaction while questioning the prohibitive application of a dualistic logic that separates "between the human perceiver and the world" by highlighting the real-world consequences this ideological dualism has on society's most vulnerable members.[53] Again, the focus here lies on class-based marginalization, yet it is framed in a way that is relevant to ecocritical questions regarding the production of landscape.

---

49 Lorimer, "Cultural Geography," 85.

50 Ingold, *The Perception of the Environment*, 155.

51 Mitchell, "Landscape," 53.

52 Ibid., 51.

53 Ingold, *The Perception of the Environment*, 154.

In the RV park, the film both narratively and visually highlights the community's close, affective, and bodily belonging to its environment. On a narrative level, the RV park almost magically appears when the protagonists' experience with actual wilderness comes to its catastrophic escalation: Will breaks his leg on his way to buy supplies, lying helplessly in a ravine for a whole night until Tom finds him. Symbolically, this plot device can be understood as a negation of Will's sense of ultimate freedom, an insistence on the harmfulness and danger of rejecting communality, and even as an extremely literal reminder that Will can never ultimately distance himself from the world around him. Tom alerts two of the park's residents who bring them to Dale's cabin. The trailer park is characterized as a "best-of-both-worlds" solution, as Pamela Hutchinson describes it in her review, meaning a composite of Tom's sense of belonging and Will's drive to freedom.[54] In contrast to the inhospitable wilderness, it emerges as a landscape in the sense of "a milieu of engagement and involvement [. . .] as a world to live in."[55] More specifically, it is a world to inhabit collectively, as the film will go on to demonstrate.

The visual moment that most strikingly encapsulates the communities' intertwining with the landscape around them, is the focus on the beehive. Tom's first encounter with the bees occurs on her first morning in the trailer park. As she walks down one of the tree-lined paths, she meets an older woman tending to the hives. Noticing the girl's interested gaze, the woman, identified as Susan (Susan Chernak McElroy) in the credits, invites Tom to open the hive. As she pulls the protective suit over Tom's head, she explains: "When I open this, the bees are gonna come up. But they're not coming out to hurt you. When a bee stings, it dies. So they don't wanna sting you. They wanna come up and land on you and just get to know you." The film then cuts to a close-up of the hive and the swarming bees inside. A ray of sunlight on the right side of the frame conveys warmth and brings out the earthy brown color of the hive, thus supporting the beekeeper's insistence on the bee's inherent peacefulness.

"It's kinda nice to have the trust of a whole box of creatures that have the power to come out and kill you if they wanted to. So, it means a lot to me that I have their trust. I worked hard to get it," Susan continues. She then proceeds to drop some of the bees on Tom's outstretched, gloved hands, establishing a connection between her, Tom, and the bees. This is an instance in which "boundaries between person and place, or between self and the landscape, dissolve alto-

54 Pamela Hutchinson, "Film of the week: Leave No Trace grieves for the wild at heart," *Sight & Sound* (December 28, 2018), https://www2.bfi.org.uk/news-opinion/sight-sound-magazine/reviews-recommendations/leave-no-trace-debra-granik-wild-heart.

55 Wylie, *Landscape*, 149.

gether."[56] In this respect, the scene mirrors Ree's reaching for her father's remains in the climactic scene of *Winter's Bone*. In both films, these moments suggest instances of cooperation and the promise of community—also, both scenes feature strong matriarchal figures and a disengagement with problematic fathers. In *Leave No Trace*, however, there is obviously a more optimistic connotation. The significance of the bees as a form of animal collective serves as a clear analogy to Tom's sense of belonging to the communal trailer park.

This parallelism is even more strongly and knowingly reaffirmed in the scene when Tom introduces her father to the beehives. At this point in the narrative, Tom attempts to convince Will, who plans to leave as soon as possible, of the merits of the trailer park's loose communality. Thus, Tom herself, not just the film on a subtextual level, makes use of the bees as a metaphor for the park's "best-of-both-worlds" compromise to support her position of remaining in the trailer park. The apparent ease with which Tom now handles the hive suggests she has spent a considerable amount of time with the motherly Susan—carefully, she opens the box and invites her father to engage with it: "If you put your hand over it, you can feel the warmth of the hive." Will complies and holds out his hands; a reaction shot of his face implies an emotional reaction but due to Ben Foster's subtle acting, both the viewers and Tom are left guessing regarding his feelings: is he touched, overwhelmed, scared? Tom suspects the latter as she explains: "A person can withstand 500 stings" and goes on to take off her gloves and drop some of the bees on her father's hands like the beekeeper did with her in the previous scene. The bees crawl over her own hands which are soaked with honey. "So you don't need to be scared", she adds and this time, there is a peaceful smile on Will's face which seems to suggest, falsely as it turns out, his gradual acceptance of their new home.

It is a touching scene as it represents Tom's desperate, emotional attempt to convince her father of the benefits of an alternative sort of collectivism that should not be as threatening to him as the futuristic city, the strictures of social services, or the rigidly structured tree farm. The motive of beekeeping is, however, not without its problematic implications. Paveck criticizes the film specifically for its central use:

> Even the beehive, itself a figure of (nonhuman) community, opens out onto close-ups of honey-soaked hands: a moment of tenderness between father and daughter. In doing so, the film reduces honeybees—a species recently under threat from exposure to insecticides—to a mere symbolic vehicle for human-to-human connection. For a contemporary film about a retreat to the forest, this anthropocentric approach to the representation of living with non-human animals and the natural environment feels not only reductive, but untimely.[57]

---

56 Ingold, *The Perception of the Environment*, 56.
57 Paveck, "Care at the Margins."

I agree with Paveck insofar as the film does not fulfil the ecological promise of its first half here. The concrete implications and harmful effects of beekeeping are never touched upon. The fact that honeybees have dramatically declined in numbers in the US and the rest of the world due to pollution, pesticide use, eradication of green spaces as well as numerous other causes is clearly not of interest to the film here.

It is worth noting, however, that the presence of the honeybee on the North American continent is due to its import by European settlers in the seventeenth century. The insect is not a native species in the US, it has been imported for its ability to produce honey. Bees and humans have, as Donna Haraway describes, lived "entangled lives" throughout history.[58] Of course, this does not justify the bees' eradication or render it any less dramatic, yet this historic perspective does point towards the relational, interactive understanding of landscape that the film favors which goes against a concept of nature that presumes an originary state. Furthermore, the beekeeping practice visible in *Leave No Trace* is hardly indicative of the large-scale, industrial commodification of bees associated with pollination that is a substantial part of agriculture in the United States today. On the contrary, the beekeeper's comment—"It means a lot to me that I have their trust. I worked hard to get it"—contradicts Paveck's suggestion of an anthropocentric approach and, again, suggests entangled coexistence.

Therefore, the film's approach calls to mind Anat Pick's concept of "shared worldhood." In her analysis of the ecocritical film *Earthlings* (Shaun Monson, 2005), Pick stresses that shared worldhood does not deny the existing power relation between humans and animals: "we share the world with animals we eat, wear, breed, and enslave, and, like them, we too are sentient."[59] Nevertheless, highlighting the shared worldhood of humans and animals imagines "a world in which beings coexist in their commonality as earthlings."[60] This notion will become even more pressing when looking at *Beasts of the Southern Wild*. Even in *Leave No Trace*, the markedly affective attitude towards beekeeping and the highly symbolical focus on the "warmth of the hive" underlines the RV park as a community that is defined by both its humanist care as well as by its meaningful engagement with the environment. Therefore, it rejects "humanity's alienation from the natural world and its quest to dominate nature" by stressing shared worldhood, entangled lives, and in-

58 Donna Haraway, *When Species Meet* (Minneapolis, MN: University of Minnesota Press, 2008), 280.

59 Anat Pick, "Three Worlds: Dwelling and Worldhood on Screen," in *Screening Nature. Cinema beyond the Human*, ed. Anat Pick and Guinevere Narraway (New York: Berghahn, 2013), 28.

60 Ibid.

teraction.[61] While Paveck's criticism of the film's shortcomings as an entry into eco-cinema are justified, I refute her claim that the film treats the natural environment as a mere "backdrop for human concerns." On the contrary, the film makes a strong case for landscape as an interactive, social category and, crucially, as a medium to counter class-based marginalization and repression.

3 "These people, they're not that different from Us" — Race and the political landscape

While *Leave No Trace* constructs a landscape which offers "care at the margins," it also imagines a community that is exclusively white.[62] Generally, Granik's feature films so far have focused almost exclusively on the United States' white underclass. In a way, the absence of non-white characters in *Leave No Trace* is even more striking than in *Winter's Bone*. Whereas *Winter's Bone* can be understood as a reflection on the culture of a very specific region, the derogatory category "Hillbilly," and its implications of whiteness and poverty, there seems to be no tangible reason for the blatant lack of diversity in *Leave No Trace*, particularly in its quasi-Utopian RV park setting. Karen Wells has summarized these issues:

> *Leave No Trace*, like *Winter's Bone* [. . .] uses the wandering of the main protagonists to show the viewer the deep poverty of the contemporary, rural working-class US. This landscape barely features any Black or Latinx people, and there are no central black or Latinx characters. The affect is to create an almost ethnographic account of white rural working-class life and sociality devoid of any of the lines of connection or border crossings that one would anticipate in a country as diverse and large as the United States. It contrasts to the depiction of white people in films about Black life and sociality in which, while white characters do not feature prominently, they are invariably present as a device to demonstrate the lack of racial animosity of Black people towards white people. The exclusion of Black people from these narratives [. . .] reproduces the racism Black people experience in them.[63]

This omission of the intersection of class and race in the neoliberal rural landscape indeed complicates the film's political significance which is otherwise denoted by its focus on radical openness. After all, the RV park is based on equality, mutual aid, and cooperation to the degree that Dale does not ask for financial compensation from Will and Tom. Furthermore, as the final images of Tom placing a bag of supplies at the edge of the trailer park suggests—in addition to Dale's

---

61 John P. Clark and Camille Martin, *Anarchy, Geography, Modernity: Selected Writings of Elisée Reclus* (Oakland, CA: PM Press, 2013), 16.

62 Paveck, "Care at the Margins."

63 Wells, *The Visual Cultures of Childhood*, 123.

earlier mention of a similar case—Will's decision or compulsion to leave the community, or rather his inability to exist within its loose confines, does not exclude him from the inhabitants' solidarity. The RV park's openness thus even extends to those who do not wish to be immediately included. The question remains, however, why it only seems to extend to white Americans and if it indeed "reproduces the racism Black people experience" through their exclusion.[64] This final section will outline the relevance and the implications of the film's lack of diversity which seem to be at odds with the construction of its political landscape.

The curious absence of race as an aspect of neoliberal marginalization in the film allows for at least two different interpretations. The first could see *Leave No Trace* as an example of "an argument that has become commonplace among leftists and progressives" in the US.[65] In response to neoliberal marginalization through "rising inequality, lower rates of unionization, and declining wages," it proposes a progressive contestation of neoliberal policies that goes "beyond race" and focuses primarily on economic justice.[66] According to this logic, such a progressive revival could "only win broad public assent if it is framed as a universal appeal to the economic needs and interests of a multiracial, national majority."[67] Singh names the sociologist William Julius Wilson as an exemplary proponent of such a position who claims, as Singh summarizes, that "such a movement can succeed only if it rejects divisive and impractical vocabularies of race."[68] This calls to mind Paveck's accusation, that in relation to environmentalism *Leave No Trace's* "critique seems specifically calibrated to appeal to a polarized America."[69] Does the film's construction of an exclusively white community similarly attempt to make notions of a socially inclusive landscape more palatable across the political spectrum of its viewers?

If so, one would have to agree that such an attempt is seriously misguided. This is not only due to the fact, as Braedley and Luxton point out, that "neoliberalism arises out of, and advances, earlier imperialist and colonial domination by the capitalist powers" and therefore fundamentally depends "on racism and racialization."[70] It would also ignore the specific American context in which historically "the promise of economic and political democracy has been limited precisely by what might be called racist uses of race."[71] Furthermore, African Americans in par-

64 Ibid.

65 Singh, *Black is a Country*, 218.

66 Ibid.

67 Ibid.

68 Ibid.

69 Paveck, "Care at the Margins."

70 Braedley and Luxton, "Competing Philosophies," 16.

71 Singh, *Black is a Country*, 219.

ticular, Singh points out, have "throughout the post-World War II period [. . .] been the single group in the United States whose politics have regularly gone beyond self-interest and aimed at broad expansions of social as well as civil rights."[72] He goes on to paraphrase the historian C.L.R. James who argued that Black struggles for such rights "should not be viewed as a concession that the left made to Negroes [sic], but as a direct part of the struggle for socialism."[73] Struggles for racial justice and more universal concerns about neoliberal marginalization can therefore not be separated from each other, particularly in the US where "a politics of race has been at the center of every major invention and reinvention of American radicalism."[74] A Utopian safe space such as the one Granik imagines is therefore marred considerably by its racial exclusivity.

Returning to the context of landscape, it is worth considering once again Olwig's idea of landscape as a social concept which is explicitly anti-racist and anti-fascist. He argues that only "if we think of land as polity and place, and nature as complex, historically constituted concept imbued with social values, then landscape ceases to be a vehicle for environmental determinism and nature fanaticism identified with race and gender."[75] While Olwig omits, as has been discussed, specific mentions of African American experiences of landscape in his studies, he delivers a convincing definition of a converse, fascist understanding of landscape as unchanging and eternal, and culture as "layered on top."[76] This would be a "blood-and-soil" ideology which Olwig describes as such:

> A teleological narrative of nature in which the progress of culture follows a predetermined path through the body politic's stages of development. The idea then leads to the restrictive belief that only "native" people or species belong naturally to a particular area of land.[77]

It is crucial to stress at this point that *Leave No Trace* clearly has no overlap with such a prohibitive concept of landscape. On the contrary, the community the film envisions adheres to Olwig's notion of the polity in that it is built on custom and "law, not blood."[78] The "law" in this case is hospitality towards traumatized, marginalized people. The exclusion of non-white inhabitants thus seems to be at odds with the film's insistence on the RV park's radical openness to victims of trauma and marginalization.

72 Ibid.

73 Ibid.

74 Ibid.

75 Olwig, *Landscape, Nature, and the Body Politic*, 226.

76 Ibid., 225.

77 Ibid., 225–226.

78 Ibid., 214.

A scene just after Will and Tom's arrival demonstrates the existence of such a "law" of hospitality. While Will is being treated by the former army medic, Dale talks to Tom about the motives and goals of their wandering. "Where is your home?", asks Dale. "With my dad," answers Tom, thus admitting their factual homelessness. In the following scene, Dale asks her: "If your dad is messed up with something or running from someone, I really need you to tell me 'cause folks around here aren't looking to get mixed up in any trouble." "It's not that kind of trouble," responds Tom. This answer succeeds in convincing Dale that the pair's problems are not the result of violent behavior but of poverty and marginalization. She therefore decides they can be part of the polity—whether or not she consults a council of other inhabitants is not specified but the communal gatherings seen later in the film at least point towards such a possibility.

When Tom tries to convince her father to remain in the forest community, she argues with regards to the other inhabitants: "These people, they're not that different from us." As Wells points out, this remark likely refers to the RV park being "populated by people with their own traumas," who equally have been marginalized from society.[79] From the perspective of race, however, it also acknowledges a problematic notion of sameness that is reflected in the community's exclusive whiteness. Tom's identification with the other inhabitants could be based on their shared class-based oppression but might, perhaps unconsciously, also refer to their shared whiteness. One could go as far as to argue that this notion is reflected in the motive of the beehive as well which, as has been established, serves as a symbol for the community earlier on. The beehive does after all appear here as a uniform species and community. Therefore, while the film clearly rejects the idea of a restrictive, ultimately fascist concept of landscape, it exposes its alternative vision of landscape to criticism by displaying a striking racial uniformity.

The second approach to interpreting this exclusive whiteness is, however, that the film concedes the limited possibilities of a polity in the context of a country that is still plagued by harsh racial divides both socially and geographically. Returning to Wells' analysis of the film's depiction of white marginality, two of her claims are particularly striking. Firstly, she argues that the absence of encounters between white and non-white characters in the film rings false in the context of "a country as diverse and large as the United States."[80] While the United States certainly are large and diverse, regional rural communities might not be. In an article investigating rural diversity, Daniel Lichter highlights that "rural America has been home throughout its history to large numbers of racial

79 Wells, *The Visual Cultures of Childhood*, 123.
80 Ibid.

and ethnic minorities."[81] However, he continues, these minority communities "are often geographically and socially isolated from mainstream America and easily forgotten or ignored. [. . .] Rural minority populations are *spatially segregated* and invisible in ways not usually found in America's metropolitan areas."[82] This spatial segregation inevitably determines cultural representations of rural America. Secondly, Wells' blanket statement on "films about Black life and sociality" where she claims white characters are "invariably" present to "demonstrate the lack of racial animosity of black people towards white people" is simply too broad: *Dayveon, Burning Cane*, and *Hale County This Morning, This Evening* all center on rural life in the so-called Black Belt and do not feature a single white character. These films quite specifically make the point that Black rural poverty is isolated, static, and, for better or worse, a singular experience.

Leave No Trace, on the other hand, does feature one prominent Black character, contrary to Wells' claim, whose appearance seems to underline this exact divide. When Tom is sent to the Portland care home, she meets two girls her age, one of which, Tiffany (Ryan Joiner), is Black. While the white girl, Valerie (Alyssa McKay), is confrontational towards Tom throughout their entire conversation ("Are you just gonna stand there?"), Tiffany patiently explains the activity they are currently engaged in, namely crafting so-called "dream board"—collages that give them "something to look forward to. Like, for example, I want love in my future." It is a short yet heart-breaking sequence that renders any claim suggesting the film attempts to erase Black experiences less convincing.

Contrasting the only Black character's expressed hope for love in the future with the absence of Black people in the Utopian RV park seems to be a deliberate, if perhaps too subtle hint towards racial inequality and spatially segregated rural communities. In the United States, this segregation has always been "rooted in a national racial geography."[83] In US cinema, this racial geography "of urban ghettoes and suburban idylls" has consigned Black people and people of color largely to urban settings.[84] The rural RV park in *Leave No Trace* offers refuge to victims of poverty but its polity does not exist outside of this historic, racist divide. Its exclusive whiteness, from this perspective, is an admission that true solidarity is only possible once systemic racism is overcome and thus, ultimately, an admission of its failure.

81 Daniel Lichter, "Immigration and the New Racial Diversity in Rural America," *Rural Sociology* 77:1 (2012), 2.

82 Ibid. Emphasis added.

83 Singh, *Black is a Country*, 7.

84 Ibid.

Chapter Six
Landscapes in Terminal Crisis: *Beasts of the Southern Wild* (2012)

Director Benh Zeitlin's debut feature *Beasts of the Southern Wild* has amassed considerable popular attention and various prestigious awards yet has also been controversial. The film's forays into urgent topics such as the climate crisis, the intersection of race, class, and gender as well as alternative modes of living in the end times of neoliberal capitalism have caused both appraisal and fierce resistance. To complicate things, the film mixes tropes from speculative genres such as fantasy with a realist aesthetic to create, as Tavia Nyong'o suggests, a "fable for an emergent Anthropocene."[1] The term Anthropocene refers to the age in which humans "act as a geological force on the planet, changing its climate for millennia to come."[2] *Beasts* is a film about the rural American landscape in terminal crisis, on the cusp of becoming entirely uninhabitable for some of its most vulnerable inhabitants.

Landscape is the film's primary means to bind these different concerns together. It effectively evokes a relational, social understanding of landscape and community that aligns its vision with the general outlook of the New Rural Cinema. On the one hand, *Beasts* may seem like an outlier in the selection of films discussed in this book as it strays from the realist style on display in the larger cycle. David Zellner's low-budget satire *Kid-Thing* (2013) might be considered as the only other film of the cycle that dips into the fantastical; interestingly, it also imagines a rebellious young girl in a ruinous, marginal landscape that seems to hide supernatural secrets. The quick pace of *Beasts'* plot and its overall turbulent liveliness—which is mainly due to its energetic young protagonist—further distinguish it, for example, from the brooding monotony of *Ballast* or the quiet tenderness of *Leave No Trace*. On the other hand, however, the film not only shares the central understanding of landscape as interactive and communal with these other films, but it also echoes important plot points such as the absence of a parent and the displacement of precarious people by powerful controlling forces. Furthermore, it accentuates what is suggested more implicitly in the other films—for example, this is the only film discussed here in which we witness an outright, violent act of rebellion and resistance against regimes of control.

1 Tavia Nyong'o, "Little Monsters: Race, Sovereignty, and Queer Inhumanism in *Beasts of the Southern Wild*," *GLQ: A Journal of Lesbian and Gay Studies*, 21: 2–3 (2015), 256.

2 Dipesh Chakrabarty, "Postcolonial Studies and the Challenge of Climate Change," *New Literary History* 43:1 (2012), 2.

https://doi.org/10.1515/9783110779417-007

The first part of this chapter will analyze the film's depiction of marginal, rural landscape and untangle the layers of social realism and fantastical elements that make up its setting. It will consider the film's construction of "a precarious community steeped in Atlantic histories" that is subjected to the disastrous ecological processes which Rob Nixon has termed "slow violence."[3] The film's heightened mise-en-scène and its association with so-called "weird fiction" as well as mainstream fantasy and science-fiction films construct an "alternative landscape" which establishes a connection between ecocritical and postcolonial concerns. The second part is dedicated to the film's strong emphasis on relational, communal approaches to landscape and their function to counter alienated perspectives which fail to accept humanity's interdependence with the natural world. It will also consider the film's potentially transhumanist notions of being wild and beastlike in the context of climate activism and racial justice. Finally, this chapter looks at the film's political landscape, its ideas of rural community as polity in times of crisis, and at its negotiation of neoliberalism, libertarianism, and anarchism.

1 "The prettiest place on Earth" — Slow violence and alternative landscapes

Beasts, at least at first glance, has all the hallmarks of a US indie production. As Franz Lidz summarizes in an article for *Smithsonian Magazine*:

> Unruly, unbound by studios or the usual Hollywood conventions, this paean to childhood perception and human resilience exists in its own hermetically sealed world, physically and metaphorically. Zeitlin made the movie on a $1.8 million shoestring in southern Louisiana with hand-held 16-millimeter cameras, jury-rigged sets, untrained actors, and a grass-roots collective of artists from around the country.[4]

This is a fitting assessment of the film's "indieness" as it refers to both the film's textual features as well as its industrial context. It is somewhat complicated by the film's purchase at the Sundance film festival by Searchlight (formerly 20th Century Fox's, now Disney's specialty division) which positions it closer to Geoff King's category of "Indiewood," the industrial and textual zone of contact between studio mainstream and indie. In her article on the film, Erin Pearson analy-

---

3 S. Trimble, *Undead Ends: Stories of Apocalypse* (New Brunswick, NJ: Rutgers UP, 2019), 125; Rob Nixon, *Slow Violence and the Environmentalism of the Poor* (Cambridge, MA: Harvard UP, 2013), 2.
4 Franz Lidz, "How Benh Zeitlin Made Beasts of the Southern Wild," *Smithsonian Magazine* (December 2012), https://www.smithsonianmag.com/arts-culture/how-benh-zeitlin-made-beasts-of-the-southern-wild-135132724/.

ses media reception of *Beasts* and concludes that despite the film's low-budget production, its numerous accolades at indie film festivals, and unusual style, "this appears not to be enough to secure a sense of the film's uncontested legitimacy as an independent product."[5] She refers to numerous negative reviews of the film which criticized the director's privileged background as a film-student from New York City and found it "to be irreconcilable with the basic indie principles of authenticity and autonomy from external (perhaps hegemonic) controls."[6] This is relevant as context for the criticism that has been levelled at the film from various analytical perspectives as well as for its ideological inconsistencies in relation to landscape and community, which will both be explored later.

Beasts is set on a Louisiana peninsula dubbed the "Bathtub" by its multi-racial inhabitants. It follows a six-year-old Black girl named Hushpuppy (Quvenzhané Wallis) who lives with her alcoholic and, as is revealed later, terminally ill single father Wink (Dwight Henry). The film's plot, based on the play *Juicy and Delicious* (2012) by Lucy Alibar, who also co-wrote the screenplay, revolves around the arrival of a tremendous storm that causes flooding of the peninsula. This runs in parallel with the film's main fantasy element: the reawakening of a pack of extinct aurochs that is caused by the melting of the polar ice caps. Wink and some of the other inhabitants of the tight-knit community blow up the levee that separates the Bathtub from the mainland, referred to as the Dry Side, in order to drain the saltwater that is ruining their crops. In response, they are forcefully evacuated by federal agents and brought to a hospital. Eventually, Hushpuppy, Wink, and the other residents of the Bathtub escape and return to their home. There, Hushpuppy confronts the arriving aurochs and Wink dies of his unspecified illness. In the film's final images, Hushpuppy leads the remaining inhabitants of the Bathtub in what could be understood as either a funeral or a revolutionary procession. Many see the film as a fictionalized version of the impact of devastating hurricane Katrina which hit Louisiana in August 2005 and caused over 1800 deaths. Zeitlin himself states that "the storm in the film and the issues with the storm are much more inspired by [2008 Hurricane] Gustav and current land-loss in south Louisiana and the levee issues around the Mississippi and saltwater intrusion and the oil spill."[7]

From the very beginning, the film thus positions itself in an unusual transitional space between realism and a heightened, fantastical aesthetic that escapes

5 Erin Pearson, "Structuring Indie and *Beasts of the Southern Wild.* The Role of Review Journalism," in *A Companion to American Indie Film*, ed. Geoff King (Oxford: Wiley-Blackwell, 2017), 176.
6 Ibid.
7 Benh Zeitlin, "Beasts of the Southern Wild Director: Louisiana Is a Dangerous Utopia," Interview by Jeremy Butman. *The Atlantic* (June 27, 2012), https://www.theatlantic.com/entertainment/archive/2012/06/beasts-of-the-southern-wild-director-louisiana-is-a-dangerous-utopia/259009/.

simple genre definitions. Nicholas Mirzeoff has argued in a blogpost that "by mixing magical sequences with cinematic realism, [*Beasts*] does for climate resistance what *Pan's Labyrinth* did for anti-fascism."[8] While the comparison is understandable, it does not fully convince: *El laberinto del fauno (Pan's Labyrinth*, Guillermo del Toro, 2006) conjures up a complex magical world inhabited by different kinds of monsters and other creatures. In *Beasts*, however, it is not mainly the appearance of the monstrous aurochs that warrants these questions about genre and aesthetics but the design and representation of the landscape. By heightening the spectacular Louisiana landscape through grainy 16-milimeter-footage, intense colors, expressive set design, and a melodious score, the film bestows an otherworldly quality upon its setting that is much more subtle than the dark fairy tale spectacle of *Pan's Labyrinth*. At the same time, this is contrasted with more somber, almost documentarian scenes such as the reoccurring aerial shots which adopt the impersonal aesthetic of TV news footage.

Fig. 10: An aerial establishing shot depicts the setting as a collection of ramshackle huts and trailers huddled precariously on the banks of a river or bay: *Beasts of the Southern Wild* (Benh Zeitlin, 2012).

It seems more productive, therefore, to refer to *Beasts'* subtle appropriation of genre tropes as an instance of "weird fiction" rather than fantasy. One of the defining characteristics of this hard-to-define category is, as Julius Greve and Florian Zappe point out, a "*crisis of the map*": a refusal to "render the abstract

8 Nicholas Mirzeoff, "Becoming Wild," *Nicholasmirzeoff.com* (September 30, 2012) https://www.nicholasmirzoeff.com/O2012/2012/09/30/becoming-wild.

reality of geography comprehensible [. . .] and to provide safety by reliable guidance and orientation."[9] *Beasts* constantly calls into question whether it aims for a realistic depiction of life in the Louisiana bayou or if it takes place in an unspecified parallel reality. The film achieves this ambiguity not only by the above mentioned visual and aural techniques, but on a more fundamental level in the choice of its shooting locations and their representation. Early in the film, a brief aerial establishing shot of the Bathtub depicts the setting as a collection of ramshackle huts and trailers huddled precariously on the banks of a river or bay (Fig. 10). As the image is part of the rapid opening montage accompanied by Hushpuppy's voice-over, this geographic overview is only glimpsed for a few seconds before the film cuts to a shaky medium shot placed in the midst of a parade. Here, the partying residents walk past an old placename sign which reads "Isle of Charles Doucet." The name has been crossed out, however, and replaced in scribbled handwriting with "The Bathtub. Pop[ulation] 87." Later, it is revealed that Wink and Hushpuppy share the surname Doucet, suggesting their intimate involvement with the fictional environment's history. The crossed-out place name in concert with the disjointed editing already points towards the film's rejection of stable geographic markers and its adherence to Zappe and Greve's concept of the "crisis of the map." A few minutes later in the film, we get a brief glimpse of an actual map of the Bathtub and the surrounding region in schoolteacher Miss Bathsheba's (Gina Montana) house, which is, fittingly, heavily distorted from age and barely readable.

This blurring of landscape tropes is complicated even further, however, when considering the geography and history of the actual shooting location. The fictional space of the Bathtub/Isle of Charles Doucet is inspired by and partially filmed on and around the real Isle de Jean Charles in Louisiana, "a tiny island connected to the US mainland by a periodically washed-out road."[10] The mostly Native American community on this island has lost, as the Louisiana based news website *Nola* reports, "98% of the land surrounding their homes since 1955, the result of a combination of subsidence, erosion, and sea-level rise. In February 2016, it became the focus of the first federally funded program aimed at relocating residents imperiled by climate-related dangers."[11] The parallels between

9 Julius Greve and Florian Zappe, "Introduction: Ecologies and Geographies of the Weird and the Fantastic," in *Spaces and Fictions of the Weird and the Fantastic – Ecologies, Geographies, Oddities*, ed. J. Greve and F. Zappe (London: Palgrave Macmillan, 2019), 2.

10 Trimble, *Undead Ends*, 123.

11 Tristan Baurick, "How Lessons from Isle de Jean Charles Could Guide Federal Climate Migration Planning," *Nola.com* (August 16, 2020), https://www.nola.com/news/environment/article_8f6c9338-de68-11ea-9f99-534747c43bd0.html.

the fictional Bathtub/Isle of Charles Doucet and the real Isle de Jean Charles are thus more than incidental as *Beasts* adopts the ecological problems facing the real community in its depiction of the imagined, symbolic Bathtub. The ambiguity between the shooting location and its fictional mirror image sets the tone for the film's representation of rural Southern landscape as simultaneously naturalistic and surreal.

The land erosion experienced by the residents of the Isle de Jean Charles is an example of "slow violence." The term describes "attritional catastrophes" that can contribute to the displacement of communities through a gradual destruction of resources over very long periods of time, and thus challenge the traditional understanding of violence as sudden and spectacular. Nixon argues that "climate change, the thawing cryosphere, [. . .] and a host of other slowly unfolding environmental catastrophes present formidable representational obstacles that can hinder our efforts to mobilize and act decisively."[12] Indeed, *Beasts* can be read as a direct response to the representational obstacles Nixon identifies at the outset of his study. He asks: "how to devise arresting stories, images, and symbols adequate to the pervasive but elusive violence of delayed effects?"[13] The film emerges as an attempt to make visible the slow, delayed, but catastrophic effects of man-made climate change on the rural American landscape. Moreover, like Nixon's study, the film centers on "people lacking resources who are the principal casualties of slow violence" and on their resistance to these processes.[14] Nixon writes that "if the neoliberal era has intensified assaults on resources, it has also intensified resistance" and describes the communities standing up against "vastly superior military, corporate, and media forces" as "impoverished resource rebels."[15] Again, this chimes with the film's explicit focus on its rebellious protagonists' deep poverty and marginality.

In fact, the film's setting emanates a sense of insecurity and instability from its very beginning. Kyo Maclear fittingly describes its landscape as an "anarchic place of car scrap and driftwood, feral animals and driftwood shacks."[16] The first image, for example, shows Hushpuppy's small hut which rests precariously on stilts to protect it from flooding. There are holes in the walls, the cladding hangs partially off the roof, and the windows are provisionally covered with plastic film. The trees in the background shake violently from an approaching storm. In the foreground, rusted metal parts are barely visible in the dusky twilight. The

12 Nixon, *Slow Violence, 2.*

13 Ibid., 3.

14 Ibid., 4.

15 Ibid.

16 Kyo Maclear, "Something So Broken: Black Care in the Wake of *Beasts of the Southern Wild*," *ISLE: Interdisciplinary Studies in Literature and Environment* 25: 3 (2018), 603.

image immediately conveys poverty, marginality, and a sense of danger which is only slightly mitigated by the warm yellow light that starts to radiate from behind the windows towards the end of the shot. The sudden appearance of this bright yellow square in the darkness seems to signal the film's approach to overturn the expectations its audience might have in connection to the rural poverty on display. Indeed, in the very next scene the landscape is cast in bright, golden sunlight and appears idyllic. The trees are depicted in a vivid, lush green and small insects can be seen dancing in the rays of sunlight. The sense of danger is superseded by the promise of adventure and even harmony as we watch Hushpuppy engage lovingly with the animals living in the shed next to her house.

Shortly after, the film introduces the first glimpse of its heightened mise-en-scène, which contributes to the setting's otherworldly appearance. First, one of the soundtrack's major musical motifs titled "Particles of the Universe/Heartbeats" sets in, which consists of a memorable sequence of melodious notes played on a glockenspiel or toy piano. This musical theme instantly succeeds in bestowing an enchanted aural dimension onto the visible landscape. In fact, the musical motif is similar to the well-known "Hedwig's Theme" composed by John Williams for the *Harry Potter*-Fantasy franchise (2001–2011) and therefore equally alludes to a magical, childlike sense of wonder. It transforms the stark images of poverty, which, in a different context, would seem almost unbearably bleak, to take on a transcendental quality and is therefore central as an aural element in elevating the filmic landscape.

This is followed by the first appearance of Wink, Hushpuppy's father, who is seen retrieving an entire plucked chicken from a cooler using a large spanner and placing it on a makeshift barbecue. Briefly, the outside of his hut is visible, a patchwork of driftwood, metal plates with fading paint, and other salvaged materials. He proceeds to ring a bell attached to his hut by a rope and calls his daughter to attend "feed up time." Hushpuppy responds with a dog-like howl. Here, the film's subtle approach to distorting the landscape becomes apparent as small details of the mise-en-scène in combination with the music and visual style elevate the overall realistic representation. Especially the rope that connects Wink's with Hushpuppy's hut which serves as a sort of doorbell for the two "neighbors" emerges as an element of "*Verfremdungseffekt*," or nuanced alienation. It is not inconceivable, of course, that such a method could be used in real life, yet the film's slightly skewed framing of the rope connecting the two scrappy houses as well as the smoke from the barbecue entering the frame suggest another layer of reality. One is reminded of the ramshackle tree houses inhabited by the Lost Boys in Steven Spielberg's *Peter Pan* adaptation *Hook* (1991) and similar Fantasy films. Indeed, Benh Zeitlin's follow-up to *Beasts of the Southern Wild, Wendy* (2020), is a

Peter Pan adaptation that retells the story of the Lost Boys, suggesting that the director may have had this connotation already in mind.[17]

The following opening montage that introduces the Bathtub and its residents contains further elements of mise-en-scène that fit the film's ambivalent "weird" style. Most of all, this is visible in the residents' means of transportation. Wink's boat, for example, is build out of the rusty rear of an old truck, an unusual prop, which speaks both of poverty and of resilient inventiveness. Furthermore, we see Wink and his friends dancing and drinking on a kind of parade float that consists of a tractor adorned with driftwood spikes, ropes, and old metal parts. The model here might be post-apocalyptic films in the vein of the *Mad Max* franchise (1979–2015) or *Waterworld* (Kevin Reynolds, 1996), which often feature rusty, reassembled vehicles used by the inhabitants of a post-crisis wasteland. *Waterworld*, while entirely different in tone and scope, seems to be a particular narrative and stylistic point of reference for *Beasts*. The film is set in a future where most of Earth is covered by water after the polar ice caps have melted. Survivors live in ramshackle towns built on the open sea that are not dissimilar to the architecture of the Bathtub. Not only is there a common ecocritical subtext, both films also focus on a young girl as an almost messianic figure who leads her community into a potentially more hopeful future.

Another crucial moment contributing to the film's eclectic style happens just before the arrival of the momentous storm. After an intense fight, which leads Hushpuppy to set fire to her hut, Wink aggressively reprimands his daughter. She responds, "I hope you die and after you die, I will go to your grave and eat birthday cake all by myself" and hits him on the chest. The hit causes Wink to stop in his tracks. Hurt and shocked he gazes back at his daughter. Thunder begins to rumble in the background. The omnipresent cicadas suddenly stop singing. Wink sinks to the ground, his body twitching in convulsions. A sudden cutaway scene takes us to the South Pole, where a colossal glacier partially sinks into the sea, eventually revealing the frozen, menacing aurochs. Dark storm clouds gather over Hushpuppy. A close-up shows the bay water rising to cover her wellingtons. "Mama, I think I broke something," she screams, addressing her absent mother. This conflation of coming-of-age elements—the rebellious act against the father, the longing for an absent mother—with the awakening of a fantastic beast and the slow erosion of a magical realm is strongly reminiscent of another well-known fantasy film: Wolfgang Petersen's adaptation of Michael Ende's classic novel *The NeverEnding Story* (1984). The design of the aurochs is clearly inspired

17 *Wendy* is an interesting companion piece to *Beasts* insofar as it applies a very similar style and evokes a similar atmosphere yet locates itself much clearer within the fantasy genre while retaining a certain ambivalence between what is real, and what is supernatural or imagined.

by this film's antagonist, the wolf-like creature Gmork, who is narratively associated with "The Nothing," a malevolent force that slowly devours the film's magical realm, Fantasia. One of the film's central scenes in which Gmork explains his intentions to the hero Atreyu even cuts between close-ups of the creature and gathering dark storm clouds in a way that is very similar to the described scene in *Beasts*. Returning to Greve and Zappe's outlining of "weird" fiction, they argue that this genre, like all fantastical genres since the 1960s "can be read as reflection of the creeping awareness of fundamental ecological and geological crises."[18] As such, the ambiguous "weird" landscape in *Beasts* can be understood as an explicit response to a growing awareness of the extreme severity of the ecological problems threatening impoverished, marginalized people in rural America and the rest of the world. The film can, thus, be said to directly respond to the question posed by Nixon: "How can we turn the long emergencies of slow violence into stories dramatic enough to rouse public sentiment and warrant political intervention?" The answer presented by *Beasts* is to subtly heighten and stylize both what is at stake, the landscapes that will be irretrievably lost, and the threat itself which takes physical shape here in the monstrous form of the aurochs.

This particular landscape vision fulfils a second purpose, however, that pertains to the Bathtub as "a precarious community steeped in Atlantic histories," and its postcolonial context.[19] The film's shooting location, the Isle de Jean Charles, has a history as a "way station for [Creole] smugglers; a place for those seeking to evade political and economic control through which the United States began securing its territory in the aftermath of the Louisiana purchase" as well as for "refugees who fled the Haitian Revolution and settled in Louisiana."[20] Furthermore, the Isle de Jean Charles was and still is inhabited by members of the Biloxi-Chitimacha-Choctaw Tribe, who moved to the island in the 1830s to escape the Indian Removal Act and the so-called Trail of Tears. These unspoken colonial histories are reflected in the Bathtub's multi-ethnic community in which people of all races and ages live peacefully together and share a strong sense of communal solidarity. S. Trimble argues that "the film registers the colonial history of the island while, at the same time, making space to speculate on the silences in that history."[21] Landscape here is not only a medium representing present and future ecological threats, but also an implicit indicator of a colonial past.

Rural landscapes in US cinema inevitably take on a different meaning in a film that, like *Beasts*, employs African American main characters. In Black history, ru-

18 Greve and Zappe, "Introduction," 3.

19 Trimble, *Undead Ends*, 125.

20 Ibid., 124.

21 Ibid., 125.

rality is inextricably connected to slavery and the plantation system and therefore, as Nixon puts it, more "a place of eviction and historical hauntings than of redemptive silence."[22] There is, however, a Black literary tradition which is invested in "altering the conventional images of place that link black environments with low social status and spiritual despair," on which Melvin Dixon focuses in his study of Black perspectives on American wilderness.[23] African American art, he argues, "is replete with [. . .] spatial images that invert these assumptions about place and endow language with the power to reinvent geography and identity."[24] *Beasts,* while directed and written by white filmmakers, undertakes such a reinvention from the perspective of its two main characters and attempts to tap into the tradition of "alternative landscapes."

Dixon traces this tradition back to slave gospel songs, the earliest surviving examples of African American folk art, in which wilderness plays a significant role both as a metaphysical place of salvation and a concrete way of escaping from the confines of the plantation. He argues:

> Music creates a landscape, defines a space and a territory the singer and protagonist can claim. The slave songs create [. . .] self-creating acts, including resistance and escape that ultimately defeat that inertia of place identity upon which the institution of slavery has thrived.[25]

He follows this line of thought through the writings of, among others, Martin Luther King Jr., James Baldwin, and Toni Morrison and concludes that "Afro-American writers, often considered homeless, alienated from mainstream culture, and segregated in negative environments, have used language to create alternative landscapes where Black culture and identity can flourish apart from any marginal, prescribed 'place.'"[26]

This utopian argument calls to mind Wink's description of the Bathtub as "the prettiest place on Earth" in spite of its obvious disintegration. Nyong'o makes a similar point when he argues that *Beasts* "aligns its vision with an alternative, nonsovereign relationship to land and world" and tells its story "from the side of the displaced, vagrant, and subaltern."[27] Zeitlin has explicitly stated in interviews

---

22 Nixon, *Slow Violence*, 258.

23 Melvin Dixon, *Ride Out the Wilderness: Geography and Identity in Afro-American Literature* (Champaign, IL: University of Illinois Press, 1987), 2.

24 Ibid.

25 Ibid., 14.

26 Ibid., 2.

27 Nyong'o, "Little Monsters," 252.

that it is the film's "goal that people will get behind the Bathtub and accept a lot of things that they've preconceived as bad."[28] As such, the film's fantastical disposition is essential in its aim to create an alternative landscape, which radically subverts negative assumptions about Black rural poverty and its prescribed spaces. Hence, it emerges that the film's enchanted landscape images serve as an attempt to bridge the gap between postcolonial and ecocritical concerns.

This strategy is perhaps best summarized by Dipesh Chakrabarty's conclusion to his essay "Postcolonial Studies and the Challenge of Climate Change" (2012). In the Anthropocene, he argues, "humans, collectively, now have an agency in determining the climate of the planet as a whole."[29] Thus, he suggests, there arises a need for unity that is almost impossible to fulfil: "in an age when the forces of globalization intersect with those of global warming, the idea of the human needs to be stretched beyond where postcolonial thought advanced it."[30] Similar to Nixon, Chakrabarty stresses how the sheer magnitude and scale of these implications exceeds the scope of current human understanding. Nevertheless, he concludes, as the survival of humanity is at stake, "all progressive political thought, including postcolonial criticism, will have to register this profound change in the human condition."[31] *Beasts'* construction of a "weird" landscape oscillating between ecological destruction and multi-racial utopia is an attempt to visually think through this profound change and to rise up to the challenge of ecological collectivism.

2 "Who the Earth is for" — Community, embeddedness, transhumanism

As argued in the previous section, the film's "weird" mise-en-scène works as an expression of the collective, interactive emergence of landscape as opposed to merely illustrating Hushpuppy's childlike perspective. In this section, I want to explore further how the film conveys the Bathtub as a "milieu of involvement," a perpetually emerging social concept caused by the interaction of community and environment.[32] This is strikingly illustrated in the film's opening montage. The second part of this section will look at the role animals play in this environment and how, and why, the film works to blur the human-animal distinction.

---

28 Zeitlin, "Dangerous Utopia," Interview by Jeremy Butman.

29 Chakrabarty, "Postcolonial Studies," 9.

30 Ibid., 14–15.

31 Ibid., 15.

32 Wylie, *Landscape*, 161.

Hushpuppy's voice-over monologue in the opening montage is mostly held in the first-person plural. She begins: "They [the inhabitants of the Dry Side] built the wall that cuts *us* off. They think *we* all gonna drown down here. But *we* ain't going nowhere." Clearly, Hushpuppy thinks of the Bathtub as a collective that is inseparably connected to its environment through custom and history. This line is followed by the aforementioned celebratory procession that begins on the narrow connecting road from the mainland and will eventually lead into the heart of the Bathtub, the square in front of the communal bar. From the very beginning, the Bathtub's residents are presented as a tight-knit solidary community that constantly engages in convivial, social acts. This is the main aim of the opening montage as a whole—to characterize the Bathtub as a landscape that arises through the custom-based interaction of a close-knit community with the environment. It revels in moments in which the "boundaries between person and place, or between self and the landscape, dissolve altogether" and thus falls into line with Olwig's notion of landscape as polity and place as opposed to mere scenery.[33]

As the procession seen at the beginning starts to merge with a drunken festivity, the opening montage cuts with increasing frequency between partying Bathtub residents of different ages and races played by local non-professional actors. The camera moves shakily, or drunkenly, and often comes very close to the dancing, singing, and drinking characters while a raucous Cajun folk tune plays in the background. The viewer is thus visually and aurally immersed in the community's festivities. In a brief, quieter, cutaway scene, Hushpuppy remarks in her voiceover: "One day, the storm is gonna blow, the ground's gonna sink, and the water's gonna rise up so high, there ain't gonna be a Bathtub. Just a whole bunch of water." This melancholic interjection serves to render the following ecstatic images as even more defiant of the outlined threat. The response to inherent danger of flooding and displacement here is not worry, complaint, or preparation, but rather an intensification of collectiveness and joy.

In concert with the beginning of the film's dramatic main theme, the film cuts to overexposed images of Hushpuppy, Wink, and other Bathtub residents running through the night holding burning roman candles. The flying sparks, the thick smoke, and the rapid sequence of cuts visually merges the characters with their surroundings. Once again, Ingold's claim that "through living in it, the landscape becomes part of us, just as we are part of it"[34] becomes tangible here. Especially Ingold's focus on the performance of everyday activity within an environment that is historically constituted by such activities over time comes into focus in this sequence.

33 Ingold, *The Perception of the Environment*, 56.
34 Ibid., 191.

For *Beasts* as for Ingold, landscape is, as Wylie summarizes, "both performative sensorium and site and source of cultural meaning."[35] Furthermore, Ingold's notion that "landscape is the world as it is known to those that dwell therein" is underlined by Hushpuppy's final line of voice-over before the display of the title card:[36] "But me and my daddy, we stay right here. *We is who the earth is for.*" With this rebellious line, the score crescendos into its leitmotif, which accompanies the images of eccentrically dressed Bathtub residents celebrating and rejoicing in a clearing lit by colorful fairy lights.

The powerful, immersive quality of this opening montage effectively conveys the bodily, emotional relation and the sense of attachment between inhabitants and the environment. One is reminded of Tilley's definition of landscape as "embodied sets of relationships between places, a structure of human feeling, emotion, dwelling, movement and practical activity," all of which are on display in the communal cooking, fishing, playing, and dancing portrayed in these introductory scenes.[37] The joyfulness of the opening montage is as crucial as the visible hardship in understanding how the landscape "as a physical place [is] [. . .] the manifestation of the polity's local custom."[38] The unity and inseparability of community and landscape that is inherent in Olwig's notion of *Landschaft* is expressed perhaps more explicitly in these opening minutes than in any of the other films discussed here. Similarly, Ingold argues that "the landscape takes on its form through a process of incorporation, not of inscription" and it is precisely this process the film seeks to illustrate.[39]

This is of particular importance in a film that, as has been argued, employs its landscape vision with ecocritical intent. The nuance the film manages to stress in this context is the distinction between its notion of landscape as a result of interaction and incorporation, on the one hand, and the conservationist fetishizing of nature as originary state, on the other hand. As in *Leave No Trace*, the polity here is clearly distinguished from an imagined pastoral idyll that might invite associations to fascist *Lebensraum* ideologies. Nixon puts forward that "the emotional power generated by attachments to place can be an invaluable resource for environmental mobilization. Yet [. . .] they can induce [both] a conservative, bigoted environmental ethic or a progressive, inclusive one."[40] The film obviously aims for the latter as it eschews attributing essential, unchanging characteristics

35 Wylie, *Landscape*, 161.

36 Ingold, *The Perception of the Environment*, 193.

37 Tilley, *The Materiality of Stone*, 25.

38 Olwig, *Landscape, Nature, and the Body Politic*, 214.

39 Ingold, *The Perception of the Environment*, 162.

40 Nixon, *Slow Violence*, 242.

to both the environment and the Bathtub's residents and instead favors diversity, interactivity, and solidarity between people of different races.

The question that arises is to what degree this solidarity extends to the non-human inhabitants of the Bathtub. Does the film's rethinking of landscape as a social category that emerges through interaction incorporate a radical "decentering of the human," as Sarah MacFarlan suggests?[41] Does it push the New Rural Cinema's central motive of blurring boundaries between self and landscape even further by suggesting "to trouble the categorical split between humanity and nature (including nonhuman animals)?"[42] The film's title obviously aims for an unsettling of the animal-human divide and seeks to portray the human residents of the Bathtub as beasts or at least as beast-like. What is the intention of this "dehumanization" and how does it fit within the film's dialectical concept of landscape and the threat of ecological disaster?

Animals feature prominently in *Beasts* from its very first scene. When we first encounter Hushpuppy, she can be seen building a nest for a chick she is apparently nursing in her hut. It is a gesture of care and respect that immediately conveys a close emotional proximity between human and non-human animal. In the next scene, Hushpuppy lays out her thoughts regarding "nonhumankind" in her voice-over.[43] While tenderly putting her ear to the bodies of a pig, a chicken, and other domestic animals, listening to their heartbeats, she says: "All the time, everywhere, everything's hearts are beating and squirting and talking to each other in ways I cannot understand. Most of the time they probably be saying: 'I'm hungry. I gotta poop.' But sometimes they be talking in codes." Both of these early scenes bring into focus the two main aspects of the animal presence in *Beasts*. Firstly, it relates to what Pick terms the "cross-species vulnerability of bodies" which is highlighted specifically in relation to the "slow violence" of climate catastrophe.[44] Secondly, it highlights the shared agency in the interaction with the environment from which landscape emerges, described by Pick as "creaturely fellowship" and by Nyong'o as "an ecological sensibility attuned to the need for a rewilded planet in which to share sovereignty with nonhumankind."[45]

---

41 Sarah McFarlan, "The Universe Unravelled: Swampy Embeddedness and Ecological Apocalypse in *Beasts of the Southern Wild*," in *Ecocriticism and the Future of Southern Studies*, ed. Zackary Vernon (Baton Rouge: LSU Press, 2019), 66.

42 Lieber, "Spaces of Communal Misery," 187.

43 Nyong'o, "Little Monsters," 251.

44 Anat Pick, *Creaturely Poetics. Animality and Vulnerability in Literature and Film* (New York: Columbia UP, 2011), 10.

45 Ibid.; Nyong'o, "Little Monsters," 251.

Hushpuppy's interaction with the chick in her first appearance on screen makes the motif of vulnerability immediately tangible. As the storm rages outside the ramshackle hut, these two small creatures share a moment of care and bodily compassion in the midst of terrible violence. As Pick clarifies, vulnerability is not equivalent to weakness, it rather "dispassionately denotes the condition of being embodied as necessarily limited, and limited by necessity, but always already encompassing the dialogic relation between bodies that underlies caring."[46] That being said, *Beasts* does indicate in this and other scenes a particular vulnerability for its precarious protagonist that goes beyond the shared susceptibility of *all* living beings to violence. This is similar to Ree's oneiric identification with a squirrel in *Winter's Bone*. Pick points out that "when it comes to animals, power operates with the fewest obstacles," and the opening scene and its paralleling of Hushpuppy with the tiny bird suggest their shared experience of this nonsovereign exposure to power.[47] Inevitably, this is exacerbated by the casting of a Black girl in a role that in the original play is described as a white boy. Nyong'o therefore argues that the film locates the "nonsovereign aspect of the human where we are most accustomed to finding it: in the defenseless, impoverished, raced, and gendered child."[48] As a poor, Black, female child, Hushpuppy, the film suggests here, is not far removed from the defenselessness to power of the small animals that surround her.

The film goes on to further stress Hushpuppy's close connection to the animals around her when her father calls her to attend "feed-up time" to which she responds with an animalistic howl. Right after, the film cross-cuts between shots of the feeding animals and Hushpuppy eating an entire grilled chicken with her hands. Wink appears in the frame and directs his daughter to "share [the food] with the dog" as he dispenses handfuls of what looks like dry dog food pellets between them. On the one hand, this scene appears as a clear illustration of the literally dehumanizing experience of abject poverty and systemic racism. It thus points to "dehumanization as a strategy of oppression."[49] On the other hand, the film works to positively reclaim this dehumanization by exploring "the regions deemed animal [. . .] that lurk within the human itself" and identifying them as a possible ground for resistance.[50] Disregarding the horrible implications of deep poverty in this scene, it aims to establish a strong bond between Hushpuppy (and by extension the whole Bathtub community) and the animals, unifying both species as the titular feral "beasts."

46 Pick, *Creaturely Poetics*, 15.

47 Ibid.

48 Nyong'o, "Little Monsters", 252.

49 Pick, *Creaturely Poetics*, 6.

50 Ibid.

Nyong'o is among the many authors who have rightly criticized such a depiction of a Black child. He points out that such "cinematic depictions of Black (and other subaltern) people as primitives on a continuum with nonhuman animals" are in constant danger of, even if unwittingly, succumbing to the racist use of dehumanization as a tool of oppression.[51] While he appreciates the film's aim to "valorize feral human nature," he asks: "at what price is such transvaluation purchased?"[52] The appeal of transhumanism in ecocritical films such as *Beasts* that suggest a decentering of the human as a strategy of ecological resistance must confront, Nyong'o argues, the questions Black studies direct at them: "have we ever been human? And if not, what are we being asked to decenter, and through what means?"[53] As will become clear, the film's answers are rather muddled.

One scene lays out the film's philosophy of both shared vulnerability and creaturely fellowship even more explicitly, yet also demonstrates the haphazard way the film attempts its foray into posthumanism. In the scene, the Bathtub's teacher Miss Bathsheba addresses Hushpuppy and the other children in her ramshackle schoolhouse: "Meat. Meat, meat, meat. Every animal is made out of meat. I'm meat. Y'all asses meat. Everything is part of the buffet of the universe." The human-animal distinction is self-evidently ignored in this monologue, as Lieber points out, "addressing all living creatures—humans included—as animals."[54] This idea is blurred, however, as Miss Bathsheba's speech points to both shared vulnerability as well as to a somewhat contradictory survival-of-the-fittest ideology ("buffet of the universe") which is amplified by the fact that, as Lieber points out, "the human beasts continuously eat other animals" throughout the film.[55]

After the storm has caused flooding of the peninsula, this contradictory approach comes to the fore again. As the community's members are refitting their houses and gathering their remaining food and resources, Hushpuppy remarks in her voice-over: "We got enough animals to eat until the water goes down." This hardly speaks of a blurring of the boundaries between non-human and human "beasts" or of a "reversal of roles between the eating and the eaten."[56] Nevertheless, some of the film's most haunting images—the bloated corpse of a cow lying face-down in the contaminated salt water, dead fishes and birds surrounding Wink and Hushpuppy's boat—seem to again point towards the shared vulnerability of precarious human and animal bodies in the context of the climate crisis.

51 Nyong'o, "Little Monsters," 251.

52 Ibid.

53 Ibid., 266.

54 Lieber, "Spaces of Communal Misery," 186.

55 Ibid.

56 Nyong'o, "Little Monsters," 252.

The image calls to mind Elisée Reclus' statement in defense of vegetarianism: "How much difference is there between the dead carcass of a cow and that of a man? Their severed limbs and entrails mixed in with one another look quite similar."[57] This disturbing image aims for a similar comparison.

Finally, it is the aurochs, originally introduced as monstrous antagonists that provide the missing link between Hushpuppy's alleged "embeddedness within a multispecies community" and the film's framing of landscape as polity.[58] After they have been shown running violently through the submerged Louisiana landscape throughout the film, the climactic scene has them finally arriving in the Bathtub. Unexpectedly, Hushpuppy's confrontation with the "undead" extinct animals does not play out in the form of a battle but as reconciliation. "You are my friend, kind of," whispers Hushpuppy at the creature upon which the aurochs retreat. In relation to this scene, Lieber argues:

> [Hushpuppy] knows to relate to nonhuman animals—and nature, more generally—as something that she and her community need to live with in solidarity [. . .] This transformation of the relationship with nature is, in short, what *Beasts* suggests as necessary in the face of climate change.[59]

Nyong'o similarly suggests that the "rebirth of the aurochs augurs the coming of a feral humankind" equipped to stand up to the forces of marginalization and ecological destruction.[60]

However, whereas the film succeeds in embedding its alternative community within the landscape and demonstrating the emergence of landscape as polity through bodily interaction and custom, its attempts to expand this theme across the species boundary fall flat. "I gotta take care of mine," says Hushpuppy to the fearsome beast as she turns to her friends in the climactic scene. Visually, the film "never assume[s] the Aurochs' perspective on her," as Lieber points out, which suggest a lack of the supposed interspecies solidarity and instead demonstrates how "care for one's own trumps the solidarity with the other, and the common 'creatureliness' is undermined."[61] Therefore, despite its own and others' claims, *Beasts* is not a transhumanist text. Its controversial attempts to make its protagonists "less than human" may succeed in illuminating the dehumanizing effects of poverty and racism under "inhuman" neoliberal capitalism and suggest a sort of resistant wild-

57 Elisée Reclus, "On Vegetarianism," [1901], translated by John Clark and Camille Martin, quoted in Clark and Martin, *Anarchy, Geography, Modernity*, 159.

58 McFarlan, "The Universe Unravelled," 70.

59 Lieber, "Spaces of Communal Misery: The Weird Post-Capitalism of *Beasts of the Southern Wild*," 186.

60 Nyong'o, "Little Monsters," 260.

61 Lieber, "Spaces of Communal Misery," 187.

ness, yet it does not, as Pick puts it, "grant animals a share in our world of subjectivity" and remains safely in anthropocentric territory.[62]

3 "The black flag of anarchy?" — The political landscape of the Bathtub

In his review of *Beasts* in the *Los Angeles Review of Books*, critic Kelly Candaele identifies what he calls "troubling social messages"[63] in the film's subtext. His concern is primarily directed at the film's final scene in which Hushpuppy leads a procession of Bathtub inhabitants along the road connecting the peninsula to the mainland, suggesting a continuation of their activism against the federal government. Candaele is especially concerned about one member of the group who "carries a black flag" which causes him to ask if it might be "the black flag of anarchy."[64] Either way, he concludes, the film's "political message seems dangerously hedonist—an apolitical, individualist hedonism with a tacked-on ending suggesting an incipient social movement."[65] It seems exaggerated that the author perceives this spontaneous, vague social justice movement as inherently dangerous and bizarrely describes it as "political" and "apolitical" in the same sentence.

I include this exemplary reaction at the outset of this section to demonstrate two things. Firstly, the film is very effective in evoking a powerful, if vague sense of political activism that is specifically tied to Mitchell's idea of a "struggle for landscape;" secondly, its confused political ideas which are solidified in its cinematic landscape in turn provoke confused critical readings.[66] As the framework of anarchism is remarkably prevalent in many of these analyses, I will read the film's political land-

---

62 Pick, *Creaturely Poetics*, 6; Again, the film's approach seems to chime with Elisée Reclus' approach to ecocriticism, specifically his outlook on the relationship between humans and other species. In a letter to the British nature writer Richard Heath, he writes: "For my part, I also include animals in my feeling of socialist solidarity. But I also say to myself: everything comes in degrees and our primary obligations begin immediately around us. [. . .] I am [however] firmly confident that our harmonic society should embrace not only humans but also beings that have consciousness of their lives." (Elisée Reclus, "Letter to Richard Heath," [no specific date, 1884] in *Correspondance Vols. 1 & 2* (Paris: Libraire Schleicher Frères, 1911), 325, quoted in Clark and Martin, *Anarchy, Geography, Modernity*, 32.)

63 Kelly Candaele, "The Problematic Political Messages of *Beasts of the Southern Wild*," *Los Angeles Review of Books* (August 9, 2012), https://lareviewofbooks.org/article/the-problematic-political-messages-of-beasts-of-the-southern-wild/.

64 Ibid.

65 Ibid.

66 Mitchell, "Cultural Landscapes," 788.

scape in this section with reference to the perhaps most influential anarchist geographer, Elisée Reclus (1830–1905). The film attempts to counter neoliberal governance's absence or retreat of government by, perhaps naively, suggesting that the liminal spaces created by this retreat open the possibility for "the birth of a society in which there are no more masters" as advocated by Reclus and other Anarchist thinkers.[67] I rely here mainly on Camille Martin and John P. Clark's book on Reclus, which both collects his most important texts and delivers insightful analyses.

The relevance of Reclus' writing for this book is immediately recognizable in his fundamental refusal to, as Clark and Martin summarize, "depict the natural world as a mere backdrop for human history."[68] As for Ingold and Olwig after him, landscape for Reclus is "always an active presence, both encompassing humanity and remaining in intimate dialectical interaction with humanity throughout history."[69] His most succinct description of this interactive approach to landscape comes in his essay *History of a Mountain* (1880), where he writes:

> Every people gives, so to speak, new clothing to the surrounding nature. By means of its fields and roads, by its dwellings and every manner of construction, by the way it arranges the trees and the landscape in general, the populace expresses the character of its own ideals.[70]

The specific relevance of Reclus in the context of *Beasts*, however, arises as a result of his self-conception as a "libertarian socialist or, to be more precise, a communist anarchist."[71] Coincidentally, Reclus was heavily influenced in his lifelong anti-racist, anti-capitalist activism by a trip he took as a young man to the Mississippi Delta in Louisiana, where he was appalled by his first-hand experience of slavery and the plantation system. It was this experience, among other things, that inspired his personal and professional pursuit of anarchism as the ideal political expression of his dialectical, interactive understanding of landscape and his rejection of the "inhumanity of capitalism."[72] The question that arises here is how in the specific case of *Beasts* where the rural polity is framed as an ecocriti-

67 Elisée Reclus, "L'Anarchie," [1894] in *Les Temps Nouveau* 18 (May 25–June 1 1895), trans. John Clark and Camille Martin, quoted in Clark and Martin, *Anarchy, Geography, Modernity*, 120.

68 Clark and Martin *Anarchy, Geography, Modernity*, 5.

69 Ibid.

70 Elisée Reclus, *The History of a Mountain*, trans. Bertha Lilly and John Lilly (New York: Harper and Brothers, 1881), quoted in Clark and Martin, *Anarchy, Geography, Modernity*, 26.

71 Elisée Reclus, "Letter to M. Roth," [no specific date, 1904] in *Correspondance Vol. 3* (Paris: Alfred Costes, 1925), 285–286, trans. John Clark and Camille Martin, quoted in Clark and Martin, *Anarchy, Geography, Modernity*, 6.

72 Clark and Martin, *Anarchy, Geography, Modernity*, 11.

cal, solidary, and politically active community, Reclus' Utopian vision of community intersects with Olwig's notion of *Landschaft*.

Similar to *Leave No Trace*, *Beasts* attempts to visualize the *processes* of neoliberal marginalization as well as the results—in other words, it illustrates the takeover of an "understanding of landscape as spatial scenery, and the displacement of the original concept of landscape as place and region" *in action*.[73] A striking example of this strategy is the depiction of the Bathtub residents' displacement from their home after they have blown up the levee to the Dry Side. Aurally announced by the faint roar of a helicopter, the Bathtub is suddenly invaded by anonymous white men who, after promising "food and shelter" are attacked by the Bathtub's defensive inhabitants. Wink and his friends are then physically restrained by the federal agents and brought (off-screen) to the "Open Arms" hospital which is described on the sign above the entry as a "processing center for disaster relief and response."

The first image of the hospital complex immediately conveys the stark contrast to the Bathtub's milieu of engagement where, as Lieber puts it, "dwellings consisting of waste and natural materials are organically integrated into the landscape of the southern wild."[74] By comparison, the hospital building appears industrial, factory-like and vaguely suggests a "quasi-genocidal efficiency," which is reinforced by the ominous, technical description as a "processing center."[75] The next shot takes us inside the structure. The camera is tilted upwards, emulating Hushpuppy's perspective, and glides over the sterile, white surfaces which stand in harsh contrast to the mainly Black bodies of the patients. "It didn't look like a prison," Hushpuppy describes in her voice-over. "It looked more like fish tank with no water." Hence, as Lieber argues, "the beasts can no longer move like fish in water, because they exist in a place that is alienated from their essence; [. . .] it is not a place that allows subjects to dwell."[76] The film paints a grim picture of the state's biopolitics in this scene—in what Lieber describes as "a Foucauldian critique of modern institutions in an *anarchist* spirit"[77]—that seems to decide at whim over its citizens' life and death. The limited space of the hospital on the Dry Side becomes a symbol for everything the Bathtub's "anarchic band of stragglers" reject: control, sovereignty, order.[78]

Furthermore, the scene calls to mind Reclus' critique of capitalist technocracy which foreshadows neoliberalism's expansion of economic rationality to every di-

73 Olwig, *The Meanings of Landscape*, 78.
74 Lieber, "Spaces of Communal Misery," 188.
75 Ibid.
76 Ibid.
77 Ibid. Emphasis added.
78 Nyong'o, "Little Monsters," 252.

mension of human life. In his pamphlet *To My Brother the Peasant* (1893) he writes:

> We are in an age of science and method, and our rulers, served by an army of chemists and professors, are preparing a social structure for you in which all will be regulated as in a factory. There, the machine controls everything, even men, who are simple cogs to be disposed of.[79]

This chimes not only with the hospitals factory-like appearance but also with Hushpuppy's comment regarding one Bathtub resident connected to a life support machine which she describes as being "plug[ged] into the wall." Shortly after, Wink resists treatment for his unspecified illness and attacks one of the doctors. In response, he is violently restrained by security guards. Here, the film evokes an overwhelming feeling of entrapment as the Bathtub's "beasts'" bodies are subjected to a "system of regimentation and control."[80] The scene culminates in a disturbing image: Hushpuppy, now groomed and dressed in an old-fashioned blue dress, watches her semi-conscious father being brought out of surgery in a wheelchair, plastic tubes protruding from his nostrils. The "beasts," it is suggested, have inevitably lost the struggle for their landscape, or rather for their *Landschaft*, of which, of course, their own bodies are integral parts as well.

It is illuminating to compare this intense sequence at the hospital with a similar narrative moment in *Leave No Trace*, i.e. Will and Tom's "assessment" at social services after they have been removed from Forest Park. In Granik's film, the "displacement of the original concept of landscape as place and region" and its replacement with a restrictive, scenic understanding is spelled out even more directly through the set design in the social services' office where father and daughter are taken from their idyllic home.[81] As described in the previous chapter, there are numerous framed pastoral woodland paintings in the office, one wall is even entirely covered with a forest-print wallpaper. Landscape is thereby transformed from place to space, from interactive environment to mere representation depicted from a controlling gaze. However, the social workers themselves are not presented as anonymous accessories to the dehumanizing process but, at least in the case of Jean, as compassionate people trying to operate as best as they can within the limited resources of social infrastructure.

This is where the two films differ and where *Beasts'* gesturing towards anarchist positions opens the film up to accusations such as Lieber's. He argues that

---

79 Elisée Reclus, "To My Brother the Peasant" [1893], trans. John Clark and Camille Martin, quoted in Clark and Martin, *Anarchy, Geography, Modernity*, 87.

80 Clark and Martin, *Anarchy, Geography, Modernity*, 87.

81 Olwig, *The Meanings of Landscape*, 78.

the almost fascist iconography of the hospital renders the film's stance here "almost indiscernible from libertarian ideology and neoliberal demands to end the state's responsibility for the wellbeing of its citizens."[82] Unlike *Leave No Trace*, which is careful to level its critique at the specific system of neoliberal welfare, not at the concept of social welfare itself, *Beasts'* attempt at illustrating the dissonance between marginalized citizens and governmental biopolitics is indeed heavy-handed. Nevertheless, I find Lieber's critique of the film too strong here. His claim that the film's political landscape is "indiscernible from libertarian ideology" seems polemical and oblivious of the difference between (leftist) anarchism and (rightist) libertarianism. This is crucial in this case because while both are essentially anti-statist ideologies, anarchism is generally founded on "natural solidarity to encourage voluntary co-operation" whereas right-wing libertarianism is exclusively "based on rational self-interest"[83] and is thus entirely compatible with neoliberalism's tenet of individualism.

The political and physical landscape that *Beasts* creates, however, is clearly one of cooperation and solidarity. For one, this is explicitly spelled out in Miss Bathsheba's monologue after the devastation of the storm. "That's the most important thing I can ever teach y'all," she tells Hushpuppy and her friends. "Y'all gotta learn to take care of people smaller and sweeter than you are." Furthermore, and unlike, for example, the disjointed geography in *Winter's Bone*, which renders cooperation and solidarity almost impossible, *Beasts'* focus on community and collaboration is also echoed in the film's landscape. The film is replete with instances of social gatherings and council—in the school building, the bar, and the "square" in front of it—which clearly mark the community as a polity or *Landschaft* in Olwig's definition. If we think of, for example, the strong identification of the Bathtub residents with their place and the rituals and festivities connected to it, we can certainly apply Olwig's notion that customary law is "inscribed and memorized in the material fabric of the *Landschaft*."[84]

Could this *Landschaft* also be described as an "anarchist commune"? As the film remains vague about the Bathtub's actual structure and is generally anchored in traditional social, particularly gender structures, this is certainly far-fetched. However, if we again turn to Reclus who, as Clark and Martin argue, generally remained vague in the "details of future social organization" in his writings, we might understand the film's "anarchism," like Reclus', more as an "inspiring social

82 Lieber, "Spaces of Communal Misery," 189.

83 Peter Marshall, *Demanding the Impossible. A History of Anarchism* (New York: HarperCollins, 1993), 14.

84 Olwig, *The Meanings of Landscape*, 27.

ideal that could give direction to present-day struggles."[85] Clark and Martin argue that for Reclus, "the achievement of anarchy thus means simply the creation of a[n] [. . .] egalitarian society to replace the existing oppressive, hierarchical, and competitive one."[86] This is clearly suggested in the film's final scenes which refute Lieber's asserted indiscernibility between the film's political landscape and right-wing libertarianism. Even if the film hardly thinks through the implications of communal organization and political collectivism, it is indeed flying the "black flag of anarchy" in the sense that it follows Reclus' "dialectical view of the relationship between humanity and nature and [. . .] [his] grasp of the importance of nondomination."[87] How is this reflected, then, in the film's final images which Candaele criticizes in his above-quoted article?

The film's final scenes take place after Wink's body is cremated in a funeral pyre floating on a boat into the bayou—mirroring Ree's father's watery grave in *Winter's Bone*. As the Bathtub residents' funeral prayer can be heard in the background, Hushpuppy stares out into the bayou. Then, her voice-over sets in, culminating in the passage: "I see that I'm a little piece of a big, big universe. And that makes things right. When I die, the scientists of the future, they're going to find it all. They're gonna know that once there was a Hushpuppy that lived with her daddy in the Bathtub." As she speaks off-screen, the remaining "beasts" of the Bathtub march towards the camera on the washed-out road to the mainland. Waves are licking at the asphalt, seemingly about to flood the road for good this time (see Fig. 11). The group of Bathtub residents are led by Hushpuppy and three other young girls which suggests, in concert with the symbolic death of the overbearing father, a distinctively female future for their unspecified movement.

On the one hand, the film's ending is unsatisfying. *Leave No Trace's* ending, by comparison, gives some concrete insight into the community's strategies in coping with their marginal position. By contrast, *Beasts'* final image leaves its community in disarray on a crumbling stretch of land and seems to naively acknowledge their self-destructive denial of government aid, as Sarah McFarlan argues, "as a powerful form of agency and an outright disregard of the [. . .] capitalistic [. . .] factors that precipitate climate change."[88] Unlike *Leave No Trace*, *Beasts* thus builds on a romanticized vision of rural poverty, yet ultimately fails to imagine *either* a bold utopian vision *or* a more practical, realistic approach to everyday life in the face of ecological threat and deep poverty.

85 Clark and Martin, *Anarchy, Geography, Modernity*, 54.

86 Ibid.

87 Ibid., 27.

88 McFarlan, "The Universe Unravelled," 70.

Fig. 11: The "beasts" march towards the camera in the final image of *Beasts of the Southern Wild* (Benh Zeitlin, 2012).

On the other hand, *Beasts'* ending seems to transmit that even when the Bathtub finally disappears into the bay, its anarchist vision of landscape will live on and serve to counter neoliberalism's "governing rationality" that is visually reflected in the sterile, white space of the "processing center."[89] As Hushpuppy and her friends are walking towards the camera, they appear to be heading towards us, out of the screen, and into the real world. This chimes with Silvia Federici's argument that resistant acts of landscaping which "are created under emergency conditions do not disappear without leaving some traces."[90] While she makes this argument in the context of political movements, the same could be said about the Bathtub since it similarly contains "a perspective anticipating in an embryonic way a world beyond capitalism."[91] Furthermore, the film's magical, heightened mise-en-scène and its childlike perspective chime with Federici's concept of "re-enchanting the world" which she describes as "the discovery of reasons and logics other than those of capitalist development."[92] This, she claims, is "a practice that [. . .] is central to most anti-systemic movements and a precondition for resistance to exploitation."[93] Just like the film's "enchanted" landscape, its elliptic ending en-

---

89 Brown, *Undoing the Demos*, 30.

90 Federici, *Re-enchanting the World*, 5.

91 Ibid., 4.

92 Ibid., 188.

93 Ibid.

courages its viewers to reflect on more inclusive ways of thinking about human interaction with the environment and resistance to exploitation. While one can be justifiably suspicious of the film's off-hand assumption of, as Nyong'o describes it, a "color-blind planetary solidarity in the face of climate change," its employment of landscape emerges as a striking contribution to a growing awareness of the crises caused by neoliberal capitalism and the role landscape plays both in its mechanisms of marginalization and its potential contestation.[94]

94 Nyong'o, "Little Monsters," 255–256.

Chapter Seven
Vestiges of Oppression: *Ballast* (2008)

By situating its narrative about Black rural poverty in the Mississippi Delta, Lance Hammer's debut feature *Ballast* taps into a complex history of Black life in the US South and its cinematic representations. In US popular discourse, the Delta, a flat stretch of land situated between the Mississippi and the Yazoo River in the northwest of the state, has developed over time into a shorthand for both "the rural South" as a culturally constructed geographic entity and for African American rural life in particular. Historically, this is due to the region's concentration of large cotton plantations from the beginning of the nineteenth century onwards, which was accompanied by an exponentially growing slave population living in horrendous conditions. After the Civil War, during the Reconstruction era, and even far into the twentieth century, these conditions only changed marginally for the better, resulting in the common perception of the Delta, as James Cobb argues, "as an isolated, time-warped enclave whose startling juxtaposition of white affluence and Black poverty suggested the Old South legacy preserved in vivid microcosm."[1] Already in 1935, sociologist Rupert Vance referred to the Delta as "the deepest South," basing this description on what he euphemistically called the region's "cotton obsessed, Negro obsessed" character.[2] Today, historians such as Cobb describe the Delta at the turn of the twentieth century more accurately as "the domain of an exceptionally prosperous, powerful, and socially and politically conservative planter elite," which ruled over an oppressed class of mainly Black sharecroppers through the brutal application of the racist Jim Crow segregation laws.[3]

Throughout the twentieth century, the Delta, on the one hand, has thus been understood as a symbol for the atrocious living conditions African Americans escaped when they migrated in large numbers to urban centers after the Second World War. On the other hand, it has also functioned as a place of longing in Black culture. This positive connotation was influenced by both an abstract "lure of a mythical South," by the legacy of Black music, literature, and activism as well as by more concrete desires to maintain family ties and to lay, as literary scholar Thadious M. Davis has observed, "claim to a culture and to a region that, though

---

1 James Cobb, *The Most Southern Place on Earth: the Mississippi Delta and the Roots of Regional Identity* (Oxford: Oxford UP, 1992), vii.

2 Rupert Vance, *Geography of the South* (New York, 1935), 266, 270, quoted in Cobb, *The Most Southern Place on Earth*, 153.

3 Cobb, *The Most Southern Place on Earth*, 125.

https://doi.org/10.1515/9783110779417-008

fraught with pain and difficulty, provides a major grounding for identity."[4] These desires were in part responsible for the trend of remigration of African Americans to the South beginning in the 1970s and reaching its peak in the 1990s.

These contrasting associations "as both a place of refuge and a site of oppression" and complex historical developments have also influenced the cinematic depictions of Black life in the Delta.[5] Over the past thirty years, films as varied as *Mississippi Masala* (Mira Nair, 1991), *Down in the Delta, Once Upon a Time . . . When We Were Colored* (Tim Reid, 1996), *Mississippi Damned* (Tina Mabry, 2009), and *Mudbound* have addressed the region's significance for Black history in the United States. However, hardly any of these films focus on the dire material conditions presently existing in the Mississippi Delta. A 2012 BBC news report drastically described the region as "the poorest corner of the poorest state in America."[6] In his cultural history of the region, Cobb mentions how common derogatory terms for the impoverished Delta such as "America's Third World" or "America's Ethiopia" suggest "a region that had somehow been bypassed by the progressive [. . .] forces that seemed to have had such a positive influence on American society at large."[7] Like Cobb, economist Joyce Allen-Smith rejects these notions when she argues that this persistent poverty is "entrenched in the fabric of rural society" by the historical injustices and practices of oppression suffered by African Americans in the Delta.[8]

Ballast, made by a white director in close cooperation with local non-professional actors, is one of the very few contemporary films that registers the extent of Black poverty in the Delta and attempts to make visible Allen-Smith's notion of poverty as "entrenched" in the rural landscape during two centuries of oppression and underdevelopment. One of the film's many positive reviews described it as "the most dignified dramatization of Black poverty in America since Charles Burnett's *Killer of Sheep* (1977)."[9] As such, it differs from many other films set in the Delta (or other rural Southern places), which often either romanticize the intense emotional connection of Black characters to the physical environment or approach the region from a strictly historical perspective.

---

4 Zandria Robinson, *This Ain't Chicago. Race, Class, and Regional Identity in the Post-Soul South* (Chapel Hill: University of North Carolina Press, 2014), 3; Thadious M. Davis, "Expanding the Limits: The Intersection of Race and Region," *Southern Literary Journal 20* (Spring 1988), 6.

5 Terrence Tucker, "Healing the (Re)Constructed Self: The South, Ancestors, and Maya Angelou's *Down in the Delta*," *CLA Journal* 58:1 (2014), 92.

6 BBC.co.uk. "Poverty and Progress in the Mississippi Delta," (January 4, 2012), https://www.bbc.co.uk/news/magazine-16385337.

7 Cobb, *The Most Southern Place on Earth*, 333.

8 Allen-Smith, "Blacks in Rural America," 10.

9 Chris Fennell, "10 Great Films Set in the Deep South," *BFI* (November 14, 2013), https://www.bfi.org.uk/lists/10-great-films-set-deep-south.

Both kinds of films rely on familiar "Black southern tropes like family, history, feminine power, [. . .] land/earth and community."[10] *Ballast*, whilst not outright rejecting these tropes, is in many ways more in line with Zandria Robinson's observation that "Black southerners [are] located on the margins of both southern and Black identity" since it presents its characters as geographically and socially isolated.[11]

The film constructs the Delta as a barren, ruinous landscape to contextualize its characters' conditions of possibility both within the violent history of the region and within present intersecting identities of class and race under neoliberal capitalism. *Ballast* traces the devastating consequences of a reactionary, scenic understanding of landscape to its logical endpoint, namely when landscape entirely "ceases to be thought of in terms of historically constituted substantive polities and places."[12] The first section will look at the depiction of spatial landmarks highlighted in the film such as the radio station and the country store, which historically have special communal significance in Black Southern history. The film articulates the region's history of oppression and underdevelopment almost exclusively through its landscape. The second part of the chapter argues that *Ballast*, like other contemporary films focused on Black rural poverty, complicates an interactive understanding of landscape, in that its characters' attempted "embodied acts of landscaping" largely fail to establish an intimate relation between inhabitants and the land.[13] Finally, the absence of community and democratic institutions suggests an understanding of *Ballast* as an illustration of the argument that, as Sue Ruddick summarizes, "contemporary practices identified with neoliberalism [. . .] were already long present in the rural South" and evaluate the film's identification of the "Black Family" as a potential site of contesting rural marginalization.[14]

1 The absence of Black infrastructure

Ballast's narrative begins in the aftermath of a tragedy: a concerned neighbor (Johnny McPhail) finds petrol-station owner Lawrence (Michael J. Smith) in a state of shock. Lawrence has just discovered the body of his twin brother Darrius, who has killed himself by taking an overdose of sleeping pills, possibly in reaction

---

10 Robinson, *This Ain't Chicago*, 50.

11 Ibid., 7.

12 Olwig, *The Meanings of Landscape*, 199.

13 Lorimer, "Cultural Geography," 85.

14 Sue Ruddick, "The Sun Never Set Upon the Blues: Reading and Honouring Clyde Woods," *Antipode* (2012), https://antipodeonline.org/wp-content/uploads/2012/12/woods_3_ruddick.pdf.

to a terminal illness, as is suggested at one point. Shortly afterwards, Lawrence also attempts to commit suicide by shooting himself in the chest. He is taken to a hospital, where he is narrowly saved from death. At the same time, the late Darrius' 12-year-old son James (JimMyron Ross) gets involved with a gang of violent drug dealers. After James buys crack from them, the gang blackmails him for more money. In desperation, he robs his uncle Lawrence at gunpoint, who has just been released from the hospital. However, there is still not enough money to pay off the drug dealers who violently attack James and his mother Marlee (Tarra Riggs) in response. Afraid of further repercussions, Marlee moves them into Darrius' house, which stands directly opposite of Lawrence's. Marlee's relationship with her brother-in-law is initially fraught due to a past fallout after Darrius abandoned her and her son. Over the course of the film, however, Marlee and Lawrence become friends again. When she is fired from her cleaning job, Lawrence provides her and James with groceries. Marlee takes up work in the twin brothers' petrol station while the still deeply traumatized, reclusive Lawrence starts home schooling James. The film's ending indicates that the three main characters form a new nuclear family. The narrative closes with the discovery that James has thrown away the bullets to Lawrence's gun in order to prevent his uncle from attempting to commit suicide again.

The film's foregrounding of landscape as a medium to mirror the characters' conditions of possibility as well as to reflect the region's "history of white brutality against black people" has been acknowledged by Hammer as well as by the film's producer, Nina Parikh.[15] In an interview with *Southern Quarterly*, Parikh explains how the film aims for "the emotion of the characters to be shown through the production design and the landscape."[16] She elaborates on the specific mise-en-scène of the physical environment the director and crew were creating when she points out that:

> [They] didn't shoot when it was sunny [. . .] [S]hooting in January and February in the Delta, it's still pretty bleak as you can see. [. . .] The place was brutally cold, but that was important to the story and had a truly cold effect on the actors and the crew.[17]

There are obvious visual parallels here to the depictions of the Missouri Ozarks in *Winter's Bone* and Upstate New York in *Frozen River*: all three films employ a stark, wintry iconography and sound design to counter popular imaginations of the rural as pastoral and to highlight their characters' hardship. It is these visual

15 Lance Hammer, "Down in the Delta," Interview by Rob Nelson, 40.

16 Parikh, "An Interview with Mississippi Film Producer Nina Parikh," Interview by Phillip Gentile, 87.

17 Ibid.

features as well as the film's slow pace, on-location production, and its employment of non-professional actors that, on a textual level, clearly identifies *Ballast* as belonging to the same tradition of regional, rural indie filmmaking as *Winter's Bone, Frozen River,* and earlier examples like *Heartland* and *Spring Night, Summer Night.*

Ballast goes further than most of these examples, however, in communicating its characters' circumstances through the landscape and only rarely through dialogue or plot and as such resembles the experimental documentary form of *Hale County This Morning, This Evening*. *Ballast* depicts the Delta as a vast expanse of fallow fields crossed by power lines, train tracks, and fences. Tree stumps, gas tanks, abandoned cars, and ruinous buildings stand under an almost constantly overcast sky. The scattered trailers and prefabricated houses are separated by long, lonely stretches of country road. Through its editing, the film imagines the Delta's geography as disrupted and fractured: characters often simply appear in certain locales without the film depicting their journey. There are very few establishing master shots or similar visual techniques employed to create a sense of place at the outset of the film. In fact, the film actively works against the forming of a coherent geographical image of its setting and instead presents the region as a loose collection of scattered locations. Even more so than in *Frozen River* and *Winter's Bone*, this appears as a geography that renders communal gatherings and collective agency nearly impossible and therefore, as I shall argue further below, denies the Delta the possibility of becoming a *Landschaft* in Olwig's sense. Even before the narrative addresses the characters' financial situations in more detail, the landscape itself already emanates a sense of deprivation, lack, and isolation.

In the depiction of its characters' living conditions, by contrast, the film is mostly subtle about visual markers of poverty and aims for an iconography that foregrounds the functional, lived-in, and preowned look of props and interiors – which, as we have seen, is common in the New Rural Cinema. It refuses to deliver images of squalor and instead focusses on the day-to-day experience of living on the breadline in a rural area lacking infrastructure. In the first longer scene set in James and Marlee's trailer home, for example, the camera focusses on James as he watches a cartoon on an old television set. To his right we can make out a hi-fi system which is old, yet functional. To his left, there is a stretch of crumbled, yellowed wallpaper visible as well as a small shelf stuffed with trinkets. The window in the background is partially covered with a crooked sun blind. The image then cuts to a profile shot of James eating cereal from a bowl. In the background, Marlee is getting ready to leave for work. The camera catches a brief glimpse of a small but clean kitchen area, pictures and mirrors hanging on the walls, a mobile heater placed centrally in the living room.

The impression conveyed here is of a single mother just barely getting by yet doing her best to provide a safe environment for her son. In contrast to the drug dealers' house briefly glimpsed a bit later, there are no signs of neglect or dilapidation here. This is a tidy, even cozy room decorated in warm colors that speaks of an ability to make do with limited means. Some luxury items such as James' Xbox gaming console as well as his small motorbike suggest a more financially stable past, possibly the time when Marlee and Darrius were still together. As will become apparent, however, this is a highly precarious situation: when Marlee is fired from her cleaning job later in the film and James is blackmailed by the gang, the threat of having no money to buy even the most essential necessities suddenly becomes very real. Even before this dramatic development, the prospect of a twenty-dollar membership fee for James' basketball club is clearly an expense that needs to be carefully considered.

As the co-owner of the petrol station and store, Lawrence's financial situation appears to be slightly more stable. His house, which is first seen from the inside after he returns from the hospital, is more spacious than Marlee's trailer. Small details such as the wood-paneled walls make this a more comfortable, yet hardly luxurious home. We later learn that Lawrence owns the property the two houses are built on which certainly provides him with more stability. According to Allen-Smith's study, this difference between Lawrence and Marlee conforms to actual socio-economic data in so far as "the poverty rate [among rural African Americans] is higher for families headed by a female with no spouse present [. . .]. If the female-headed family contains dependent children, the poverty rate is especially high."[18] As the bright red patch of his own blood left on the wall from the suicide attempt calls to mind, however, Lawrence's situation is only minimally less dire. After he returns from the hospital, traumatized and apparently unable to communicate with his neighbor, he steps out of his door and stares blankly into the flat, greyish landscape. Even if Lawrence compared to Marlee is less directly threatened by the most extreme effects of poverty—ultimately either starvation or utter vulnerability at the hands of violent gangs—he is still trapped in an impoverished, hopeless environment. One is reminded in this somber scene of Bonnie Bedics' claim that "rather than truly living, the rural poor merely exist."[19] As he stares out into the vast expanse of the Delta, the film illustrates how the absence of opportunity and hope is made solid in the physical environment.

18 Allen-Smith, "Blacks in Rural America," 12.

19 Bonnie Bedics, "The History and Context of Rural Poverty," *Human Services in the Rural Environment* 11:1 (1987), 14.

In addition to this visual, spatial approach to poverty, however, *Ballast* also illustrates, as Rob Nelson argues, how "the effects of racism are [. . .] embedded in the very landscape of the Delta."[20] The continuity of the South and particularly the Mississippi Delta as a region characterized for over two centuries by racist exploitation and oppression as well as by deep and persistent rural poverty is pointed out by Allen-Smith. She argues:

> The heavy concentration of rural Blacks in specified areas, notably the Mississippi Delta and the Black Belt, has its roots in plantation agriculture and the systems of slavery and sharecropping that provided a cheap input, labor. For decades, many counties in these areas have been among the poorest in the country.[21]

This context is visible *exclusively* in the film's landscape, not in racist acts committed by people or institutions on screen. On the contrary, the film's two white characters are both presented in a generally positive light: Dixon, Lawrence's neighbor supports him after his failed suicide attempt and the white lawyer Marlee visits after her husband's death offers free legal advice. One may wonder if the film is too forgiving towards the white population of a region that is well-known for "the pervasiveness of racial violence against Blacks" and has seen abhorrent instances of racially motivated murder far into the twentieth century.[22]

In response, one could argue that Lawrence's guarded reaction to Dixon's offers of support implicitly acknowledges this history and reflects a continuation of the "deferential and submissive role" African Americans assumed towards whites under Jim Crow rule out of fear for violent reprisal.[23] Furthermore, there is an even more expressive moment when Lawrence visits Dixon following his invitation to dinner. Dixon's house is first visible from the window of Lawrence's small bungalow. It is a large old manor possibly built in the nineteenth century and, hence, an explicit reminder of racial power structures physically persisting in the present. Hammer has commented on his intention to illustrate this contrast when he described his approach "to capture the way the geography speaks of history—the relationship between the tenant houses and the older manors that are these vestiges of a system that's dead now, but still has long fingers."[24]

As the handheld camera tracks Lawrence on his brief walk from his house to Dixon's through the dusky twilight, the brightly lit manor remains constantly out

20 Nelson, "Down in the Delta," 41.

21 Allen-Smith, "Blacks in Rural America," 9.

22 Stephen A. Berrey, "Resistance Begins at Home: The Black Family and Lessons in Survival and Subversion in Jim Crow Mississippi," *Black Women Gender & Families* 3:1 (2009), 76.

23 Ibid., 78.

24 Hammer, "Down in the Delta," Interview by Rob Nelson, 40.

of focus and appears almost like a mirage in the distance. The blurry shape of the imposing two-story structure seems both like an apparition from a traumatic past and, at the same time, like inhabiting a parallel world separated from Lawrence's everyday life. The detail that Dixon serves porterhouse steak and a bottle of red wine reinforces the class difference to the Black characters who are mostly seen eating cheap ready meals throughout the film. It is also notable that Lawrence refers to his neighbor as "Mister Dixon" whereas Dixon calls Lawrence by his first name. The connection between the historic experiences of slavery and Jim Crow as symbolized by the imposing manor, on the one hand, and the visible economic inequalities of the present, on the other hand, is however mainly represented through the use of landscape, not through overt racist actions. While Dixon emerges as a positive, helpful character, he is nevertheless unable or unwilling to escape these spatial vestiges, to use Hammer's term, of the region's racist history.

Apart from this instance of directly highlighting the discrepancies between Black and white Delta residents' living conditions, the film's landscape vision is centered on illustrating the decline of places of former collective significance to the Delta's Black community. Firstly, it is crucial to note the near total absence of agriculture in the film's mise-en-scène which takes on special significance in the context of the Delta. Whereas rural life for African Americans was for a long time equivalent to farming—first as slaves, then as only minimally more self-determined sharecroppers—the gradual transformation of the United States from "an agrarian to an urban, industrial-service economy" resulted in the fact that in the mid-1990s, "only 3.1 percent [of rural Blacks] [. . .] [were] farm residents."[25] In some places in the Delta, "between 1960 and 1984, the number of farms [. . .] fell by 90 percent" while the remaining large farms became increasingly industrialized and mechanized.[26] Social scientists contend that the long-term economic disadvantages for African Americans in rural contexts stem from the ineffectiveness of social and agricultural institutions during and after this economic shift. For example, economist Lester Thurow argues that public social institutions "did essentially nothing to plan for decline or to help those leaving agriculture" and thereby facilitated mass unemployment and wide-spread poverty.[27]

From the very first evocative image of James running towards a flock of geese on a barren, empty field the iconography of uncultivated farmland is cen-

25 Allen-Smith, "Blacks in Rural America," 9.

26 Cobb, *The Most Southern Place on Earth*, 273–274.

27 Lester Thurow, "Agricultural Institutions and Arrangements Under Fire," in *Social Science Agricultural Agendas and Strategies: Social Science Agricultural Project*, ed. G.L. Johnson (East Lansing: Michigan State UP, 1991), quoted in Allen-Smith, "Blacks in Rural America," 9.

tral to the film's portrayal of the Delta. These images carry a multitude of meanings. Not only do they suggest the decline of traditional agriculture in the rural South, but they also call to mind the traumatic history of cotton plantation slavery specific to the region. The images of fallow fields are often interspersed in between the film's more plot-driven scenes, for example directly after Lawrence's dinner with Dixon, and thus interrupt the narrative flow and draw attention to the landscape and its history. Again, this is a similar visual technique to RaMell Ross' use of cotton fields in the afore-mentioned experimental documentary *Hale County This Morning, This Evening*. While Ross' film shows the fields in rural Alabama in full bloom and juxtaposes them with the foley sounds of playing children, the effect is nevertheless similar. Both films suggest a haunted quality of the landscape, a layer of history that is impossible to escape. One of the intertitles interrupting the flow of the images in Ross' film could serve just as well as a description of *Ballast*'s post-Civil-Rights-era Delta landscape: "What happens when all the cotton is picked?" The answer the film gives is a multifaceted one. There is no sense of nostalgia as the past is fraught with injustice, yet also no sense of direction as there are no available economic or cultural opportunities. The result is an overarching feeling of stasis, of a precarious community in limbo.

One of the film's most striking images, which is also used for many of the accompanying poster designs, produces a similar effect. It shows Lawrence facing the derelict local radio station where he and his brother used to host a radio show (see Fig. 12). As the film does not use any flashbacks, we only know of this background from a single line of dialogue in which Lawrence mentions the show to James. A little later we see him visiting the dilapidated place, now clearly no longer functional. As the image's promotional use underlines, this is one of the film's central markers for the decline of its *Landschaft*. The symbolic reasons are obvious: not only does the radio station from Lawrence's perspective stand for a more hopeful time spent with his now-deceased twin brother and, therefore, for an overwhelming feeling of grief, the metaphoric dimension of radio silence also signals the creeping disintegration of community infrastructure. A third meaning is grounded in the historical importance of local radio stations for rural Black life as pointed out by Valerie Grim.

In her article on rural Black culture in the first half of the twentieth century, Grim argues that "the adoption of communication technology provided opportunity for rural African Americans to express themselves culturally and socially."[28] One of

---

28 Valerie Grim, "African American Rural Culture, 1900–1950," in *African American Life in the Rural South, 1900–1950*, ed. R. Douglas Hurt (Columbia, MO: University of Missouri Press, 2003), 125.

Fig. 12: Lawrence (Michael J. Smith) facing the derelict local radio station in *Ballast* (Lance Hammer, 2008).

her interviewees, Edward Scott, explains: "The radio was a fantastic thing 'cause we could, then, hear different things from' round the whole state and Delta."[29] Radio shows provided the Delta's residents with news, public service announcements, weather forecasts, entertainment, and communal organization as it enabled the possibility to announce "organized picnics, musicals, and parties to celebrate the positive image of Blackness."[30] Known as the birthplace of the Blues, the Delta in addition has a special affinity with African American musical traditions. The Blues as a form of music—be it in its original musical form or its more recent generic mutations into R&B and Hip-Hop—but also as its more complex interpretation namely as a diasporic "philosophical system [developed by] working-class African Americans in the nineteenth-century rural South" is another glaring absence in *Ballast*'s (aural) landscape.[31] This falls into line with the film's aim of highlighting the fractured, isolated experience of racialized marginality under neoliberalism considering, as Clyde Woods points out in his essay on "blues geography" that "the blues tradition has consistently served to unite working-class communities across different spatial scales."[32] Accordingly, Blues broadcasts were another staple of Mississippi radio stations. It is hardly an overstatement, then, when Grim argues that "the radio came to symbolize hope. [. . .] With the radio, rural African

29 Edward Scott, interview by author [date not specified], quoted in Grim, "African American Rural Culture," 125.

30 Grim, "African American Rural Culture," 125–126.

31 "'Sittin' on Top of the World.' The Challenges of Blues and Hip Hop Geography," *Black Geographies and the Politics of Place*, ed. K. McKittrick and C. Woods (Toronto: Between the Lines, 2007), 50.

32 Ibid., 53.

Americans felt less isolated; they had plugged into the rest of the world."[33] At least in the early days of radio, listening was also often a communal experience as another interviewee explains: "our friends could come over and listen. This was our recreation, and we learned something at the same time."[34]

The central image of the defunct radio station in *Ballast* therefore takes on a crucial, catastrophic meaning for the film's landscape. Certainly, the decreasing importance of radio can more generally be ascribed to the rise of technologies such as television and the internet and is as such not specific to the Mississippi Delta. Considering the historic significance of radio in the Delta and other rural areas as well as the local specificity and communal aspect of radio shows, however, the image and its devastating meaning for the culture and customs of the rural African American community become clear. Considering Grim's assertion that the introduction of the radio in the early twentieth century symbolized hope for an isolated, oppressed community, the shuttered building is a powerful indicator of hopelessness and stasis. By connecting Lawrence's personal tragedy to the demise of the radio station, the film makes this infrastructural decline felt on a direct, emotional level.

A further notable absence in the film's landscape is the church. While there is a brief mention of a nearby community center, which might be church-owned, church is neither directly brought up in dialogue nor do church buildings feature prominently in the landscape. This is significant because church was and is one of the most important places for Black rural communities and features prominently in most other film's depicting Black rural life—*Down in the Delta* is a telling example. The importance of the church for Southern Black communities in particular is immense. Generally, as Terrence Tucker points out, "African Americans have historically survived, and indeed resisted, the impact of white supremacist hegemony through the creation and maintenance of African American cultural and expressive traditions."[35] The Black church was one of the most important hubs of these traditions as even during slavery, it constituted a space in which Black communities could gather and hold (often coded) council with comparatively little interference from their white oppressors.

More specifically, it served a vital function as an organizational center for the community throughout Black history. Grim notes how "in the Mississippi Delta [. . .] the school and the church combined to play a vital role in establishing literacy" by organizing events for both children and adults where, for example, "poetry,

33 Grim, "African American Rural Culture," 126.

34 Ella Hearon, interview by author, Memphis, Tennessee, July 3, 1989, quoted in Grim, "African American Rural Culture," 126.

35 Tucker, "Healing the (Re)Constructed Self," 102.

Scripture, and stories by Black writers were read."[36] Furthermore, preachers and deacons "gave the names of families in need to those who had a surplus of food, clothes, bedcovers, and other items and who could afford to share"[37] and thereby helped to diminish the effects of poverty. Churches organized cultural events such as weddings, funerals, baptisms, and carnivals which facilitated the expression of social and religious customs and "encouraged rural African American's energy and talents in different ways."[38] Finally, "announcements, read at church in loud tones and with much energy and humor, informed those living throughout the community of [. . .] significant events [. . .]. The church association took on a carnival atmosphere."[39] The church, in many ways, was at the very center of Black rural culture.

Its absence in Hammer's film is therefore an additional indicator of how social and communal life is reduced to a bare minimum in the impoverished environment. Firstly, the above-mentioned social functions of the church are entirely absent in *Ballast*'s landscape. Social gatherings in *Ballast*, if they occur at all, are held briefly in private houses, and then quickly disperse. There is no sense of collective agency and even the thought of communal events and festivities as described by Grim seems impossible in the landscape the film captures. By extension, this suggests the at least partial collapse of the Black cultural and expressive traditions Tucker describes as modes of resistance to white supremacy.

Secondly, Grim's description of "the spirit of fellowship, celebration, and worship" associated with Black churches and the joyful "carnival atmosphere" accompanying it stands in strong contrast to *Ballast*'s overall sense of grief, numbness, and defeat.[40] It is impossible to imagine the film's Black characters engulfed in celebration. Indeed, their behavior and emotional state is mirrored in a passage from a report on rural poverty from 1967 quoted in Cobb's cultural history of the Delta. It describes northbound refugees from the plantation system under Jim Crow law as carrying with them "a chronic state of mind, a form of withdrawn, sullen behavior that the word 'depression' only begins to describe."[41] This is an apt description of how particularly Lawrence and his nephew James behave throughout the film. Therefore, it would be limiting to say that the barren land-

36 Grim, "African American Rural Culture," 114.

37 Ibid., 115.

38 Ibid., 116.

39 Ibid.

40 Ibid., 117.

41 Subcommittee on Employment, Manpower and Poverty, *Examination of the War on Poverty: First Session on Hunger and Malnutrition in America* (1067), 53, quoted in Cobb, *The Most Southern Place on Earth*, 275.

scape is merely a metaphor for their state of mind—the absence and impossibility of communal solidarity and joyful congregation contained in the landscape engenders its residents' behavior and emotions in a very real sense.

One historically significant place for rural Black communities that does feature prominently in the film, if in a different form, is what Grim calls "the country store."[42] It appears in the form of "Lucky's 49," the petrol station and convenience store Lawrence and Darrius used to run together. Paralyzed by grief, Lawrence has given up on the store at the outset of the film. Only upon Marlee's initiative do they eventually reopen the store together. The country store, as Grim points out, "was a cultural hub where [. . .] white and Black men [sic] sat on the porch discussing the latest developments."[43] Grim does explicitly not suggest that the country store porch was somehow exempt from the hegemonic racial power structures: "when both races sat together, white men initiated and dominated the conversation [. . .] The store's porch was where societal norms often reminded Black people of their place."[44] Nevertheless, the occasional absence of white people generated opportunities for council, exchange, and social interaction. For example, "Black women met on the store porch and generally conversed about their families [. . .] [F]or single adult Black women, the store porch served as a meeting place [. . .] to see who they could meet and to engage in conversations about possible relationships."[45] The store porch took such a central part in Black rural life that Grim speaks of "porch culture."[46] Therefore, it features prominently in many films about the rural South and the Delta, most recently in Dee Rees' historical drama *Mudbound*.

There are no traces left of this "porch culture" in *Ballast's* depiction of "Lucky's 49." While the store does serve as the family's best and only hope from a financial perspective, the element of a communal hub has been completely lost. The interactions Marlee and James have in the store are entirely functional. In one instance, they are selling petrol to a customer, in another scene, there is a friendly but formal conversation with the grocery delivery men. Thus, while the store possibly fulfils an important function for the rural community as a supplier of petrol and groceries, *Ballast* eschews any notions of the store porch as a meeting place. In a way, this is the final straw in the film's depiction of the area's demise from a communal, substantive perspective. The store's function here falls in line with a purely commercial, individualist rationality that provides customers

42 Grim, "African American Rural Culture," 119.

43 Ibid.

44 Ibid.

45 Ibid., 119–120.

46 Ibid., 120.

with goods and the owners with an income yet does not offer any social function extending beyond this economic basis. It does not emerge as Olwig's "symbolic heart of the landscape," where a community may establish and order the "relationships between place, space, body, and polity"[47] but only further illustrates the desolation of its landscape.

Ballast is very effective in highlighting the structural deficiencies of its landscape and positions its marginalized characters at the intersection of class and race by alluding to the region's history of oppression and underdevelopment. If anything, one may wonder if *Ballast* is not too effective in doing so. The film's relentless depiction of the landscape as monotone and barren, and its characters as numb and hopeless risks falling into line with a problematic tradition of characterizing "African American rural culture as vulgar and unexpressive."[48] If one were to read the film's narrative divorced from its historical, racial, and material background, the landscape and its residents' behavior might seemingly emerge as evidence of a rural "low culture" that is inherently uncreative and impoverished.[49] There is evidence that the film has indeed been read in such a decontextualized, post-racial way. In his review, the late film critic Roger Ebert, for example, notes after mentioning the film's Delta setting:

> Be honest. When I wrote "Mississippi Delta," you immediately thought of poor Black people. You know you did. The race of these characters has no relevance to the story. Lawrence and Marlee are not poor. Hell, they have a gas station and a store. They're having a hard time right now, because the store is closed, and they are sad and angry, but you can see from the insides of their houses that while they're far from rich, they have what they need, and a little more. James has his own motor scooter.[50]

While the review is positive and Ebert even included the film in his "Best Of 2008" list, the disavowal of the importance of class and race and the addressing of the imagined readers' stereotypes is puzzling. Seen from this demonstratively class- and color-blind perspective, the characters' "sad and angry" emotions become mere quirks, the living conditions simply expression of humble (or "low") country culture.

By concentrating entirely on the characters' everyday lives and by referring to, to use the director's own words again, the "history of white brutality against black people" only implicitly through the landscape, the film allows for such a

47 Olwig, *Landscape, Nature and the Body Politic*, 215; ibid., 214.
48 Grim, "African American Rural Culture," 110.
49 Ibid., 109.
50 Roger Ebert, "The Very Life of Life," *RogerEbert.com* (October 29, 2008), https://www.rogerebert.com/reviews/ballast-2008.

decontextualized reading.[51] However, the context of white supremacy does come to the fore, explicitly in the brief glimpse of the white neighbor's spacious home as well as implicitly through the suggested spatial contingency from slavery to contemporary Black poverty. Therefore, the film refutes notions of an *inherently* low Black rural culture and instead suggests, in accordance with Grim, that this "'low culture' evolved from the conditions in which Blacks lived" throughout history, even if this history is never explicitly mentioned.[52]

2 The Delta as scenery

The absence or abandonment of places of historical communal significance to rural African Americans in *Ballast* results in a landscape that seems largely devoid of custom or, in fact, any signs of collective dwelling. It is crucial to remember here that custom, as Olwig argues in his description of the *Landschaft*, is "inscribed in the land through physical practice. The landscape [. . .] as a physical place was thus the manifestation of the polity's local custom and common law."[53] Similarly, Ingold defines landscape as "a pattern of activities 'collapsed' into an array of features."[54] Whereas the previous section looked at the film's landscape in terms of its spatial markers of lack, this section will focus on the near absence of interactivity between residents and physical environment which is indicative of a profound alienation from their place of dwelling. While the other films discussed in this book all feature moments in which the boundaries between landscape and inhabitants' bodies seem to temporally dissolve, *Ballast* often draws attention to moments in which such attempts at incorporation fail. To use Olwig's words, this indicates that *Ballast* portrays a landscape in which the "process by which space appropriated place" is nearly completed.[55] Looking at the few other examples belonging to the New Rural Cinema which focus on Black experiences – *Dayveon, Burning Cane, Hale County This Morning, This Evening* – it further seems that there is a reluctance to embrace an interactive understanding of landscape. However, there are brief moments to be found in which *Ballast* does highlight the embodied vision of its characters and thus their active engagement with the world around them.

51 Hammer, "Down in the Delta," Interview by Rob Nelson, 40.

52 Grim, "African American Rural Culture," 109.

53 Olwig, *Landscape, Nature and the Body Politic*, 214.

54 Ingold, *The Perception of the Environment*, 198.

55 Olwig, *Landscape, Nature and the Body Politic*, 217.

Ballast opens with a short, striking scene seemingly detached from the following narrative. A shaky tracking shot shows James walking in a fallow field under an overcast sky. He is walking towards a large gaggle of geese in the process of ascending into the air. The soundtrack consists entirely of the geese's distant quacking which gains in intensity as the hundreds of birds suddenly all begin to collectively rise from the ground. When this happens, James starts to run towards the animals. Then, as if realizing he can neither reach them nor follow them into the sky, he stops and stares blankly at the disappearing birds. Abruptly, the film cuts from the scene and its now deafening soundtrack of bird calls to a silent landscape image over which the film's title is displayed in somber white letters. The prominent positioning of a scene that, considering its autonomy from the rest of the narrative, could conceivably be inserted at any point in the film, suggests its key significance for the film's landscape vision. Nelson reads the film's opening, which he compares to the famous final scene of Francois Truffaut's *Les quatre-cents coups (The 400 Blows*, 1959), as an early indication of James' "desire for freedom and community."[56] He describes the scene as "the boy running towards a school of geese as if yearning to fly."[57] James' desperate pursuit of the geese also speaks of an intense yearning to belong to a collective that, however, remains hopelessly intangible and elusive. This dynamic first scene with its shaky tracking shot and its focus on the fast-moving animals is followed by a static shot of an empty stretch of road which underlines the central themes of stasis, loneliness, and yearning from the very beginning.

This opening scene invites comparisons to various instances from the other films discussed in this book, all of which suggest a quite different relationship to both the physical environment as well as to animals. Most notably, the beekeeping scene from *Leave No Trace* comes to mind here. Both films use groups of animals to comment on the living situations of their young protagonists, yet in *Leave No Trace*, the beehive by contrast signals the protagonist's successful joining of a community. As Tom extends her hands into the hive, the bees crawl peacefully over her fingers, indicating her integration into the trailer park's polity and the dissolving of boundaries between herself and the landscape. I have pointed out similar readings for the dream sequence in *Winter's Bone*, which has Ree identify with a squirrel as her dream avatar, as well as for Hushpuppy in *Beasts*, who lives in close contact with the animals of the Bathtub and takes pleasure in listening to their heartbeats.

---

56 Nelson, "Down in the Delta,", 41.
57 Ibid.

These scenes refer to customs and tasks which suggest "the rich intimate ongoing togetherness of beings and things which make up landscapes and places, and which bind together nature and culture over time."[58] In *Ballast's* opening, however, this togetherness is interrupted: the birds fly away, the uniform greyness of the overcast sky and the muddy field suggests an invisible barrier between James and his surroundings. If landscape is, as Wylie puts forward, "the close-at-hand, that which is both touching and touched, an affective handling through which self and world emerge and intertwine," then this interactive understanding of landscape is literally out of reach in the opening of *Ballast*.[59] Furthermore, the scene draws attention to the lack of community experiences available to James and how his desire to join a community sets the film's narrative in motion: his wish to join the basketball team is initially thwarted due to his mother's limited financial means and when he engages with the only other community available to him, the gang of drug dealers, violence ensues. The departure of the birds in the opening scene is a striking illustration of the transformation of landscape from interactive, communal place to mere scenery—a "make-believe landscape" that resists interaction.[60] As mentioned before, the scene also calls to mind a similar moment in *Dayveon*, in which the young main character is attacked by a swarm of bees. Black experience of landscape here is not only isolating, but physically dangerous, a sentiment that is reflected in the violent death of Dayveon's older brother and his subsequent decision to join a violent gang.

The motif of a removed, inaccessible natural world is repeated throughout in *Ballast*, particularly in relation to animals. At the outset of the film, James seems to be surrounded by artificial imitations of animals which again stand in notable contrast to the real, tactile interspecies interactions experienced by the characters in the other films discussed here. Firstly, there are the cartoon animals James repeatedly watches on television such as, for example, a classic cartoon rendition of the old nursery rhyme character Little Bo-Peep and her sheep.[61] The short clip featured in the scene offers a brief, colorful glance into a stylized, romanticized vision of US rurality and agriculture that bears little resemblance to the barren rural landscape James inhabits. The Disneyesque pastoral idyll makes his actual

58 Cloke and Jones, "Dwelling, place, and landscape," 651.

59 Wylie, *Landscape*, 167.

60 Olwig, *Landscape, Nature and the Body Politic*, 216.

61 *Little Boy Blue* (1936). The fact that this particular cartoon is used and not a more contemporary TV show might be attributed to the free availability of the clip due its expired copyright, but certainly also links back to the time of its release when Jim Crow laws were still very much in place in the Mississippi Delta–not least because the chosen extract focusses on Little Bo-Peep's only black sheep.

physical surrounding seem like a wasteland by comparison. Secondly, the film returns twice to the image of several plastic reindeer, presumably a Christmas decoration, placed in the middle between Darrius' and Lawrence's houses. They emit a similar feeling of a "make-believe landscape" that has lost its meaningful connection to actually existing animals.[62] Both of these commodified representations of animals signify the impossibility of *Ballast's* version of the Delta's landscape to emerge as a place; if, as Wylie argues, "landscape and place conjoin intimacy, locality, and tactile inhabitation," this reciprocal relation to the land and to fellow living creatures is permanently interrupted.[63]

In order to find moments which do feature some form of interaction between the characters and their surroundings, one needs to consider the aimless, mostly solitary walks James undertakes. These walks, like the opening scene, are shot in close, shaky tracking shots which illustrate his subjective, embodied vision on the landscape around him and are dispersed throughout the film. In one scene—significantly, one of the rare moments of sunshine in this otherwise grey, rainy film—James explores an abandoned, decrepit house, playing with the former residents' left-behind furniture and personal belongings. Another moment shows him gazing blankly at the passing cargo trains, again implicitly suggesting a desire to leave his surroundings and at the same time underlining his own stasis. These scenes are significant because, as Wylie puts it, the impoverished, fragmented landscape here "ceases to be understood as a static, framed gaze, and becomes instead the very interconnectivity of eye, body, and land, a constantly emerging perceptual and material milieu."[64] The film identifies James in these moments as an active participant in the emergence of landscape mainly through his vision. Wylie summarizes this idea when he writes: "It is the fact that I belong to the landscape [. . .] that enables my seeing—it is my seeing which enables me to witness that belongingness."[65] Unlike the other case studies, *Ballast*'s protagonists' intertwining with their surroundings is illustrated almost exclusively through their gaze on the landscape.

The most interactive "intertwinings of self and world" could be said to take place on an otherwise uneventful walk James takes with his uncle and his uncle's dog, Juno.[66] Not only do we see James walking as part of a group for the first time, there is a certain sense of ease in the conversations between uncle and nephew and in the relaxed atmosphere of the walk that has been largely absent from the film up to this point. Wylie's assertion that "to speak of [. . .] gazing

62 Olwig, *Landscape, Nature and the Body Politic*, 216.
63 Wylie, *Landscape*, 167.
64 Ibid., 177.
65 Ibid., 152.
66 Ibid., 177–178.

upon landscape, is [. . .] to speak about an intertwining through which observer and observed are assembled as such" is particularly tangible here.[67] Up to this scene, most gazes on the landscape have been characterized by unfulfilled longing, grief, or nostalgia and, therefore, by a sense of alienation from the physical world. For the first time, the film suggests an "attunement with landscape" that is based both on the characters' perception of the landscape as well as on the sense of community and companionship between the two humans and their dog.[68] Significantly, the scene ends with the two characters shrouded in near-darkness, visually blending in with the landscape. James breaks up branches and throws the little pieces into a small pond. It is, at first glance, an entirely mundane, insignificant scene which, however, offers a glimpse at a minimal form of direct interaction between characters and their physical surrounding. It also serves as a first hint at the developing bond between James and Lawrence which, by extension, suggests the forming of a new nuclear family that I will explore further below.

To summarize, while there are brief moments which hint at the characters' perception of the environment as embodied landscape vision, the film's landscape generally resists the affective engagement that, for example, *Beasts'* vision of the Louisiana bayou foregrounds so intensely. In order to grasp why this distinct separation between people and their surroundings is significant for the film's political implications, it is worth briefly reiterating the difference between place and space as defined by Tuan and Olwig. Place, as Tuan argues in his influential study on space and place, "is a unique entity [. . .] [that] has a history and meaning. Place incarnates the experiences and aspirations of a people."[69] Olwig builds his exploration of *Landschaft* and polity as instances of place on this definition and goes on to argue that gradually, space has supplanted place in our current understanding of landscape. The idea of landscape as space—meaning as scenery, map, and other perspectival representations—is utilized to exercise top-down, hegemonic power and control, according to Olwig, whereas place suggests affective attachment to landscape as well as an active local community. The fact that the characters in *Ballast* are largely unable to interact and engage with their environment, let alone experience an intense blurring of boundaries as Hushpuppy or Ree do, suggests the absence of "places" in *Ballast*'s version of the Delta and presents an environment that has become pure "space." The film thereby draws attention to the absence of communal life and custom, which speaks of a lingering

67 Ibid., 178.

68 Ibid., 152.

69 Tuan, "Space and Place," 213.

influence of the historic systems of control "entrenched in the fabric of rural society."[70] James and his family live in an environment that not only appears as impoverished and lacking infrastructure, but one that largely prevents them from becoming part of a collective signified by the impossibility of a bodily, tactile engagement with their surroundings.

In addition, this reluctance to picture Black characters as visually blending in with their surroundings, which we can also observe in some of the other films focusing on Black protagonists, might be partially rooted in a reaction against the history of racist thinking which often reduced enslaved Black people to mere elements of the environment. This history problematizes the notion of embodied acts of landscaping from a Black perspective. The sheer "masses of Blacks who toiled on the great estates of the Delta" around the turn of the twentieth century, for example, were commonly portrayed as a somehow natural occurrence embedded in the physical environment.[71] Cobb quotes from the 1910 Census of Agriculture's conclusion:

> The plantation system is probably more firmly fixed in the Yazoo-Mississippi Delta than in any other area of the South. The fertile soil and climatic conditions favorable for cotton raising, together with the large negro population, make the plantation the dominant form of agricultural organization in the Delta.[72]

The "fertile soil" and "the large negro population" are both presented here as economically advantageous features of the landscape that arise from a seemingly rational, scientific observation of landscape. In fact, they are indicative of a white supremacist view of landscape as scenery. Dissolving the boundaries "between person and place, or between self and the landscape" is therefore a potentially more fraught prospect from an African American perspective.[73]

Nevertheless, it is worth noting here, there are older films which do suggest such an interactive, historical relation between the Southern landscape and Black bodies. For example, Maya Angelou's *Down in the Delta* sees the South, as Tucker summarizes, as "an important regenerative space for African Americans, a place where Blacks can re-establish connections to their roots and encounter a supportive community that pushes back against the crushing isolation [. . .] of Northern, urban spaces."[74] Hence, Aneglou's film makes for a productive comparison to *Bal-*

70 Allen-Smith, "Blacks in Rural America," 10.

71 Cobb, *The Most Southern Place on Earth*, 98.

72 Department of Commerce, Bureau of the Census, *Thirteenth Census of the United States* 5 (Washington 1914), 884, quoted in Cobb, *The Most Southern Place on Earth, 98.*

73 Ingold, *The Perception of the Environment*, 56.

74 Tucker, "Healing the (Re)Constructed Self," 92.

last for several reasons. Firstly, it is striking to see how two films made exactly 20 years apart from each other conjure up such intensely different visions of the same setting, both from a visual as well as from a symbolic perspective. Secondly, there is an equally notable difference in how both films engage with the historical importance of Southern rural landscape for Black identity through respectively emphasizing or denying their characters' bodily connection to the Delta landscape. The differences between the two films' use of landscape in their portrayal of marginalized communities serve to emphasize *Ballast*'s affiliation to a New Rural Cinema in the US.

Down in the Delta envisions the return of a single mother and her two troubled children from a drug- and crime-riddled Chicago cityscape to the pastoral family home in the Delta. The natural environment is portrayed in luscious, golden-tinted colors and the landscape is characterized by many of the places and institutions—the church, the local diner, etc.—that are absent in *Ballast*. Furthermore, there are several moments which suggest an intimate entanglement between characters and their environment. For example, a central scene revolves around a tree planted on the family's enslaved ancestor's grave, which reaffirms the family's ties to the land and their survival in spite of the historic trauma of slavery and racism. *Down in the Delta* "celebrates the rural South and its potential in the post-Civil Rights moment to act as regenerative space" by establishing a historical, deeply affective connection between the landscape and Black bodies.[75] However, as Robinson points out, the film entirely "obscures [. . .] the prevalence of southern Black poverty" and only refers tentatively to the reality of Southern communities as "relatively impoverished places, devastated by unemployment and deindustrialization."[76]

Ballast's reluctance, then, to engage in romanticized notions of characters being "reborn in the pastoral space" through a tactile rediscovery of Southern roots, can be understood in the context of these socio-economic realities which are absent in Angelou's film.[77] This insistence on "actually existing neoliberalism," to use Brenner and Theodore's term, and its "socially regressive and politically volatile trajectories of [. . .] spatial change" is what marks out *Ballast* as a film following a new perspective on US rurality that seeks to make rural decline and poverty visible on screen.[78] The absence of bodily interaction, which is at the core of Olwig's substantive understanding of landscape as a social category, is directly related to the devastation of rural communities under neoliberal capitalism

75 Ibid., 101.

76 Robinson, *This Ain't Chicago*, 51; ibid., 53.

77 Tucker, "Healing the (Re)Constructed Self," 95.

78 Brenner and Theodore, "Cities," 349.

that becomes visible in *Ballast*'s landscape. In contrast to *Beasts*, which envisions a rebellious Black protagonist embedded in a multi-racial community struggling to defend their customs and polity, *Ballast* depicts a deindustrialized landscape shaped by "two centuries of active underdevelopment" inhabited by isolated characters apparently unable to become active in the community, let alone resistant to the forces of marginalization.[79] The miniscule traces of an embodied landscape vision featured in the film, however, also point towards a similarity with *Down in the Delta*: both films center on the Black family as the main institution of resilience, if not resistance to white supremacist, capitalist power structures embedded in the Southern landscape.

3 The Black family — protection and subversion

In the near absence of a local community and social institutions, family in *Ballast* becomes central as an entity that provides some form of protection from the lawlessness and impoverishment of the Delta's landscape. The film begins just after the suicide of Darrius, James' father, whose lifeless body is seen for a brief moment when Dixon comes to check in on Lawrence at the beginning of the film. Therefore, similar to *Winter's Bone*, *Frozen River*, *Shotgun Stories*, *Joe*, and other films of the New Rural Cinema, the death or disappearance of a problematic father figure forces the characters to rethink their notion of family and to assume roles previously unfamiliar to them. In *Ballast*, it is Darrius' twin brother, Lawrence who has to come to terms with his responsibility for his nephew and sister-in-law. This focus on the family in *Ballast* falls into line with what Stephen Berrey has termed "the Black family" and its history as "a critical institution for protecting children from racial violence and for planting the seeds of subversion."[80] The Black family, in Berrey's definition, goes back to protection from the experiences of "lynching, rape, and other forms of physical violence endured by African Americans in the Jim Crow South" and crucially included "not only parents but additional relatives, neighbors, and other adults in the community."[81] The Black family in *Ballast* provides a similar function in response to the effects of neoliberal marginalization in the rural South. These effects culminate, as Ruddick summarizes, in the destruction of "any alternative infrastructures or organizational

79 Ruddick, "The Sun Never Set," 4.

80 Berrey, "Resistance Begins at Home," 66.

81 Ibid., 65–66.

supports developed by the Black community," some of which have been addressed in the first part of this chapter and must thus be understood as the outcome of a systemic form of racism under neoliberal capitalism.[82] I will finally focus on the question how effective the subversion of these neoliberal practices might be within the film's context of the nuclear family considering that neoliberal ideology places "an idealized family at its center" and the film, therefore, risks feeding into these reactionary tendencies.[83]

Singh has defined racism under neoliberalism as a form of prejudice that eschews overt claims of racial inferiority and is instead "filtered through a logic of neoliberal discipline that vehemently opposes government intervention into the 'natural' workings of the marketplace."[84] It has worked to undermine programs designed to achieve racial equality in historically underdeveloped Black communities such as the Mississippi Delta on the basis of neoliberalism's "'one size fits all' model of policy implementation that assumes that identical results will follow the imposition of market-oriented reforms."[85] Inequality is thereby divorced from spatial and historical differences and is implicitly and effectively blamed on those struggling. Woods argues that such "post-racial rhetoric is one of the pillars of neo-liberalism [sic]. It is the glue that binds the dominant economic powers with the billions who are still suffering the effects of historic racialized colonialism and modern forms of marginalization."[86] This resonates with the world presented by *Ballast* in which white supremacy as racist aggression is completely absent yet, as argued above, manifested in the landscape through the absence of Black social institutions and the lingering architectural influence of the plantation regime.

In his article on "blues geography," Woods goes as far as claiming that the economic structure and social organization of the Mississippi plantation regime "provided neo-liberalism with its core organizing principles."[87] Specifically, he argues that "the fragmented neo-plantation model of governance has been rebuilt and expanded globally based on the privatization of critical state resources, the elimination of state subsistence guarantees, and the devolution of national and local state responsibilities."[88] Cobb makes a similar point without explicitly referring to neoliberalism:

82 Ruddick, "The Sun Never Set," 4.

83 Kim Moody, *Workers in a Lean World* (New York: Verso, 1997), 120.

84 Singh, *Black is a Country*, 11.

85 Brenner and Theodore, "Cities," 353.

86 Woods, "'Sittin' on Top of the World," 49.

87 Ibid., 56.

88 Ibid., 57.

> Recent statistical trends pointing to rapidly widening gaps in income and opportunity throughout the United States suggest that the economic and social polarization that is synonymous with the Mississippi Delta may be observed wherever [. . .] the pursuit of wealth [. . .] overwhelms the ideals of equality, justice, and compassion [. . .]. As socioeconomic disparity and indifference to human suffering become increasingly prominent features of American life, it seems reasonable to inquire whether the same economic, political, and emotional forces that helped to forge and sustain the Delta's image as the South writ small may one day transform an entire nation into the Delta writ large.[89]

The world Cobb and Woods describe here is visible in the physical environment of *Ballast*'s vision of the Delta. This is a world from which the State and its institutions have receded, in which rural community infrastructure is devastated due to joblessness and, more generally, neoliberalism's "core-periphery polarization and socio-spatial inequality" that favors the urban as the space for its "forces of production."[90] Woods goes on to argue that the Blues, not only as a form of musical expression but as a "philosophical system [developed by] working-class African Americans in the nineteenth-century rural South," enables "the construction of new communities, institutions, and social practices" that continues to provide an "antithesis of the plantation tradition and all of its manifestations."[91] As we have seen, however, this idea of the Blues as a potential cultural site of resistance is absent from *Ballast*'s landscape of "actually existing neoliberalism," meaning the "embeddedness of neoliberal restructuring projects" within the physical environment.[92]

The only available institution within the film's world that provides safety and stability is the family, consisting in this case of a mother, her son, and the deceased father's twin brother. The film presents only two other possible communities which are either inaccessible or undesirable for the protagonists. There is, on the one hand, the community of affluent whites represented by Dixon and the lawyer. On the other hand, there are the drug dealers, who are not overly demonized—even though one can certainly criticize the film for their one-dimensional portrayal, especially in comparison to *Dayveon*'s empathic view on criminal life at the margins—yet clearly constitute a precarious collective based solely around profit and, if necessary, brutal violence. The film's overall narrative ark, the re-establishment of a nuclear family, is presented as crucial for the protagonists' safety and, more specifically, for James' urge to join a community. It is striking how the film narrows down this community to blood-relatives only, however.

89 Cobb, *The Most Southern Place on Earth*, 333.

90 Brenner and Theodore, "Cities," 353.

91 Woods, "'Sittin' on Top of the World," 50; ibid., 59; ibid., 56.

92 Brenner and Theodore, "Cities," 351.

There is a brief moment, namely when we see from James' perspective how Marlee learns of her husband's death, in which the film hints at a community existing outside of the family. James watches from within the trailer as a man and a woman deliver the tragic message. Since James and the camera are positioned behind the window, their conversation is inaudible and clearly removed and separated from the domestic space of the family. The couple speak to Marlee, give her a brief hug, then return to their truck to drive away. These unnamed friends or neighbors do not reappear and are never mentioned again throughout the film.

As mentioned above, Berrey's concept of the Black family explicitly includes "not only parents but additional relatives, neighbors, and other adults in the community."[93] Clearly, this openness is reduced to relatives in *Ballast*. Berrey situates this concept within the historical context of the South from the late nineteenth century onwards in which the Jim Crow segregation laws were "cemented [. . .] within virtually every aspect of Southern life. Indeed, Jim Crow rule represented far more than a series of laws and customs, or of political and economic practices" and instead permeated everyday life to an overwhelming degree.[94] In this culture of inequality and simmering violence, the Black family "functioned as a critical institution for protecting children from racial violence and for planting the seeds of subversion."[95] If one assumes, as Woods does, that certain structures of oppression have persisted in the rural South from the plantation regime to the post-Civil Rights present, it seems logical to conclude that traces of Berrey's concept of the Black family as a protective, subversive institution have survived as well to counter these circumstances. Considering that direct racist aggression is absent from the film, this will inevitably take on different forms than the ones described by Berrey in relation to everyday life under Jim Crow. Let us look at both of these aspects—protection and subversion—separately in order to gauge how and if *Ballast* engages with them.

The protective aspect of the family in *Ballast* takes several forms in relation to the infrastructural devastation surrounding them. First, there is the literal protection from physical harm which is most explicitly encountered in James' confrontation with the drug dealers. After the gang physically attack mother and son, Marlee moves them to Darrius' house in order to protect them from further assaults. Indeed, the drug dealers do not make an appearance in the film after this. Similarly, James' use of crack which he has bought from the gang is never mentioned again, either. Seen on its own, this narrative development does suggest a

93 Berrey, "Resistance Begins at Home," 66.
94 Ibid., 69.
95 Ibid., 66.

socially conservative position in which the domestic space serves as a safe haven from violent external forces. This is reinforced by the impersonal depiction of the drug dealers, who appear as a collective of aggressive Black men and are never granted their own motivations. Without denying the problematic nature of this depiction, this is somewhat qualified by the film's landscape. The way the film places the drug dealers within the decaying architecture of the Delta—James first encounters them in an abandoned house strewn with rubbish and later in a dark, neglected flat—does not portray them as faceless antagonists, but rather as one of the potential futures awaiting James. Their aggression is presented as a result of the conditions, namely the "dismantling of public infrastructure supporting families [and] children" that the family in *Ballast* seeks to mitigate.[96]

This mitigation is primarily reflected in Marlee's efforts to provide James with an education and a more stable family unit. It is crucial that both aspects develop out of Marlee's decision to home-school her son and her plan to split the teaching between herself and Lawrence since they "can't be worse than the teachers you already have," as she puts it. Presumably, she is referring to an inadequate local education system here, which the film does not investigate further. We only get a brief glimpse of James' school when Marlee delivers the paperwork to deregister him. Nevertheless, this is a striking illustration of how "gender subordination is intensified [. . .] by neoliberalism"[97] as the dismantling of public infrastructure "penalizes women to the extent that they remain disproportionately responsible for those who cannot be responsible for themselves."[98] Brown argues that it is precisely this compensation for inadequate social infrastructure by women that makes "familialism [. . .] an essential requirement, rather than an incidental feature" of the neoliberal privatization and elimination of public services.[99] The protection from the presumably negative influence of an underfunded education system James' home-schooling seeks to provide thus demonstrates the role of the family in neoliberal ideology as the sole provider of the "practices that make and sustain human life."[100]

Furthermore, this again calls to mind Berrey's research into the function of the Black family under Jim Crow and underlines the continuity of oppression in the rural South suggested by Woods. Berrey argues that under Jim Crow "beyond the involvement of some Black teachers, at times parents went to great lengths to

96 Brown, *Undoing the Demos*, 105.
97 Ibid.
98 Ibid.
99 Ibid., 106.
100 Ibid., 107.

overcome the educational setbacks imposed on Black schools."[101] While Berrey is referring here to the setbacks connected to segregation and to the possibility in home-schooling "to introduce children to positive images and Black role models," which are absent in *Ballast*, this is an indication that the protective function of the Black family persists in the film.[102] The difference is that in the Delta of the twenty-first century *Ballast* depicts, the Black family serves as "the invisible infrastructure sustaining a world of putatively self-investing human capitals," where visible social infrastructure has largely disappeared.[103]

Finally, it is worth noting that the protective function of the family in *Ballast* extends beyond James' well-being and explicitly extends to Marlee and Lawrence as well. Thanks to the newly formed family union, Marlee is able to escape the drug dealers' threats and to start work in her husbands' store, thus escaping her precarious former employment as a cleaner. However, I want to focus here specifically on Lawrence, whose storyline opens and closes the film: it begins with his failed, but nearly successful suicide attempt in the aftermath of his brother's death and ends with another suicide attempt which is, however, prevented by James. After Lawrence has attempted to become intimate with Marlee, an attempt she categorically rejects, he sinks back into the deep depression that he had just begun to escape. He locks himself in his house and when he finally does answer Marlee's knocking on the door asks her to "please leave me alone." When she has left for the store, he visits the abandoned radio station, staring silently at the crumbling building that symbolizes both his personal loss and grief as well as the hopelessness and stasis of his surroundings. This might be the moment, we later realize, when he again decides to commit suicide. In a brief cut-away scene, we see James approaching Lawrence's house through the pouring rain. Later, Lawrence sits silently in his dark flat, then gets up to get his gun. Upon realizing that the bullets are missing, he rushes over to the neighboring house, grabs James violently by the neck and asks his nephew to show him where he hid the bullets. James leads him across the adjacent muddy field where they find the bullets in a puddle, wet and unusable (see Fig. 13).

The scene is crucial, not only because it is such an affective, understated display of James' emotional intelligence and care, but because it is arguably the only moment in the film where community, family, and land physically converge. The close-up image of the bullets, half-buried in the wet earth and muddy water is evocative in a way that resists an easy interpretation. Perhaps it is best to under-

101 Berrey, "Resistance Begins at Home," 80.
102 Ibid.
103 Brown, *Undoing the Demos*, 107.

Fig. 13: Lawrence's bullets in a puddle, wet and unusable. *Ballast* (Lance Hammer, 2008).

stand it as a mirror image of the above-mentioned scene from *Down in the Delta,* which focuses on the tree planted by one of the family's enslaved ancestors. In both cases, the Delta's soil represents the survival of a traumatized Black family in spite of their hostile surroundings as well as some form of belonging and mutual care. Certainly, the scene in *Ballast* is much less romanticized and symbolic than its counterpart, and focuses more on the factual, acute rescue of one family member from serious harm, probably death. Therefore, I would not go as far as Nelson in his assessment that this scene is indicative of the protagonists' "spiritual revitalization."[104] However, it does chime with Berrey's assertion that "the Black family served as a source for nurturing and protecting Black children" in response to the everyday experience of oppression and hopelessness and expands this protective function to the adults as well.[105]

Can this depiction of the Black family also be understood as equivalent to the subversive tendencies Berrey ascribes to it in the context of the Jim Crow era? Berrey claims that while it is difficult to draw a direct historical connection from the racial lessons experienced by Black children in the family to concrete political resistance later in life, it is "nonetheless clear that the Black family played a pivotal role for many Black children in establishing a foundation for challenging the dominant ideologies, laws, and customs. The Black family not only nurtured and protected, but it also promoted subversion."[106] This is because in the family context, they heard "messages that rejected ideas of racial inferiority" and, in a more general

104 Nelson, "Down in the Delta," 41.
105 Berrey, "Resistance Begins at Home," 76.
106 Ibid., 84.

sense, because "the lines between family and community [. . .] [were] blurred as various individuals took on the responsibilities of nurturing [. . .] the children" thus producing the experience of a solidary collective.[107] Both aspects are clearly absent from *Ballast*'s depiction of Black family life. The family members do not discuss or comment on their living situation in a way that would suggests the rejection of dominant ideologies, let alone their overt subversion. Furthermore, as the family here is a minimal social unit limited to close relatives only, there is no sense of a solidary local community, especially considering the neighbors' brief, silent appearance discussed above which seems to remain on a purely functional level.

The only attempt at resistance to the forces of marginalization, perhaps, lies in the continued cooperation between Lawrence and Marlee even after she has rejected his sexual advances. Especially the final scene suggests, as Francesco Sticchi puts forward in his discussion of the family under neoliberalism, the family as "a minimal space of solidarity and mutual care where precarious subjectivities try to negotiate and respond to their marginality."[108] In the scene, Marlee drives away from their house to go to work at the petrol station with James in the passenger seat. Just when they have reached the road, Marlee reverses the car. The next shot shows that she has returned to invite Lawrence to come with them, visibly to James' contentment. The newly united family drives off and the film ends with a black screen. The fact that this is a social unit emphatically based around cooperation and mutual care, not around traditional heteropatriarchal values positions the film's ending as a minimal attempted resistance to dominant ideologies and circumvents an affirmation of the traditional nuclear family. As such, we can do away with the distinction between protection and subversion within *Ballast*'s vision of the Black family; protection here is the only subversive act available to its characters.

The film draws attention to questions "about what holds families or societies together in neoliberal regimes."[109] Situated within a fractured landscape that offers no possibilities to congregate with others and to strengthen the "link between community [. . .] and place," an ambiguous form of family arises in *Ballast* that is neither equivalent to Berrey's historical concept of an open collective including neighbors and friends, nor to the idealized nuclear family of conservative ideology.[110] The film's ambiguous representation of the family thus reflects neoliberal ideology's "fundamental incoherence" in relation to family as a social unit, which

---

107 Ibid.; ibid., 83.

108 Francesco Sticchi, *Mapping Precarity in Contemporary Cinema and Television. Chronotopes of Anxiety, Depression, Expulsion/Extinction* (London: Palgrave Macmillan, 2021), 140.

109 Brown, *Undoing the Demos*, 102.

110 Olwig, *The Meanings of Landscape*, 23.

Brown has pointed out: "if the family is the ultimate operative unit, the site of freedom, and the perspective from which we judge social arrangements, then the individual cannot be, and vice versa."[111] One might even go as far as to interpret the film's enigmatic title as a reference to the incoherent position family takes in neoliberal ideology: followed to its logical endpoint, the neoliberal individual would have to view vulnerable family members such as Lawrence as mere ballast. However, family in *Ballast* is a protective arrangement in absence of social infrastructure, which the film makes clear in its construction of landscape. That its members provide care to each other despite this somewhat functional arrangement, is the small form of everyday resistance the film holds out towards the overwhelming forces of white supremacy, neoliberal restructuring, and devastation embedded in the landscape of the Mississippi Delta.

111 Brown, *Undoing the Demos*, 100; ibid., 100–101.

Conclusion
Towards a "Landscape Consciousness"?

In this book, I have examined the representation of rural poverty in recent US indie cinema as well as developing a novel way of analyzing cinematic landscapes that goes beyond the pictorial and foregrounds interactivity and communality. I mainly base this understanding of landscape on texts by Tim Ingold and Kenneth Olwig. Both argue for an approach to landscape that refutes fixed notions of "setting" or "scenery" and instead favor the idea of landscape as the constantly evolving result of the interplay between habitation, or dwelling, and environment. These two perspectives align in what I have called the New Rural Cinema, a recent cycle of US indie films that emphasizes such relational, social approaches to landscape in order to find ways of relating the deep rural poverty experienced across the nation. The novelty of this cycle emerges upon examining previous representations of US rurality and rural poverty, which, whilst linked to the new films in many ways, have tended to focus on a scenic view of the US landscape. This scenic approach is limited insofar as it ignores, in the best case, the cooperative, communal aspect of landscape and is thus caught in a static understanding of the environment that inevitably reproduces essentialist landscape tropes. At its worst, landscape scenery may be used to actively advocate for nationalist, exclusionary ideologies that seek to mystify the interactive historicity of the landscape.

The intervention in cinematic landscape studies this book undertakes, consists furthermore in the identification of an enduring tradition of landscape thinking based on interactivity and collectiveness that finds expression in the four films discussed here and the cycle at large. Their communal landscape visions make visible the connections between Olwig's historical description of the Renaissance European *Landschaften*, Reclus' anarchist conception of landscape as well as Silvia Federici's understanding of the commons. This common thread can best be summarized as the radically democratic, socialist potential of creating communal places resistant to forces of exploitation and domination through conscious interactivity between community and environment. For example, Federici argues that the recent intensification of social and economic injustice as well as the dismantling of the public sphere forces "millions of people to act collectively" and names the Occupy movement and the protests against the Dakota Access Pipeline as two contemporary examples of collective social action in the United States.[1] She continues:

1 Federici, *Re-enchanting the World*, 5.

https://doi.org/10.1515/9783110779417-009

> Appropriations of urban and rural spaces are being constantly re-enacted, resulting in an increasing number of settlements where space and resources are shared, decisions about daily reproduction are collectively taken, and family relations are redefined.[2]

Even if these developments are temporary, she argues, "the *commoning activities* that are created under emergency conditions do not disappear without leaving some traces."[3] The term "commoning activities" demonstrates the compatibility of her understanding of the commons with Olwig's conception of the *Landschaft* as formed through custom, community, and bodily activity. This, in turn, leads back to Reclus' formulation of the interactivity of landscape:

> Every people gives, so to speak, new clothing to the surrounding nature. By means of its fields and roads, by its dwellings and every manner of construction, by the way it arranges the trees and the landscape in general, the populace expresses the character of its own ideals.[4]

Reclus also stresses the importance of everyday life in his anarchist conception of landscape, specifically among marginalized people: "Where anarchist practice really triumphs is in the course of everyday life among common people who would not be able to endure their [. . .] struggle for existence if they did not engage in spontaneous mutual aid."[5] There is, thus, a long-running tradition of collective, solidary landscape thinking (and practice) that these films bring to light and reinterpret for the contemporary context.

Furthermore, I have argued that the four exemplary films of the New Rural Cinema cycle—*Ballast*, *Winter's Bone*, *Beasts of the Southern Wild*, and *Leave No Trace*—employ similar stylistic and narrative devices to respond to the challenge of capturing experiences of marginalization under neoliberalism, where old forms of resistance such as unionization, industrial action, or protest do not seem viable anymore. In addition, the four films are connected to each other by their depiction of young protagonists searching for community in rural landscapes that often appear as ruinous and impoverished. All of them include central moments of entanglement with the landscape which, in some cases, herald the successful integration into solidary communities, yet remain more ambiguous in others.

The individual chapters have laid out if and how such "embodied acts of landscaping" as forms of resistance to neoliberal marginalization can work in their respective environments. The chapter on *Winter's Bone* sought to demonstrate how

2 Ibid.

3 Ibid. Emphasis added.

4 Reclus, *The History of a Mountain*, quoted in Clark and Martin, *Anarchy, Geography, Modernity*, 26.

5 Reclus, "L'Anarchie," quoted in Clark and Martin, *Anarchy, Geography, Modernity*, 128.

the film establishes a solidary female community that, through a radical, bodily act of cooperation, manages to resist the forces of marginalization by successfully protecting the main character Ree's family home from repossession. However, the film also concedes that this cooperation is kept from potentially developing into more Utopian practices by both the deindustrialized, fragmented terrain of the Ozark mountain community as well by an alliance of patriarchal traditions and neoliberalism's inherent gender hierarchy. In the chapter on *Leave No Trace*, I have argued that the film presents its viewers with various types of landscape that reveal prevalent attitudes to rural landscape in the United States. The opening setting Forest Park in particular invites reflections on the problematic "invention" of wilderness in the United States by means of violent displacement—the forceful removal of all traces of human, particularly indigenous habitation, and interaction. The film's final setting, the RV park, by contrast, imagines a collective, hospitable relation to the environment and arguably emerges as the most positive, communal landscape vision discussed in this book as well as in the New Rural Cinema at large.

Beasts of the Southern Wild encapsulates the notion of landscape as a "milieu of involvement" precisely by diverging from the realist style employed by the other three films.[6] I have shown that the film's spectacular, heightened images of the Louisiana bayou landscape transmit the idea that landscape arises through the interaction of community and environment. At the same time, it extends this concern with landscape interactivity to both ecological and postcolonial questions, even if it exchanges *Leave No Trace*'s Utopian gesture for a more abstract rebellious spirit. Finally, in the chapter on *Ballast*, I have demonstrated how the historical injustices of slavery are ingrained into the film's vision of the Mississippi Delta and thwart any form of communal cooperation. The landscape that presents itself here lacks, as Olwig puts it, a "symbolic heart" and therefore offers its impoverished African American protagonists no opportunity to resist their marginalization.[7] The only hope here lies in the forming of the most miniscule collective, an unconventional nuclear family, to find protection from neoliberalism's destruction of infrastructure and the lingering traces of racist landscaping.

The question that presents itself at the close of this endeavor is where this loose cycle of films and their longing for landscape as inclusive and cooperative lead us. I want to begin answering this question by juxtaposing two partially contrasting perspectives on the real word effectiveness of radical social visions in (indie) cinema. At the outset of this book, I examined Kevan Feshami's article on indie cinema and neoliberalism. In the text, the author concludes that "just as

6 Wylie, *Landscape*, 161.

7 Olwig, *Landscape, Nature and the Body Politic*, 215.

with all other facets of life, independent cinema is not autonomous in relation to the determinations of capitalism."[8] He goes on to argue:

> A supposedly progressive or oppositional set of practices which turns on a currency of individuality opposed to collective authority—be it the state, the major studios, or whatever else—not only has the potential to run counter to pursuits of social justice but can undercut social protections which vulnerable populations depend on.[9]

However, Feshami admits, by relating positively to the work of indie filmmaker John Sayles, that indie films are indeed able to offer "compelling visions of collective struggle that eschew the kind of individualism celebrated by (neo)liberalism" as well as "oppositional potential" to neoliberal ideology.[10]

This chimes with Francesco Sticchi's conclusion to his investigation of precarity in contemporary cinema and television. He argues that films like *Beasts of the Southern Wild* remind us that "we need to learn to walk again in this precarious reality in order to start re-inhabiting it collectively, and there is nothing more powerful than cinema's affective storytelling in teaching us how to do it."[11] This is precisely the approach I identify in the New Rural Cinema. Even though the cycle is concerned with deep poverty, misery, and even utter hopelessness in the face of overwhelming ecological crises and the uninhibited power of capital, its films emphasize care, hospitality, and solidarity—and, crucially, demonstrate how these ethical values can be furthered through an understanding of landscape that is oppositional to neoliberal individualism. To quote from Sticchi's insightful conclusion again, this approach to film landscape suggests "how travelling into precarious film maps and interacting with the subjectivities inhabiting them has meant *more* than simply recognizing the pain of the characters and establishing with them detached and compassionate relations of sympathy."[12] While Sticchi understands this "more" as the forming of a new precarious class consciousness, I see it in the context of the New Rural Cinema as the potential for an intersectional "landscape consciousness" that incorporates the awareness of spatial marginalization on the basis of class, race, and/or gender, as well as ecological concerns.

An indication that such a consciousness is indeed pushing its way into the cultural mainstream can be found in the ongoing wave of popular US films dealing with rurality, poverty, and marginalization based on race and gender. This is where the delineation of the cycle starts to become especially complicated. These

8 Feshami, "US Independent Cinema," 51.

9 Ibid., 53.

10 Ibid., 54.

11 Sticchi, *Mapping Precarity*, 247.

12 Ibid., 252. Emphasis added.

most recent films can be considered part of the New Rural Cinema from a thematic perspective, yet clearly dispense with most of the more radical, communitarian aspects found in the films discussed in this book, and adopt a far more conventional, individualist outlook as well as a more polished aesthetic. For example, the 2021 Academy Awards nominees included such films as *Hillbilly Elegy* (Ron Howard, 2021), *Minari* (Lee Isaac Chung, 2020), and *Nomadland* (the latter won the Best Picture Award), all of which deal with specific aspects of rural poverty and landscape. Furthermore, one might add such recent indie/studio hybrids as *The Glass Castle* (Destin Daniel Cretton, 2017), *Captain Fantastic* (Matt Ross, 2016), and *Land* (Robin Wright, 2021) (see list at the end of this book). I want to briefly summarize some of their approaches to rural landscape in order to gauge how the New Rural Cinema's landscape sensibility may further develop.

Minari approaches rural American landscape from an immigrant perspective as it follows a Korean family starting a farm in 1980s rural Arkansas. The film's title refers to a particular Korean herb (called water celery in English), which serves to symbolize the family's difficult integration into US culture. While father Jacob's (Steven Yeun) plans to grow and sell produce eventually fail, the *minari* planted by his mother-in-law Soonja (Yuh-Jung Youn) continues to successfully grow at a creek near the family farm. The import of a foreign species of plant serves to equate US landscape and society: both have historically evolved through the integration of "imported" people, plants, and animals. The act of planting the *minari* can be seen as, to refer back to Cloke and Jones, an instance of "the rich intimate ongoing togetherness of beings and things which make up landscapes and places, and which bind together nature and culture over time."[13] This certainly aligns the film with the landscape consciousness I have identified in the New Rural Cinema. The film's largely uncritical celebration of this well-known civic credo of the United States, however, clearly separates it from the bleaker tone of the four films discussed in this book. The hard-working Yi family's struggles are presented as tough, but certainly manageable, and overall, they are welcomed into US society with open arms by the eccentric townspeople.

Hillbilly Elegy is based on the successful memoir by author J.D. Vance, who was elected to the US senate in 2022 and whose right-wing platform was officially endorsed by Donald Trump. The adaptation similarly offers a heavily romanticized view of rural America. It looks back at the main character—a fictionalized version of Vance—in his teenage years in mid-nineties rural Kentucky. The film's first images, accompanied by an evangelical preacher's sermon on the American Dream, consist of fast tracking shots moving through the sunlit, green landscape.

13 Cloke and Jones, "Dwelling, place, and landscape," 651.

Certain markers of rural poverty such as an old, rusted car stick out, but quickly disappear in the fast-moving montage that builds up to the introduction of young Vance. Pontificating about his rural background in the voice-over, grown-up Vance (Gabriel Basso), a law student at Yale in the film's present-day timeline, muses: “Ask me where I feel most at home, that's the hill country, Jackson, Kentucky. [. . .] It's where my people come from.” The soundtrack, which consists of melodious violin sounds in this opening montage, suggests nostalgia, a simpler time. This nostalgia is reinforced by the close-knit and exclusively white mountain community the film introduces in this scene. After this pastoral introduction, the film goes on to center on the enduring conflict between Vance and his abusive mother Bev (Amy Adams) as well as on the supportive role played by his late grandmother Mamaw (Glenn Close). It is mainly the caricature-like figure of Bev, a violent alcoholic and drug-addict that caused the film to be widely rejected by critics—the book had already caused similar negative reactions at its release.

Katie Rife, for example, writes in her review of the film for the website *AV Club* that it “views its subjects as zoo animals, offering [. . .] enduring stereotypes about Appalachia—namely, that it's full of people too ignorant to realize that they're being victimized by their own bad choices.”[14] She goes on to argue that while the film correctly identifies pressing issues for rural America—the opioid epidemic, poverty, teenage pregnancy—it “ties itself into knots in order to make those factors a matter of personal responsibility” instead of focusing on larger political issues.[15] She concludes that the film is “bootstrapping poverty porn; *Hillbilly Elegy* just reinforces the stereotypes it insists it's illuminating.”[16] This tendency is also reflected in the film's depiction of landscape which remains pure scenery throughout. It is depicted as an unchanging bright green background, the stage on which the family drama is performed. There is no sense that what is happening to the Vance family is somehow part or expression of the environment surrounding them. As such, we might compare it to the function of landscape Olwig identifies in the scenery of the plays, or “masques” performed at Renaissance British courts: it “was used to present a scene shaped in imitation of natural law. This scene represented a fragment of a cosmos whose natural laws were thought to govern the realms of nature and humanity.”[17] Reframed for our times, this suggests that the film accepts rural poverty and misery as a somehow “natural” oc-

14 Katie Rife, “May Hillbilly Elegy Mark the End of Trump-Era Myth-Making about the White Working Class,” *AV Club* (November 10, 2020), https://www.avclub.com/may-hillbilly-elegy-mark-the-end-of-trump-era-myth-maki-1845625283.

15 Ibid.

16 Ibid.

17 Olwig, *Landscape, Nature and the Body Politic*, 80.

currence from which one can easily distance oneself, as Vance does, by leaving and starting afresh in the city. Like *Minari*, the film ultimately endorses a version of the Horatio-Alger-myth and its ideological belief in unfettered class mobility.

Nomadland, finally, is closer to the vision of rurality laid out in this book, yet, just as the other two films mentioned here, ultimately also represents a more conciliatory, "watered-down" approach. Its director Chloé Zhao has previously made two films that have been mentioned in this book—*Songs My Brothers Taught Me* and *The Rider*—as they clearly fall in line with this book's focus on poverty, marginality, and an interactive landscape vision. *Nomadland* follows Fern (Frances McDormand), a widow in her sixties, who is living in her customized van as she drives across the United States, looking for work and meeting other outcasts of US society. While the film's focus on mobility and its road-movie-sensibility separate it from the stasis prevalent in most other stories of the New Rural Cinema, it is connected to them by its keen eye for the real-world conditions of marginalized communities.

I want to highlight one scene in particular, in which Fern joins a solidary community and support "bootcamp" of other "vandwellers" called the "Rubber Tramp Rendezvous", which is organized yearly by real-life YouTube celebrity Bob Wells in Arizona. The temporary camp in the desert is strongly reminiscent of the communal RV park in *Leave No Trace*. There is a sense of solidarity between the participating outsiders who share helpful tips, food, stories, and equipment between each other. Wells himself is shown giving a passionate speech against the conditions of neoliberal capitalism ("the tyranny of the marketplace"), particularly the negative impact of precarious work. This temporary community briefly seems to achieve a resistant agency against the forces of marginalization—its interaction with the sparse desert environment suggests the possibility of creating "something from nothing," of establishing a polity based on interaction and cooperation in the face of extreme exploitation.

Overall, however, the film's treatment of landscape remains staunchly individualist even if it does tap into the "embodied vision" favored by landscape phenomenologists such as Ingold. The film's striking, contemplative moments in which the boundaries between bodies and their surroundings appear to blur are experienced alone and are presented solely as instances of personal reflection, not of community. One of these moments occurs when Fern's acquaintance Swankie, a terminally ill, elderly woman, sends Fern a video which the film inserts full screen into the flow of images accompanied by mournful piano music. The video depicts Swankie's POV-shot from a canoe in a little river bay. From the nests on the rocks beside her, hundreds of swarming swallows seem to engulf and surround her. Earlier, Swankie had told Fern that she wanted to experience precisely this situation one last time before she died. The scene is deeply moving and calls to mind the opening of *Ballast*, in which James seeks to, perhaps, experience a very similar animal encounter, yet fails to do so. Another brief scene in which the boundaries between "the self and the landscape dissolve altogether" can be found in a melancholic montage after Fern has left the "Rubber Tram Rendezvous".[18] Driving through a national park—it is not specified which one—Fern can first be seen standing on a cliff, surrounded by a breath-taking view of the surrounding land, shouting her own name into the abyss (see Fig. 14). Briefly afterwards, she submerges herself fully naked into a mountain stream, her closed eyes suggesting peacefulness and contemplation. As I have argued elsewhere, "her intimate connection to nature is depicted [. . .] as a respite from her precarious work and as an almost mythical ritual to potentially overcome the grief for her dead husband."[19]

Fig. 14: Fern (Frances McDormand) shouts her name into the abyss. *Nomadland* (Chloé Zhao, 2020).

These touching moments suggest, as Wylie puts it, that the characters "perceive through an attunement with landscape."[20] This approach, he proceeds, presupposes that landscape is "an ongoing process of intertwining [. . .]. It is the fact that I belong to the landscape of visible things that enables my seeing—it is my seeing which enables me to witness that belongingness."[21] In the context of the characters' extremely marginalized position in relation to US mainstream culture, such a focus on "belongingness" and intertwining with the landscape can certainly be under-

18 Ingold, *The Perception of the Environment*, 161.

19 Tim Lindemann, "Travelling the Scenic Landscape: Community, Nationalism and Precarity in Nomadland (2020)," *Empedocles* 13:1 (2022), 33.

20 Wylie, *Landscape*, 152.

21 Ibid.

stood as politically empowering. However, the reoccurring images of overwhelming natural beauty as well as the final narrative twist, in which Fern rejects the invitation to permanently live in her friend Dave's (David Strathairn) son's guest house, also suggest a fascination with the freedom of the nomad lifestyle that can only be experienced solitarily. This is not inherently problematic yet does suggest a quite different concept of landscape compared to the four films discussed in this book as well as to Zhao's earlier films. Therefore, one could level at *Nomadland* the critique that has been directed at phenomenological landscape studies as well, namely, as Catherine Nash puts forward, that "they constitute a retreat from [. . .] the politics of the body in favor of the individualistic and universalizing sovereign subject."[22] While *Nomadland* is much more specific about working conditions than any of the four films discussed here, it paradoxically appears vaguer in its focus on rural landscape. This is because it is too fascinated with the wide-open spaces, and, thereby, a scenic understanding, of the American landscape. Therefore, as Wylie puts it, it "appears to neglect the constraining and determining effects of forms of power" as they present themselves in the environment.[23]

These three examples demonstrate how the New Rural Cinema is in the process of gradually shedding its radical focus on collectiveness and, in some cases, even embraces neoliberal individualism as it moves towards and potentially merges with mainstream cinema. While all three films, to varying degrees, contain valid critiques of rural marginalization, they are clearly more interested in establishing an ideological consensus that connects with a larger audience and that has successfully enabled greater profitability. A comparison of, for example, *Nomadland's* ending and its celebration of individualist landscape experience with the inclusive conception of community presented in the final scene of *Leave No Trace*, reinforces Geoff King's assessment that "scope for radical departure is usually closely tied to an industrial position at a distance from the more commercial mainstream."[24] *Nomadland*, while produced independently, was acquired, and distributed by Disney; its individualist response to neoliberal marginalization is thus mirrored by its position within, or at least close to the industrial mainstream.

Nomadland as well as the other films discussed in this conclusion therefore fall into line with King's definition of Indiewood, which not only refers to films produced by Hollywood studios' specialty divisions like Disney's Searchlight Pictures but can also "include certain films made or distributed by the major studios themselves [. . .] confected consciously to buy into the market opened up by the

22 Catherine Nash, "Performativity in Practice: Some Recent Work in Cultural Geography," *Progress in Human Geography*, 24:4 (2000), 660.

23 Wylie, *Landscape*, 181.

24 King, "Introduction," 4.

independent sector."[25] These films may embrace textual qualities, as King continues, "from institutionally non-studio-affiliated directions that appear designed specifically with potential indie/mainstream cross-over in mind."[26] Considering that Zhao was at the time of *Nomadland*'s production already considered to direct Disney's comic-book blockbuster *Eternals* (2021), one is furthermore reminded of King's argument that for the major studios, "involvement in the Indiewood/indie/specialty sector [. . .] enables them to bring emerging new filmmaking talent into their orbit, potentially to go on to serve mainstream duty."[27] At the time of writing, the three directors of the case studies discussed in this book have not undertaken the leap into the studio mainstream; the same goes for Phillip Youmans, Amman Abasi and even Kelly Reichardt who, while certainly a prominent auteur of US indie cinema, remains dedicated to small-scale productions. Others, like David Gordon Green (*Undertow, George Washington*) and Jeff Nichols (*Shotgun Stories, Mud*) have made the transition to Hollywood cinema, but have largely left their interest in rural poverty behind. It is clear, however, that the tropes of the New Rural Cinema have been identified by the studios as textual qualities recognizable enough to serve as content for mainstream/indie crossover projects. It is therefore of limited interest if one wants to argue for or against their inclusion into the original cycle; they undoubtedly respond to the same discourses surrounding rurality and poverty, yet their ability to instigate progressive debate is diminished by their firm position within the mainstream.

Finally, as briefly suggested in the introduction, it is worth pointing out here that the Covid-19 pandemic has already dramatically exacerbated the circumstances for many already vulnerable people in the rural United States. The reason why rural areas are generally hit harder than urban regions, as J. Tom Mueller and colleagues suggest in their article, lies precisely in the infrastructural destruction and underdevelopment fostered by neoliberal austerity politics that the films of the New Rural Cinema make visible. They summarize:

> Many of the dramatic impacts documented in urban locales and on the national stage are just as prominent as, and in some cases even more pronounced, in the most geographically sparse region of the United States. As these rural regions have poorer hospital access, more vulnerable labor markets, and heightened levels of material hardship compared to urban areas, these dramatic impacts likely indicate an even more difficult road to recovery. These vulnerabilities of rural areas are reflected in our findings of significant increases in unem-

25 King, *Indiewood USA*, 4–5.
26 Ibid., 4.
27 Ibid., 6.

> ployment, heightened use of unemployment insurance, negative impacts to mental health, and currently poor perceptions of local economic health.[28]

It is likely therefore that rural poverty will remain an urgent problem in the United States, which will continue to be addressed in popular culture and, thus, also in cinema. The question that remains is whether an interactive, collective approach to landscape will continue to reverberate through these representations.

---

28 Tom J. Mueller, Kathryn McConnell, Paul Berne Burow, Katie Pofahl, Justin Farrell and Alexis A. Merdjanoff. "Impacts of the COVID-19 Pandemic on Rural America," *PNAS* (January 15, 2021), https://www.pnas.org/content/118/1/2019378118.

Bibliography

Allen-Smith, Joyce E. "Blacks in Rural America: Socioeconomic Status and Policies to Enhance Economic Well-Being." *The Review of Black Political Economy* 22:4 (1994), 7–24.

Anderson, Benedict. *Imagined Communities. Reflections on the Origin and Spread of Nationalism*. London/New York: Verso, 2003.

Andersson, Johan and Lawrence Webb. "American Cinema and Urban Change: Industry, Genre, and Politics from Nixon to Trump." In *The City in American Cinema: Film and Postindustrial Culture*, ed. Johan Andersson and Lawrence Webb. London: Bloomsbury, 2019, 1–42.

Andrews, Malcolm. *Landscape in Western Art*. Oxford: Oxford UP, 1999.

Alston, Phillip. "Statement on Visit to the USA, by Professor Philip Alston, United Nations Special Rapporteur on Extreme Poverty and Human rights." *The Office of the High Commissioner for Human Rights* (2017), https://www.ohchr.org/en/statements/2017/12/statement-visit-usa-professor-philip-alston-united-nations-special-rapporteur.

Badley, Linda. "Down to the Bone: Neoliberalism and Genre in Contemporary Women's Indies." In *Indie Reframed: Women's Filmmaking and Contemporary American Independent Cinema*, ed. L. Badley, C. Perkins, and M. Schreiber. Edinburgh: Edinburgh University Press, 2016, 121–137.

Bandy, Mary Lee and Stoehr, Kevin. *Ride, Boldly Ride: The Evolution of the American Western*. Berkeley: University of California Press, 2012.

Banner, Stuart. *How the Indians Lost Their Land: Law and Power on the Frontier*. London/Cambridge, MT: Harvard UP, 2005.

Baron, Cynthia and Yannis Tzioumakis. *Acting Indie. Industry, Aesthetics, and Performance*. London: Palgrave Macmillan, 2020.

Barrow, Clyde W. *The Dangerous Class. The Concept of the Lumpenproletariat*. Ann Arbor: University of Michigan Press, 2020.

Baurick, Tristan. "How Lessons from Isle de Jean Charles Could Guide Federal Climate Migration Planning." *Nola.com* (August 16, 2020), https://www.nola.com/news/environment/article_8f6c9338-de68-11ea-9f99-534747c43bd0.html.

Bazin, André. *What is Cinema? Vol. 2*, trans. Hugh Gray. Los Angeles/Berkeley: University of California Press, 2004.

BBC.co.uk. "Poverty and Progress in the Mississippi Delta" (January 4, 2012), https://www.bbc.co.uk/news/magazine-16385337.

Bedics, Bonnie. "The History and Context of Rural Poverty." *Human Services in the Rural Environment* 11:1 (1987), 12–14

Bell, David. "Anti-Idyll: Rural Horror." In *Contested Countryside Cultures: Rurality and Socio-Cultural Marginalisation*, ed. Paul Cloke and Jo Little. London: Routledge, 1997, 91–105.

Bell, James. "Meth and the Maiden." *Sight & Sound* 20:10 (2010), 29–30.

Bellah, Robert, William M. Sullivan, Richard Madsen, Ann Swidler, and Steven Tipton. *Habits of the Heart: Individualism and Commitment in American Life*. Berkely: University of California Press, 1985.

Berger, John. *Ways of Seeing*. London: Penguin, 2008.

Berger, Martin A. "Overexposed: Whiteness and the Landscape Photography of Carleton Watkins." *Oxford Art Journal* 26:1 (2003), 1–23.

Bernstein, Maxine. "OUT OF THE WOODS. POLICE RESCUE FATHER, GIRL WHO SAY FOREST PARK WAS THEIR HOME FOR FOUR YEARS." *The Oregonian* (May 20, 2004) section A1, 1–6.

Berra, John. "Rural Crimewave: Reconfiguring Regional Spaces through Genre in US Indie Cinema." In *A Companion to American Indie Film*, ed. Geoff King. Oxford: Wiley-Blackwell, 2017, 325–347.

https://doi.org/10.1515/9783110779417-010

Berrey, Stephen A. "Resistance Begins at Home: The Black Family and Lessons in Survival and Subversion in Jim Crow Mississippi." *Black Women Gender & Families* 3:1 (2009), 65–90.

Blake, Linnie. *The Wounds of Nations. Horror Cinema, Historical Trauma and National Identity.* Manchester: Manchester UP, 2013.

Bonnemaison, Sarah and Christine Macy. *Architecture and Nature: Creating the American Landscape.* London: Routledge, 2003.

Braedley, Susan and Meg Luxton. "Competing Philosophies. Neoliberalism and Challenges for Everyday Life." In *Neoliberalism and Everyday Life*, ed. Susan Braedley and Meg Luxton. Montreal: McGill-Queen's UP, 2010, 3–22.

Brenner, Neil and Nik Theodore. "Cities and the Geographies of 'Actually Existing Neoliberalism'." *Antipode* 34:3 (2002), 349–379.

Brown, Wendy. *Undoing the Demos. Neoliberalism's Stealth Revolution*. New York: Zone Books, 2015.

Campbell, Neil. *Post-Westerns: Cinema, Region, West.* Lincoln/London: University of Nebraska Press, 2013.

Candaele, Kelly. "The Problematic Political Messages of Beasts of the Southern Wild." Los Angeles Review of Books (August 9, 2012), https://lareviewofbooks.org/article/the-problematic-political-messages-of-beasts-of-the-southern-wild/.

Catsoulis, Jeanette. "A Small-Town Buzz About the Missing." *The New York Times* (August 30, 2012), https://www.nytimes.com/2012/08/31/movies/the-tall-man-a-thriller-directed-by-pascal-laugier.html?ref=movies.

Chakrabarty, Dipesh. "Postcolonial Studies and the Challenge of Climate Change." *New Literary History* 43:1 (2012), 1–18.

Cicchetti, Pasquale. "'I Ain't Going Nowhere.' The House, the Mobile Hero and the Frontier in *Winter's Bone*." In *Spaces of (Dis)Location*, ed. Rachael Hamilton, Alison Macleod, and Jenny Munro. Newcastle upon Tyne: Cambridge Scholars, 2013, 73–90.

Clark, John P. and Camille Martin. *Anarchy, Geography, Modernity: Selected Writings of Elisée Reclus.* Oakland, CA: PM Press, 2013.

De Cleyre, Voltairine. "Anarchism and American Traditions." [1932] In *Exquisite Rebel: The Essays of Voltairine de Cleyre*, ed. Sharon Presley and Crispin Sartwell. New York: State University of New York Press, 2005, 91–102.

Cloke, Paul and Owain Jones. "Dwelling, place, and landscape. An Orchard in Somerset." *Environment and Planning* A33 (2001), 649–666.

Clover, Carol. *Men, Women, and Chainsaws. Gender in the Modern Horror Film*. 2nd ed. Oxford: Princeton UP, 2015.

Cobb, James. *The Most Southern Place on Earth: the Mississippi Delta and the Roots of Regional Identity.* Oxford: Oxford UP, 1992.

_____ *The Brown Decision, Jim Crow, and Southern Identity*. Athens, GA: University of Georgia Press, 2005.

Cole, Thomas. "Essay on American Scenery." [1836] *University of Virginia* http://xroads.virginia.edu/~HYPER/DETOC/hudson/cole.html.

Coleman, Nancy. "Why We're Capitalizing Black." *The New York Times* (July 5, 2020), https://www.nytimes.com/2020/07/05/insider/capitalized-black.html.

Cosgrove, Denis. "Prospect, Perspective and the Evolution of the Landscape Idea." *Transactions of the Institute of British Geographers* 10:1 (1985), 45–62.

Cubitt, Sean. "Ecopolitics of Cinema." In *The Routledge Companion to Cinema and Politics*, ed. Yannis Tzioumakis and Claire Molloy. London: Routledge, 2016, 40–49.

Current, Karen. *Photography and the Old West.* New York: Abradale Press, 1986.

Daniels, Stephen. *Fields of Vision: Landscape Imagery and National Identity in England and the United States*. Oxford: Princeton UP, 1993.

Davis, Thadious M. "Expanding the Limits: The Intersection of Race and Region." *Southern Literary Journal 20* (Spring 1988), 3–11.

Denby, David. "Thrills and Chills." *New Yorker* (May 7, 2010), https://www.newyorker.com/magazine/2010/07/05/thrills-and-chills.

Dixon, Melvin. *Ride Out the Wilderness: Geography and Identity in Afro-American Literature*. Champaign, IL: University of Illinois Press, 1987.

Donnar, Glen. "'Ah, You Lose You in There': Gothic Masculinities, Specters of Vietnam and Becoming Monstrous in *Southern Comfort*." In *War Gothic in Literature and Culture*, ed. Agnieszka Soltysik Monnet and Steffen Hantke. London: Routledge, 2015, 136–156.

Duncan, Cynthia. *Worlds Apart. Poverty and Politics in Rural America*. 2nd ed. New Haven/London: Yale UP, 2014.

Ebert, Roger. "The Very Life of Life." *RogerEbert.com* (October 29, 2008), https://www.rogerebert.com/reviews/ballast-2008.

Edelman, Marc. "How Capitalism Underdeveloped Rural America." *Jacobin* (January 26, 2020), https://jacobinmag.com/2020/01/capitalism-underdeveloped-rural-america-trump-white-working-class.

Edsall, Thomas Byrne. *The New Politics of Inequality*. London/New York: Norton, 1985.

Fargo, Jamison, Vincent Kane, Dennis Culhane, Ellen Munley, George Sheldon, Elizabeth Ann Montgomery, and Stephen Metraux. "Prevalence and Risk of Homelessness Among US Veterans." *Preventing Chronic Disease*, 9: E45 (2012), https://www.ncbi.nlm.nih.gov/pmc/articles/PMC3337850.

Farragher, John Mack. *Rereading Frederick Jackson Turner. "The significance of the frontier in American history," and Other Essays*. New Haven, CT: Yale UP, 1998.

Farrigan, Tracey. "Poverty and Deep Poverty Increasing in Rural America." *Amber Waves (ERS)* (March 4, 2014), https://www.ers.usda.gov/amber-waves/2014/march/poverty-and-deep-poverty-increasing-in-rural-america.

____ "Extreme Poverty Counties Found Solely in Rural Areas in 2018." *Amber Waves (ERS)* (May 4, 2020), https://www.ers.usda.gov/amber-waves/2020/may/extreme-poverty-counties-found-solely-in-rural-areas-in-2018.

____ "Rural Poverty and Well-Being." *ERS* (2021), https://www.ers.usda.gov/topics/rural-economy-population/rural-poverty-well-being/#howis.

Federici, Silvia. *Re-enchanting the World. Feminism and the Politics of the Commons*. Oakland, CA: PM Press, 2019.

Fennell, Chris. "10 Great Films Set in the Deep South." *BFI* (November 14, 2013), https://www.bfi.org.uk/lists/10-great-films-set-deep-south.

Feshami, Kevan. "US Independent Cinema and the Capitalist Mode of Production: Complicating Discourses of Independence and Oppositionality." In *Contemporary Cinema and Neoliberal Ideology*, ed. Ewa Mazierska and Lars Kristensen. London: Routledge, 2018, 42–56.

Fowler, Catherine and Gillian Helfield. "Introduction." In *Representing the Rural. Space, Place and Identity in Films about the Land*, ed. Catherine Fowler and Gillian Helfield. Detroit: Wayne State UP, 2006, 1–16.

French, Philip. *Westerns: Aspects of a Movie Genre*. London: Secker and Warburg, 1977.

Fusco, Katherine and Nicole Seymour. *Kelly Reichardt*. Chicago: University of Illinois Press, 2017.

Galandi-Pascual, Julia. *Zur Konstruktion amerikanischer Landschaft*. Freiburg: Modo, 2010.

Gallaher, Carolyn. "Anti-Statism." In *Key Concepts in Political Geography*, ed. Carolyn Gallaher. London/ Los Angeles: Sage, 2009, 260–273.

Gilbey, Ryan. "Vanishing Point." *Sight & Sound* 28:7 (2018), 46–48.

Gonzales, Rachel, Larissa Mooney, and Richard Rawson. "The Methamphetamine Problem in the United States." *Annual Review of Public Health* 31:1 (2009), 385–398.

González, Jesús Ángel. "New Frontiers for Post-Western Cinema: Frozen River, Sin Nombre, Winter's Bone." Western American Literature 50:1 (2015), 51–76.

Grandin, Greg. *The End of the Myth. From the Frontier to the Border Wall in the Mind of America*. New York: Metropolitan Books, 2019.

Green, Archie. "Hillbilly Music: Source and Symbol." *The Journal of American Folklore* 78:209 (1965), 204–228.

Greve, Julius and Florian Zappe. "Introduction: Ecologies and Geographies of the Weird and the Fantastic." In *Spaces and Fictions of the Weird and the Fantastic – Ecologies, Geographies, Oddities*, ed. J. Greve and F. Zappe. London: Palgrave Macmillan, 2019, 1–12.

Griffin, Farah Jasmine. *"Who set you Flowin"?": The African-American Migration Narrative*. New York/ Oxford: Oxford UP, 1995.

Grim, Valerie. "African American Rural Culture, 1900–1950." In *African American Life in the Rural South*, 1900–1950, ed. R. Douglas Hurt. Columbia, MO: University of Missouri Press, 2003, 108–128.

Hans, Simran. "Hale County, This Morning, This Evening review – poetic and profound." *The Guardian* (January 20, 2019), https://www.theguardian.com/film/2019/jan/20/hale-county-this-morning-this-evening-review.

Haraway, Donna. *When Species Meet*. Minneapolis, MN: University of Minnesota Press, 2008.

Harkins, Anthony. *Hillbilly: A Cultural History of an American Icon*. Oxford: Oxford UP, 2005.

Harper, Graeme and Jonathan Rayner. "Introduction – Cinema and Landscape." *Cinema and Landscape*, ed. Graeme Harper and Jonathan Rayner. Bristol: Intellect, 2010, 13–29.

Harrington, Michael. *The Other America: Poverty in the United States*. 2nd ed. New York: Simon & Schuster, 1997.

Hazelton, John. "*Leave No Trace* director Debra Granik on carving her own niche in social-realism", *Screen Daily* (December 1, 2018), https://www.screendaily.com/features/leave-no-trace-director-debra-granik-on-carving-her-own-niche-in-social-realism/5134942.article.

Heidegger, Martin. "Building Dwelling Thinking." In *Poetry, Language, Thought*, trans. Albert Hofstadter. New York: Harper Perennial, 2001, 143–59.

Higham, John. "Multiculturalism and Universalism: A History and Critique." *American Quarterly* 45 (1992), 195–219.

Hutchinson, Pamela. "Film of the week: Leave No Trace grieves for the wild at heart." *Sight & Sound* (December 28, 2018), https://www2.bfi.org.uk/news-opinion/sight-sound-magazine/reviews-recommendations/leave-no-trace-debra-granik-wild-heart.

IndieWire. "Toolkit Case Study: How Indie Hit *Winter's Bone* Came to Be." (November 4, 2010), https://www.indiewire.com/2010/11/toolkit-case-study-how-indie-hit-winters-bone-came-to-be-244485.

Ingold, Tim. *The Perception of the Environment: Essays on Livelihood, Dwelling and the Skill*. London: Routledge, 2000.

Insdorf, Annette. "Ordinary People, European Style: How to Spot an Independent Feature." *American Film* 6:10 (1981), 57–60.

Isenberg, Nancy. *White Trash: The 400-Year Untold History of Class in America*. London: Penguin, 2017.

Kendi, Ibram X. *Stamped from the Beginning: The Definitive History of Racist Ideas in America*. London: Bodley Head, 2017.

King, Geoff. *Indiewood USA: Where Hollywood Meets Independent Cinema*. London: I.B. Tauris, 2009.

____ *Indie 2.0: Change and Continuity in Contemporary American Indie Film*. London: IB Tauris, 2014.

____ "Introduction: What Indie Isn't . . . Mapping the Indie Field." In *A Companion to American Indie Film*, ed. Geoff King. Chichester: Wiley & Sons, 2014.

King, J.C.H. *Blood and Land. The Story of Native North America*. London: Penguin, 2017.

King, Jeannine. "Memory and the Phantom South in African American Migration Film." *The Mississippi Quarterly* 63:3 (2010), 477–491.

Kitses, Jim. *Horizons West*. 2nd ed. London: BFI Publishing, 2004.

Klein, Amanda Ann. *American Film Cycles: Reframing Genres, Screening Social Problems, and Defining Subcultures*. Austin: University of Texas Press, 2011.

Knight, Arthur. "African American Cinema." *Oxford Bibliographies* (October 27, 2016), https://www.oxfordbibliographies.com/view/document/obo-9780199791286/obo-9780199791286-0213.xml.

Kuhn, Annette Kuhn and Guy Westwell. *Oxford Dictionary of Film Studies*. 2nd ed. Oxford: Oxford UP, 2020.

Langman, Larry and David Ebner. *Hollywood's Image of the South: A Century of Southern Films*. Westport, CT: Greenwood, 2001.

Lapin, Andrew. "The Real Bathtub: Back to the Bayou with Beasts Of The Southern Wild." IndieWire (June 27, 2012), https://www.indiewire.com/2012/06/the-real-bathtub-back-to-the-bayou-with-beasts-of-the-southern-wild-46302.

Lefebvre, Martin. "Between Setting and Landscape in the Cinema." In *Landscape in Film*, ed. Martin Lefebvre. London: Routledge, 2006, 19–61.

____ "On Landscape in Narrative Cinema." *Canadian Journal of Film Studies* 20:1 (2011), 61–78.

Lewis, Oscar. "The Culture of Poverty." *Scientific American* 215 (1966), 19–25.

Lichter, Daniel. "Immigration and the New Racial Diversity in Rural America." *Rural Sociology* 77:1 (2012), 3–35.

Lidz, Franz. "How Benh Zeitlin Made Beasts of the Southern Wild." *Smithsonian Magazine* (December 2012), https://www.smithsonianmag.com/arts-culture/how-benh-zeitlin-made-beasts-of-the-southern-wild-135132724/.

Lieber, Marlon. "Spaces of Communal Misery: The Weird Post-Capitalism of *Beasts of the Southern Wild*." In *Spaces and Fictions of the Weird and the Fantastic – Ecologies, Geographies, Oddities*, ed. J. Greve and F. Zappe. London: Palgrave Macmillan, 2019, 183–200.

Lindemann, Tim. "Travelling the Scenic Landscape: Community, Nationalism and Precarity in *Nomadland* (2020)." *Empedocles* 13:1 (2022), 25–40.

Lorimer, Hayden. "Cultural Geography: The Busyness of being 'More-Than-Representational'." *Progress in Human Geography* 29:1 (2005), 83–94.

Loyo, Hilaria. "Resignifiying the National Home. Gendered Domopolitics and Neoliberal Geographies of Exclusion in Debra Granik's Cinema." In *Screening the Crisis: US Cinema and Social Change in the Wake of the 2008 Crash*, ed. Juan A. Tarancón and Hilaria Loyo. New York: Bloomsbury, 2022, 163–183.

Lusted, David. *The Western*. London: Routledge, 2003.

Maclear, Kyo. "Something So Broken: Black Care in the Wake of Beasts of the Southern Wild." ISLE: Interdisciplinary Studies in Literature and Environment 25: 3 (2018), 603–629.

Marshall, Peter. *Demanding the Impossible. A History of Anarchism*. New York: HarperCollins, 1993.

Marx, Karl. *Capital Volume 1*, trans. Ben Fowkes. London: Penguin Books, 1990.

Marx, Karl and Friedrich Engels. *The Communist Manifesto*, trans. L.M. Findlay. Minneapolis, MN: First Avenue Editions, 2018.

Massood, Paula J. *Black City Cinema: African American Urban Experiences in Film*. Philadelphia: Temple UP, 2003.

Mayer, Hervé. "Neo Frontier Cinema: Rewriting the Frontier Narrative from the Margins in *Meek's Cutoff* (Kelly Reichardt, 2010), *Songs My Brother Taught Me* (Chloé Zhao, 2015) and *The Rider* (Chloé Zhao, 2017)." *Miranda* 18 (2019), http://journals.openedition.org/miranda/16672.

McCarroll, Meredith. *Unwhite: Appalachia, Race, and Film*. Athens, GA: University of Georgia Press, 2018.

McFarlan, Sarah. "The Universe Unraveled: Swampy Embeddedness and Ecological Apocalypse in *Beasts of the Southern Wild*." In *Ecocriticism and the Future of Southern Studies*, ed. Zackary Vernon. Baton Rouge: LSU Press, 2019, 66–84.

McLean, Craig, Michael Long, Paul Stretesky, Michael Lynch, and Steve Hall. "Exploring the Relationship between Neoliberalism and Homicide: A Cross-National Perspective." *International Journal of Sociology*, 49:1 (2019), 53–76.

Melbye, David. *Landscape Allegory in Cinema – From Wilderness to Wasteland*. New York: Palgrave Macmillan, 2010.

Merleau-Ponty, Maurice. *The Visible and the Invisible*. Evanston: Northwestern UP, 1968.

Mitchell, Don. "Cultural Landscapes: Just Landscapes or Landscapes of Justice?", *Progress in Human Geography*, 27: 6 (2003), 787–796.

_____ "Landscape." In *Cultural Geography*, ed. David Atkinson. London: I.B. Tauris, 2005, 49–57.

Miller, Angela. "The Fate of Wilderness in American Landscape Art." In American Wilderness – A New History, ed. Michael Lewis. New York: Oxford UP, 2007, 91–113.

Mills, Stephen. *The American Landscape*. Edinburgh: Keele UP, 1997.

Mirzeoff, Nicholas. "Becoming Wild." *Nicholasmirzeoff.com* (September 30, 2012) https://www.nicholasmirzoeff.com/O2012/2012/09/30/becoming-wild.

Moody, Kim. *Workers in a Lean World*. New York: Verso, 1997.

Moss, RaMell. "Filming the Black Belt: An Interview with RaMell Moss." Interview by Max Fraser. *Dissent Magazine* (Fall 2019), https://www.dissentmagazine.org/article/filming-the-black-belt-an-interview-with-ramell-ross.

Mueller, Tom J., Kathryn McConnell, Paul Berne Burow, Katie Pofahl, Justin Farrell, and Alexis A. Merdjanoff. "Impacts of the COVID-19 Pandemic on Rural America." *PNAS* (January 15, 2021), https://www.pnas.org/content/118/1/2019378118.

Murphy, Bernice M. *The Rural Gothic in American Popular Culture: Backwoods Horror and Terror in the Wilderness*. London: Palgrave Macmillan, 2013.

Nash, Catherine. "Performativity in Practice: Some Recent Work in Cultural Geography." *Progress in Human Geography*, 24:4 (2000), 653–664.

Nash, Roderick. *Wilderness and the American Mind*. 4th ed. New Haven, CT: Yale UP, 2001.

Nelson, Rob. "Down in the Delta." *Film Comment* 44.5 (2008), 40–41.

Newitz, Annalee and Matt Wray. *White Trash: Race and Class in America*. London: Routledge, 1997.

Nixon, Rob. *Slow Violence and the Environmentalism of the Poor*. Cambridge, MA: Harvard UP, 2013.

Nyong'o, Tavia. 2015. "Little Monsters: Race, Sovereignty, and Queer Inhumanism in *Beasts of the Southern Wild*." *GLQ: A Journal of Lesbian and Gay Studies*, 21: 2–3 (2015), 249–272.

Nystrom, Derek. *Hard Hats, Rednecks, and Macho Men: Class in 1970s American Cinema*. Oxford: Oxford UP, 2009.

Olmsted, Frederick Law. "Preliminary Report upon the Yosemite and Big Tree Grove." [1865] In *The Papers of Frederick Law Olmsted: The California Frontier, 1863–1865*, ed. Victoria Post Ranney and Gerard Rauluck. Baltimore: Johns Hopkins University Press, 1990, 488–516.

Olwig, Kenneth. *Landscape, Nature, and the Body Politic*. Madison: University of Wisconsin Press, 2002.

____ "'Natural' Landscapes in the Representation of National Identity." In *The Routledge Research Companion to Heritage and Identity*, ed. Brian Graham and Peter Howard. London: Routledge, 2008, 73–89.

____ *The Meanings of Landscape*. London: Routledge, 2019.

Ortner, Sherry B. *Not Hollywood. Independent Film at the Twilight of the American Dream*. Durham/London: Duke University Press, 2013.

Parikh, Nina. "An Interview with Mississippi Film Producer Nina Parikh." Interview by Phillip Gentile. *Southern Quarterly* 49:2/3 (2012), 83–101.

Paveck, Hannah. "Care at the Margins: Debra Granik's *Leave No Trace*." *Another Gaze* (May 19, 2018), https://www.anothergaze.com/care-margins-debra-graniks-leave-no-trace-2018.

Pearson, Erin. "Structuring Indie and *Beasts of the Southern Wild*. The Role of Review Journalism." In *A Companion to American Indie Film*, ed. Geoff King. Oxford: Wiley-Blackwell, 2017, 155–180.

Perkins, Claire. "Life During Wartime: Emotionalism, Capitalist Realism, and Middle-Class Indie Identity." In *A Companion to American Indie Film*, ed. Geoff King. Oxford: Wiley-Blackwell, 2017, 349–367.

Pick, Anat. *Creaturely Poetics. Animality and Vulnerability in Literature and Film*. New York: Columbia UP, 2011.

____ "Three Worlds: Dwelling and Worldhood on Screen." In *Screening Nature. Cinema beyond the Human*, ed. Anat Pick and Guinevere Narraway. New York: Berghahn, 2013, 21–36.

Pimpare, Stephen. *Ghettos, Tramps, and Welfare Queens. Down and Out on the Silver Screen*. New York: Oxford UP, 2017.

Pinkowitz, Jaqueline. "Down South: Regional Exploitation Films, Southern Audiences, and Hillbilly Horror in Herschell Gordon Lewis's *Two Thousand Maniacs!*" *Journal of Popular Film and Television* 44:2 (2016), 109–119.

Purvey, Lee. "Navigating Fact and Fiction: Chloé Zhao on Songs My Brothers Taught Me." *Walker Art Center Magazine* (March 1, 2016), https://walkerart.org/magazine/navigating-fact-and-fiction-Chloé-zhao-on-songs-my-brothers-taught-me.

Reichardt, Kelly, "Interview with Kelly Reichardt." Interview by Brian Sholis. *Artforum* (October 2008), https://www.artforum.com/print/200808/online-only-interview-with-kelly-reichardt-21124.

Rife, Katie. "May Hillbilly Elegy Mark the End of Trump-Era Myth-Making about the White Working Class." *AV Club* (November 10, 2020), https://www.avclub.com/may-hillbilly-elegy-mark-the-end-of-trump-era-myth-maki-1845625283.

Robinson, Zandria. *This Ain't Chicago. Race, Class, and Regional Identity in the Post-Soul South*. Chapel Hill: University of North Carolina Press, 2014.

Rogers, Alisdair, Noel Castree, and Rob Kitchin. *Dictionary of Human Geography*. Oxford: Oxford UP, 2013. Doi: 10.1093/acref/9780199599868.001.0001.

Rødje, Kjetil. *Images of Blood in American Cinema: The Tingler to The Wild Bunch*. London: Routledge, 2015.

Ruddick, Sue. "The Sun Never Set Upon The Blues: Reading and Honouring Clyde Woods." *Antipode* (2012), https://antipodeonline.org/wp-content/uploads/2012/12/woods_3_ruddick.pdf.

Savoy, Eric. "The Face of the Tenant: A Theory of American Gothic." In *American Gothic: New Interventions in a National Narrative*, ed. Eric Savoy and Robert Martin. Iowa City: University of Iowa Press, 1998, 3–20.

Schatz, Thomas. *Hollywood Genres*. New York: McGraw-Hill, 1981.

Sharrett, Christopher. "'Fairy Tales for the Apocalypse': Wes Craven on the Horror Film." *Literature/Film Quarterly*, 13:3 (1985), 139–147.

_____ "The Idea of Apocalypse in The Texas Chainsaw Massacre." Planks of Reason: Essays on the Horror Film, ed. Christopher Sharrett and Barry Keith Grant. Lanham, MD: Scarecrow Press, 2004, 300–321.

Simmon, Scott. *The Invention of the Western Film – A Cultural History of the Genre's First Half-Century.* Cambridge/New York: Cambridge UP, 2003.

Singh, Nikhil Pal. *Black is a Country. Race and the Unfinished Struggle for Democracy*. Cambridge, MA: Harvard UP, 2005.

Smith, Henry Nash. *Virgin Land: The American West as Symbol and Myth*. Cambridge, MA: Harvard UP, 1971.

Spence, Sam. "David Gordon Green talks history of *George Washington*, 20 years later." *Charleston City Paper* (November 18, 2020), https://charlestoncitypaper.com/2020/11/18/david-gordon-green-talks-history-of-george-washington-20-years-later.

Standing, Guy. *The Precariat: The New Dangerous Class*. London: Bloomsbury Academic, 2016.

Stead, Peter. *Film and the Working Class: The Feature Film in British and American Society*. London: Routledge, 1989.

Steven, Mark. *Splatter Capital*. London: Repeater Books, 2017.

Stewart, Jacqueline Najuma. *Migrating to the Movies: Cinema and Black Urban Modernity*. Berkeley: University of California Press, 2005.

Sticchi, Francesco. *Mapping Precarity in Contemporary Cinema and Television. Chronotopes of Anxiety, Depression, Expulsion/Extinction*. London: Palgrave Macmillan, 2021.

The Numbers. "Beasts of the Southern Wild." https://www.the-numbers.com/movie/Beasts-of-the-Southern-Wild#tab=summary.

Thoreau, Henry David. *Walking*. Thomaston, ME: Tilbury House, 2019.

Thurow, Lester. "Agricultural Institutions and Arrangements Under Fire." In *Social Science Agricultural Agendas and Strategies: Social Science Agricultural Project*, ed. G.L. Johnson. East Lansing: Michigan State UP, 1991, 155–164.

Thornham, Sue. *Spaces of Women's Cinema. Space, Place and Genre in Contemporary Women's Filmmaking*. London: BFI/Bloomsbury, 2019.

Tickamyer, Ann R. "Rural Poverty: Research and Policy for U.S. Families." In *Rural Families and Communities in the United States: Facing Challenges and Leveraging Opportunities (National Symposium on Family Issues*, 10), ed. Jennifer E. Glick, Susan M. McHale, and Valarie King. Cham, Switzerland: Springer Nature, 2020, 3–27.

Tickamyer, Ann R. and Emily Wornell. "How to Explain Poverty?" In *Rural Poverty in the United States*, ed. Ann R. Tickamyer, Jennifer Sherman, and Jennifer Warlick (New York/Chichester: Columbia UP), 2017, 84–115.

Tilley, Christopher. *The Materiality of Stone – Explorations in Landscape Phenomenology*. Oxford: Berg Publishers, 2004.

Tompkins, Jane. *West of Everything: The Inner Life of Westerns*. Oxford: Oxford UP, 1992.

Trahan, Erin. "Telling a Backwoods Tale with Chilling Accuracy." *Boston.com* (June 13, 2010), http://archive.boston.com/ae/movies/articles/2010/06/13/winters_bone_director_strived_for_authenticity_in_cast_script_set.

Trimble, S. *Undead Ends: Stories of Apocalypse*. New Brunswick, NJ: Rutgers UP, 2019.

Tuan, Yi-Fu. "Space and Place: Humanistic Perspective." *Progress in Geography* 6 (1974), 211–252.

_____ *Landscapes of Fear*. New York: Pantheon, 1979.

Tucker, Terrence. "Healing the (Re)Constructed Self: The South, Ancestors, and Maya Angelou's 'Down in the Delta'." *CLA Journal* 58:1 (2014), 91–104.

Turner, Frederick Jackson. *The Significance of the Frontier in American History*. London: Penguin, 2008.

Tzioumakis, Yannis. *American Independent Cinema*. Edinburgh: Edinburgh UP, 2017.

Warnick, Bryan, Heather Dawson, D. Spencer Smith, and Bethany Vosburg-Bluem. "Student Communities and Individualismin American Cinema." *Educational Studies* 46 (2010), 168–191.

Watkins, Robert. *Freedom and Vengeance on Film: Precarious Lives and the Politics of Subjectivity*. London/New York: I.B. Tauris, 2016.

Weissman, Judith, Laura Pratt, Eric Miller, and Jennifer Parker. "Serious Psychological Distress Among Adults: United States, 2009–2013." *NCHS Data Brief* 203 (2015), 1–8.

Wells, Karen. *The Visual Cultures of Childhood: Film and Television from The Magic Lantern To Teen Vloggers*. London: Rowman & Littlefield, 2020.

Wexman, Virginia Wright. "The Family on the Land: Race and Nationhood in Silent Westerns." In The Birth of Whiteness – Race and the Emergence of U.S. Cinema, ed. Daniel Bernadi. New Brunswick, NJ: Rutgers UP, 1996, 129–169.

Wood, Robin. *Hollywood from Vietnam to Reagan*. New York/Chichester: Columbia UP, 1986.

Woodrell, Daniel. *Winter's Bone*. London: Sceptre, 2016.

Woods, Clyde. "'Sittin' on Top of the World.' The Challenges of Blues and Hip Hop Geography." In *Black Geographies and the Politics of Place*, ed. K. McKittrick and C. Woods. Toronto: Between the Lines, 2007, 46–81.

Wuthnow, Robert. *The Left Behind. Decline and Rage in Small-Town America*. Princeton/Oxford: Princeton UP, 2019.

Wylie, John. *Landscape*. London: Routledge, 2007.

Zeitlin, Benh, "*Beasts of the Southern Wild* Director: Louisiana Is a Dangerous Utopia." Interview by Jeremy Butman. *The Atlantic* (June 27, 2012), https://www.theatlantic.com/entertainment/archive/2012/06/beasts-of-the-southern-wild-director-louisiana-is-a-dangerous-utopia/259009/.

Zinn, Howard. *A People's History of the United States. 1492 to Present*. New York: Harper Perennial, 2010.

Selected Filmography — New Rural Cinema

A Single Shot. Dir. David M. Rosenthal. USA/UK/Canada, 2013.
Ballast. Dir. Lance Hammer. USA, 2008.
Beasts of the Southern Wild. Dir. Benh Zeitlin. USA, 2012.
Burning Cane. Dir. Phillip Youmans. USA, 2019.
Certain Women. Dir. Kelly Reichardt. USA, 2016.
Dayveon. Dir. Amman Abbasi. USA, 2017.
First Cow. Dir. Kelly Reichardt. USA, 2019.
George Washington. Dir. David Gordon Green. USA, 2000.
Hale County This Morning This Evening. Dir. RaMell Moss. USA, 2018.
Hillbilly Elegy, Dir. Ron Howard. USA, 2020.
Joe. Dir. David Gordon Green. USA, 2013.
Kid-Thing. Dir. David Zellner. USA, 2013.
Land. Dir. Robin Wright. USA, 2021.
Leave No Trace. Dir. Debra Granik. USA, 2018.
Meek's Cutoff. Dir. Kelly Reichardt. USA, 2010.
Minari. Dir. Lee Isaac Chung. USA, 2020.
Mud. Dir. Jeff Nichols. USA, 2012.
Nomadland. Dir. Chloé Zhao. USA, 2020.
Rich Hill. Dir. Andrew Droz Palermo, Tracy Droz Tragos. USA, 2014.
Songs My Brothers Taught Me. Dir. Chloé Zhao. USA, 2015.
Stray Dog. Dir. Debra Granik. USA, 2014.
Them That Follow, Dir. Britt Poulton, Dan Madison Savage. USA, 2019.
The Rider. Dir. Chloé Zhao. USA, 2017.
Undertow. Dir. David Gordon Green. USA, 2004.
War Pony. Dir. Riley Keough and Gina Gammell. USA, 2022.
Wendy and Lucy. Dir. Kelly Reichardt. USA, 2008.
Winter's Bone. Dir. Debra Granik. USA, 2010.

https://doi.org/10.1515/9783110779417-011

General Filmography

12 Years a Slave. Dir. Steve McQueen. USA, 2013.
Albino Farm. Dir. Joe Anderson. USA, 2009.
Apache. Dir. Robert Aldrich. USA, 1954.
Broken Arrow. Dir. Delmer Daves. USA, 1950.
Cabin Fever. Dir. Eli Roth. USA, 2002.
Captain Fantastic. Dir. Matt Ross. USA, 2016.
Country. Dir. Richard Pearce. USA, 1984.
Dark Manhattan. Dir. Harry Fraser. USA, 1937.
Daughters of the Dust. Dir. Julie Dash. USA, 1991.
Dayveon. Dir. Amman Abbasi. USA, 2017.
Deliverance. Dir. John Boorman. USA, 1972.
Down in the Delta. Dir. Maya Angelou. USA, 1998.
Down to the Bone. Dir. Debra Granik, 2004.
Easy Rider. Dir. Dennis Hopper. USA, 1969.
Earthlings, Dir. Shaun Monson. USA, 2005.
El laberinto del fauno (Pan's Labyrinth). Dir. Guillermo del Toro. Spain/Mexico, 2006.
Five Easy Pieces. Dir. Bob Rafelson. USA, 1970.
Frozen River. Dir. Courtney Hunt. USA, 2008.
Get Out. Dir. Jordan Peele. USA, 2017.
Green Pastures. Dir. Marc Connelly, William Keighley. USA, 1936.
Gummo. Dir. Harmony Korine. USA, 1997.
Hallelujah. Dir. King Vidor. USA, 1929.
Harlan County, USA. Dir. Barbara Kopple. USA, 1976.
Harriet. Dir. Kasi Lemmons. USA, 2019.
Heartland. Dir. Richard Pearce. USA, 1979.
Heaven's Gate. Dir. Michael Cimino. USA, 1980.
Hillbilly Elegy. Dir. Ron Howard. USA, 2020.
Hook. Dir. Steven Spielberg. USA, 1991.
House of 1000 Corpses. Dir. Rob Zombie. USA, 2003.
Killer of Sheep. Dir. Charles Burnett. USA, 1978.
Joy. Dir. David O. Russell. USA, 2015.
Les quatre-cents coups (*The 400 Blows*). Dir. Francois Truffaut. France, 1959.
Little Big Man. Dir. Arthur Penn. USA, 1970.
Mat i Syn (Mother and Son). Dir. Aleksandr Sokurov. Russia/Germany, 1997.
Mississippi Damned. Dir. Tina Mabry. USA, 2009.
Mississippi Masala. Dir. Mira Nair. USA/UK, 1991.
Mudbound. Dir. Dee Rees. USA, 2017.
Night Moves. Dir. Kelly Reichardt. USA, 2013.
Nomadland. Dir. Chloé Zhao. USA, 2020.
Northern Lights. Dir. John Hanson, Rob Nilsson. USA, 1978.
Nothing But a Man. Dir. Michael Roemer. USA, 1964.
Norma Rae. Dir. Martin Ritt. USA, 1980.
North Country. Dir. Niki Caro. USA, 2005.
Once Upon a Time . . . When We Were Colored. Dir. Tim Reid. USA, 1996.

https://doi.org/10.1515/9783110779417-012

Southern Comfort. Dir. Walter Hill. USA, 1981.
Spring Night, Summer Night. Dir. Joseph L. Anderson. USA, 1967.
Sweet Sweetback's Baadasssss Song. Dir. Melvin van Peebles. USA, 1971.
The Battle at Eldersbush Gulch. Dir. D.W. Griffith. USA, 1913.
The Birth of a Nation. Dir. Nate Parker. USA, 2016.
The Covered Wagon. Dir. James Cruze. USA, 1923.
The Glass Castle. Dir. Destin Daniel Cretton. USA, 2017.
The Grapes of Wrath. Dir. John Ford. USA, 1940.
The Great Train Robbery, Dir. Edwin S. Porter. USA, 1903.
The Hills Have Eyes. Dir. Wes Craven. USA, 1977.
The Iron Horse. Dir. John Ford. USA, 1924.
The NeverEnding Story (Die Unendliche Geschichte). Dir. Wolfgang Petersen. USA/West Germany, 1984.
The River. Dir. Mark Rydell. USA, 1984.
The Searchers. Dir. John Ford. USA, 1956.
The Tall Man, Dir. Pascal Laugier. Canada/France, 2012.
The Texas Chainsaw Massacre. Dir. Tobe Hooper. USA, 1974.
The Texas Chainsaw Massacre, Dir. Marcus Nispel. USA, 2003.
The Wild Bunch. Dir. Sam Peckinpah. USA, 1969.
To Sleep with Anger. Dir. Charles Burnett. USA, 1990.
Two Thousand Maniacs! Dir. Herschell Gordon Lewis. USA, 1964.
Wagon Master. Dir. John Ford. USA, 1950.
Walking Tall. Dir. Phil Karlson. USA, 1973.
Waterworld. dir. Kevin Reynolds. USA, 1995.
Wendy. Dir. Benh Zeitlin. USA, 2020.
Wrong Turn. Dir. Rob Schmidt, 2003.

Index

https://doi.org/10.1515/9783110779417-013

www.ingramcontent.com/pod-product-compliance
Lightning Source LLC
LaVergne TN
LVHW050955080826
845145LV00006B/1508
* 9 7 8 3 1 1 2 2 4 7 4 8 8 *